Spies Who
Changed
History

Spies Who Changed History

The Greatest Spies and Agents of the 20th Century

Nigel West

AN IMPRINT OF PEN & SWORD BOOKS LTD
YORKSHIRE – PHILADELPHIA

First published in Great Britain in 2022 by
FRONTLINE BOOKS
an imprint of Pen & Sword Books Ltd
Yorkshire – Philadelphia

Copyright © Nigel West, 2022

ISBN 978-1-39908-632-5

Typeset by Concept, Huddersfield, West Yorkshire, HD4 5JL.
Printed and bound in England by CPI Group (UK) Ltd, Croydon CR0 4YY.

Pen & Sword Books Ltd incorporates the imprints of Aviation, Atlas, Family
History, Fiction, Maritime, Military, Discovery, Politics, History, Archaeology,
Select, Wharncliffe Local History, Wharncliffe True Crime, Military Classics,
Wharncliffe Transport, Leo Cooper, The Praetorian Press, Remember When,
White Owl, Seaforth Publishing and Frontline Books.

For a complete list of Pen & Sword titles please contact
PEN & SWORD BOOKS LTD
47 Church Street, Barnsley, South Yorkshire, S70 2AS, England
E-mail: enquiries@pen-and-sword.co.uk
Website: www.pen-and-sword.co.uk
or
PEN & SWORD BOOKS
1950 Lawrence Rd, Havertown, PA 19083, USA
E-mail: uspen-and-sword@casematepublishers.com
Website: www.penandswordbooks.com

Contents

Acknowledgements

The author acknowledges his debt of gratitude to all those who have assisted his research, among them the late Bill Williams, Roger Hesketh, David Strangeways, Noel Wild, Juan Pujol (GARBO), Roman Garby-Czerniawski (BRUTUS), Harry Williamson (TATE), Frano de Bona (FREAK), Ib Riis (COBWEB), Dusan Popov (TRICYCLE); Ivo Popov (DREADNOUGHT), Eugn Sostaric (METEOR), John Moe (MUTT), Tor Glad (JEFF), Elvira de la Fuentes (BRONX), Lisel Gärtner, Hugh Astor, Len Burt, Christopher and Pam Harmer, Cyril Mills, John Maude, Gerald Glover, Peter Ramsbotham, Tommy and Joan Robertson, Susan Barton, Enriiquetta Harris, Sarah Bishop, Joanna Phipps, Peter Hope, Jim Skardon, Eric Goodacre, John Gwyer, Dick White, Victor and Tess Rothschild, Bill Magan, Russell Lee, Michael Ryde, Anthony Blunt, Rupert Speir and Bill Luke, who shared their wartime MI5 experiences; and the late Sigismund Best, Philip Johns, Cecil Gledhill, Nicholas Elliott, Felix Cowgill, Desmond Bristow, Rodney Dennys, Cecil Barclay, Eddie Boxshall, Euan Rabagliati, Charles Seymour, Andrew King, George Blake, Lionel Loewe, Walter Bell, Fred Winterbotham, Kenneth Benton, John Codrington, Lord Tennyson, George Young, Gervase Cowell, Peter Falk, Kenneth Cohen, Pat Whinney, Robin Cecil and John Cairncross, who all served in SIS. Also, from SOE, Ronnie Seth, Peter Kemp, Jack Beevor, Brian Stonehouse, Tony Brooks and Peter Wilkinson; Al Ulmer, Bill Hood, Pete Bagley, Brian Kelley, Jack Platt, Bill Casey, Peter Sichel and Hugh Montgomery from OSS; Ken Crosby, formerly of the FBI Special Intelligence Service; Ray Batvinis, Edward Gazur, Paul Moore and David Major of the FBI; Jack Morton and Jack Prendergast, both postwar Special Branch officers; Cleve Cram, Dick Helms, Dick Walters, David Doyle, Pete Bagley and Dick Holm from the CIA, and John Taylor from NARA; also Oleg Tsarev, Oleg Gordievsky, and Oleg Kalugin from the KGB; Vladimir Rezun of the GRU. Finally, Halina Szymanska, Martin and Kim Dearden, Jenifer Hart, Rufina Philby, Michael Straight, Gunter Peis, Rob Hesketh, Erich Vermehren, David Mure, Bill Kenyon-Jones,

Jock Colville, Anthony Montague Browne, and Bill Cavendish-Bentinck, David Kahn, Marco Popov, Francois Grosjean, Ladislas Farago, John Taylor, Jennifer Scherr, Sebastian Cody, Kim and Marton Dearden, Christian Linde, Frederick Solms-Baruth, Katharine Ritter, Otto Weltzien, Jim Lee and Christopher Risso-Gill. Also Len Beurton, Ursula and Robert Kuczynsky and Wolf Kuczynsky. Finally, Charles Byford, for his online research skills.

Author's Note

Many of the documents reproduced in this volume originate from official files and have been redacted during the declassification process. Where it has been possible the redactions have been restored, but where this has not been possible the redaction is indicated thus: [XXXXXXXXXXXXX]. The author has retained the convention of printing codenames in capitals.

In the interests of consistency, some American-month/day style dates have been altered to the European day/month convention.

Abbreviations and Glossary

ACP – Austrian Communist Party
Aman – Israeli military intelligence service
ARCOS – All-Russia Co-operative Society
ASA – US Army Security Agency
B1(a) – MI5's section handling double agents
B1(b) – MI5's German espionage research section
B1(g) – MI5's Spanish section
B5(b) – MI5's investigations section
CC – Central Committee
CCNY – City College of New York
CIC – CIA Counterintelligence Center
CPGB – Communist Party of Great Britain
CPUSA – Communist Party of the United States of America
DCI – Director of Central Intelligence
DDO – Deputy Director for Operations
D/F – Direction-Finding
DSIR – Department of Scientific and Industrial Research
DSO – Defence Security Officer
DSS – Director of the Security Service, Vernon Kell
FBS – US Navy Fleet Broadcast System
FCD – First Chief Directorate
FSB – Russian Security Service
G-2 – Irish Intelligence Service
GC&CS – Government Code & Cipher School
GCHQ – Government Communications Headquarters
GIS – German Intelligence Service
GRU – Soviet (later Russian) military intelligence service
Ic – OKW intelligence liaison
ICBM – Inter-Continental Ballistic Missile
I/H – Eins Heer

I/L – Eins Luft
I/LTW – Eins Luft Technik
IDF – Israeli Defence Force
IKKI – Central Committee of the Comintern
I-M – Eins Marine
IRBN – Intermediate-Range Ballistic Missile
ISI – Inter-Service Intelligence Directorate
ISOS – Abwehr decrypts
JIC – Joint Intelligence Committee
JIOA – Joint Intelligence Objectives Agency
KGB – Soviet intelligence service
KO – KriegsOrganization
KPD – Kommunische Partei Deutschland
MI5 – British Security Service
MI6 – British Secret Intelligence Service
MI-19 – Combined Services Detailed Interrogation Centre
MIS – Iranian Ministry of Intelligence
MNVK/2 – Hungarian military intelligence service
MOPR – International Workers Relief Organization
MRBM – Medium-Range Ballistic Missile
NATO – North Atlantic Treaty Organisation
NKVD – Soviet intelligence service
OACSI – Office of the Assistant Chief of Staff Intelligence
OGPU – Soviet intelligence service
OKH/Chi – Oberkommando der Wehrmacht, Cipher Section
Ops (B) – SHAEF deception planning unit
OSS – Office of Strategic Services
PF – Personal File
RCS – Royal Corps of Signals
RDF – Radio Direction-Finding
ROF – Royal Ordnance Factory
RSS – Radio Security Service
SA – Sturmabteilung
SAVAK – Iranian security service
SD – Sicherheitsdienst
SIM – Servicio de Información Militar
SIME – Security Intelligence Middle East
SIS – British Secret Intelligence Service

SOSUS – Sound Surveillance System
TPMO – Tudeh Party Military Organization
XX – Twenty Committee
Y – Wireless interception
YCL – Young Communist League

Dramatis Personae

19th – NKVD codename for Laurence Duggan
Abel, Rudolf – Alias of Willie Fisher, KGB illegal *rezident* in New York
Abramov – Head of NKVD International Department
AE/MONOLIGHT – CIA codename for Gennadi Vasilenko
Agca, Mehmet Ali – Turkish assassin
Agranat, Simon – Former President of the Israeli Supreme Court
Akhemova, Elena – KGB officer
Albam, Jacob – KGB spy, convicted 1957
ALEK – GRU codename for Alan Nunn May
ALEKSEI – NKVD codename for Anatoli Yakovlev
Ames, Aldrich – CIA officer and KGB spy, convicted 1994
Andropov, Yuri – KGB Chairman, 1967–1982
ANGEL – Mossad codename for Ashraf Marwan
Angelov, Pavel – GRU officer in Ottawa
ANTENNA – NKVD codename for Julius Rosenberg
Appleton, Edward – Director, DSIR
Apresyan, Stepan – NKVD officer codenamed MAY
ATILLA – Unidentified NKVD spy
Aubert, Marc – Abwehr spy in French Merchant Navy, executed 1939
Bagot, Millicent – MI5 officer
Barbusse Henri – French novelist
Belovai, Istvan – MNVK/2 officer and CIA asset, arrested 1985
Ben-Gurion, David – Israeli prime minister, 1955–1963
Bendman, Yonah – Head of Egyptian Section, Israeli military
  intelligence
Beria, Lavrenti – NKVD Chief, 1938–1953
Best, Sigismund Payne – SIS officer abducted at Venlo 1939
Bethe, Hans – Atomic physicist and espionage suspect
Bethe, Rose – Wife of Hans Bethe
de Bettignies, Louise – Head of SIS spy-ring in Luxembourg
Beznikov, Andrey – SVR illegal alias Donald Heathfield, arrested 2010

Deutsch, Oscar – Arnold Deutsch's uncle and proprietor of Odeon Cinemas
Deutsch, Josefine – Arnold Deutsch's wife and radio operator
Dewé, Walther – Head of SIS's WHITE LADY train-watching network
Dickson, Jimmy – MI5 agent M/3
Dierks, Hilmar – Abwehr officer
Dollman, William – London Coroner
DRAGONFLY – MI5 double agent
Draper, Christopher – MI5 double agent
Driberg, Tom – MI5 agent M/8
DUCHE – NKVD codename for Sergei Spiegelglas
Dunbar, Nicholas – FBI special agent
Duncombe, Else – Abwehr postbox in London
Duggan, Laurence – NKVD spy codenamed 19th
Edemski, Serge – GRU officer in Washington DC
EDITH – NKVD codename for Edith Suschitsky
Eisentrager, Otto – Abwehr officer
Elitcher, Max – Soviet espionage suspect
Elliott, Nicholas – SIS officer
ERIC – NKVD codename for Engelbert Broda
Eriksson, My – Abwehr spy in London, interned 1939
FATHER – MI5 double agent
Feklisov, Aleksandr – Soviet spy codenamed CALISTRATUS
Fisher, Willie – KGB illegal *resident* in New York
Fitin, Pavel – NKVD officer
Floud, Bernard – Soviet spy
Foley, Tracey – Alias of Eleva Vavilova
Fradkov, Mikhail – SVR Director, 2007–2016
Franco, Francisco – Head of Spanish government, 1936–1975
Frankignoul, Charles – Head of SIS train-watching network
Friedman, Lizzy – Kim Philby's Austrian wife and NKVD courier codenamed MARY
Frinovsky, Mikhail – NKVD officer
Fuchs, Klaus – Physicist and Soviet spy, convicted 1950
Gedaliah, David – IDF officer
GERTA – Unidentified NKVD codename
Gerwing, Hildegard – Austrian wife of Engelbert Broda
Giebl, Ignatz – Abwehr spy in New York, indicted in 1938

Glading, Elizabeth – Percy Glading's Spanish wife

Glading, Jane – Percy Glading's daughter

Glading, Percy – CPGB National Organizer and NKVD spy codenamed GOT, convicted 1938

GLAN – NKVD codename for Vladimir Barkovsky

Glaser, Erich – US Army soldier and Abwehr spy, convicted 1938

Glasser, Abraham – NKVD spy codenamed MORRIS

Glassman, Eleanor – William Perl's former girlfriend, and Vivian's sister

Glassman, Vivian – Joel Barr's former girlfriend and espionage suspect

GNOME – NKVD codename for William Perl

Gold, Harry – NKVD spy in New York, convicted 1951

Goldschmudt, Hans – Suspected NKVD spy

Gonen, Shmuel – IDF officer

Gordievsky, Oleg – KGB defector exfiltrated from Moscow, 1985

Gore-Booth, Paul – British diplomat

GOT NKVD – codename for Percy Glading

Gouzenko, Igor – GRU defector in Ottawa, 1945

Graur, André – NKVD officer

Gray, Olga – MI5 agent M/12 and Old Bailey witness 'Miss X'

Greenglass, David – NKVD spy codenamed CALIBRE, convicted 1951

Greenglass, Ruth – NKVD spy codenamed WASP

Gregory, Jeffrey – US Army NCO and Hungarian spy, convicted 1994

GROLL – Soviet codename for Walter Krivitsky

Gruentzel, Donald – FBI special agent

GT/ACCORD – CIA codename for Vladimir Vasiliev

Gudenberg, Werner – Abwehr spy, indicted 1938

Haden-Guest, David – CPGB member

von Halban, Hans – Atomic physicist at Cambridge University

Hall, Theodor – Atomic physicist and NKVD spy codenamed YOUNG

Hancock-Nunn, Vivian – MI5 agent M/7

Hanfstangl, Ernst – Close friend of Adolf Hitler

Hanssen, Robert – FBI counter-intelligence officer and KGB spy codenamed KARAT convicted 2001

al-Haq, Mohammed Zia – President of Pakistan, 1978–1988

Hardt, Paul – Alias of Theodore Mally

Harington, John – FBI special agent

Harker, Jasper – Director, MI5's B Division

HARLEQUIN – MI5 codename for Abwehr officer Richard Wurmann

Hart, Herbert – MI5 officer
Hart, Jenifer – Home Office civil servant and Soviet spy
Heathfield, Donald – Alias of Andrey Beznikov, arrested 2010
Helfferich, Erich – Abwehr officer
HEIR – Unidentified NKVD spy in England
Helfand, Leon – Soviet diplomat and defector in 1940
Henderson, Wilfred – British naval attaché in Berlin
Himsworth, Norman – MI5 officer
Hofmann, Johanna – Abwehr courier on SS *Europa*, convicted 1938
Hohenlohe, Max – Spanish businessman and Abwehr agent
Hollis, Roger – MI5 officer
Honigmann, Georg – Lizzie Friedmann's postwar husband
Hoover, J. Edgar – FBI Director, 1935–1972
Howard, Edward Lee – CIA officer and KGB spy, defected 1985
HUGHES – NKVD codename for Al Sarant
Jaruzelsky, Wojciech – President and Prime Minister of Poland, 1981–1990
JOHN – Unidentified NKVD spy
Johnson, John – Metropolitan police detective
Jordan, Jessie – Abwehr spy in Dundee, convicted 1938
Kalugin, Oleg – KGB officer
Kapustin, Pavel – SVR illegal, alias Christopher Matsos, arrested 2010
KARAT – KGB codename for Robert Hanssen
Karetkin, Vitali – KGB officer
KASPAR – MI5 codename for Josef Lemmel
Kazankin, Gennadi – KGB officer
Keitel, Wilhelm – Chief, OKW
Kell, Vernon – Director-General of MI5, 1909–1940
Kelley, Brian – CIA counter-intelligence officer
KELLY – NKVD codename for unidentified atomic spy in London
Kercsik, Imre – Hungarian intelligence courier, convicted 1998
Kercsik, Sandor – Hungarian intelligence courier, convicted 1998
Khouri, George – Suspected spy in Cairo
Kirpichenko, Vadim – KGB officer
Klugmann, James – Soviet spy
Knight, Maxwell – MI5 officer
Koechel, Johann – Abwehr spy in Brooklyn
Kostromin, Lev – KGB officer
Kowarski, Lev – Atomic physicist

Dramatis Personae

McCredie, Ian – SIS officer in Tehran
McGough, Randall – FBI special agent
Maclean, Donald – Soviet spy and British diplomat, defected to Moscow 1951
McNutt, Russell – Soviet spy codenamed PERS and VOGEL
de Mahe, Prince – British Army officer
Mahoney, John – FBI special agent
Mally, Theodore – NKVD illegal *rezident* in London codenamed MARR
MARR – NKVD codename for Theodor Mally
Marwan, Ashraf – President Nasser's son-in-law and Mossad agent
MARY – NKVD codename for Lizzie Friedmann
Massing, Hede – NKVD defector
Matsos, Christopher – Alias of Pavel Kapustin
Maund, Mona – MI5 agent M/2
Maxse, Ernest – British Consul-General, Netherlands
May, Alan Nunn – Atomic physicist and GRU spy codenamed ALEK, convicted 1946
Merkulov, Vsevolod – NKVD officer
Milmo, Helenus – MI5 officer
Mitrokhin, Vasili – KGB defector
Molody, Konon – KGB illegal *rezident* in London, convicted 1961
MORRIS – NKVD codename for Abraham Glasser
Morrison, Philip – Atomic physicist and espionage suspect
Morrison, William – CPGB radio operator
Mortati, Tomasso – US Army NCO and Hungarian spy, convicted 1989
Mossadeq, Mohammed – Iranian prime minister deposed in 1953
Motinov, Pyort – GRU officer in Ottawa
Moxon, Peggy – Arthur Wynn's wife
Moxson, Peter – FBI special agent
Mubarak, Gamal – President Mubarak's son
Mubarak, Hosni – President of Egypt, 1981–2011
Mueller, Georg – NKVD officer
Naidoo, Kevin – Metropolitan Police detective
Nasser, Gamal Abdel – President of Egypt, 1954–1970
Nasser, Mona – Nasser's second daughter
Nebenzahl, Yitzak – Israeli State Comptroller
Nicholson, Harold – CIA officer and KGB spy, convicted 1997

Nicossof, Paul – Notional wireless operator and CHEESE's deputy
NIGEL – NKVD codename for Michael Straight
NIL – NKVD codename for Nathan Sussman
O'Donoghue, John – FBI special agent
Ogarkov, Nikolai – Soviet military strategist
OLD – NKVD codename for Saville Sax
Olsen, Jim – CIA officer in Vienna
Oppenheim, Laurie – British military attaché in The Hague
Orlov, Alexander – NKVD illegal *rezident* in London codenamed
  SCHWED
Ot, Theodor – Former Israeli judge and mediator
OTTO – NKVD codename for Arnold Deutsch
Ovakimyan, Gaik – NKVD officer
Owens, Arthur – Abwehr spy and MI5 double agent
Panetta, Leon – CIA Director, 2009–2011
Passov, Zelman – NKVD Chief of intelligence
Pateman, Fred – British journalist and CPGB member
Pelton, Ronald – NSA analyst and KGB spy, convicted 1986
Penkovsky, Oleg – GRU officer and CIA asset, arrested 1962
Perl, William – NKVD spy codenamed GNOME and YACOV
PERS – NKVD codename for Russell McNutt
PFEIL – Unidentified NKVD codename
Phieffer, Erich – Abwehr officer
Philby, Kim – SIS officer and Soviet spy
Piekenbrock, Hans – Abwehr officer
PIET – Notional South African sub-agent of CHEESE
Piguzov, Vladimir – KGB officer and CIA agent, arrested 1985
Piskunov, Valentin – KGB officer
Platt, Jack – CIA officer
Pollard, Ernest – Atomic physicist
Pollard, Graham – MI5 agent M/1
Pollitt, Harry – General Secretary, CPGB
Polonik, Mikhail – KGB officer
Polyakov, Dmitri – GRU officer codenamed ROAM by the FBI and
  TOPHAT by the CIA, arrested 1985
Poretsky, Elizabeth – Widow of Ignace Reiss
Potakova, Yelena – NKVD officer
Poteyev, Alexander – SVR officer and CIA asset exfiltrated from
  Moscow in 2010

Powers, F. Gary – CIA pilot of U-2 aircraft shot down in 1960
Prime, Geoffrey – GCHQ analyst and KGB spy, convicted 1982
PRINCE – NKVD codename for Laurence Duggan
Raev, Aleksandr – NKVD officer codenamed LIGHT
Ramsay, Roderick – US Army NCO and Hungarian spy, arrested 1990
Rantzau, Nikolaus – Alias of Nikolaus Ritter
Ranscak, Hildegard – Austrian wife of Hans Travaglio
Rastvorov, Yuri – KGB defector 1954
RAYMOND – Soviet codename for Ignace Reiss
REDWOOD – KGB defector Vladimir Kuzichkin
Reich, Wilhelm – Austrian psychologist
Reif, Ignaty – KVD illegal *rezident* in London
RELAY – NKVD codename for Joseph Chinilevsky
Revizorov, Pavel – KGB officer
Rezun, Vladimir – GRU defector
Ribbentrop, Joachim – German foreign minister
Ritter, Nikolaus – Abwehr officer, alias Dr Rantzau
ROAM – FBI codename for Dmitri Polyakov
Rochford, Mike – FBI counter-intelligence officer
Rommel, Erwin – Commander, Afrika Korps
Rondeau, Jeffrey – US Army NCO and Hungarian spy, convicted 1994
Roozbeh, Khosto – Tudeh Party leader
Rosenberg, Ethel – NKVD spy codenamed ETHEL, convicted 1951
Rosenberg, Julius – NKVD spy codenamed ANTENNA and
    LIBERAL
Ross, Louise – Al Sarant's wife
Ross, Victor – Al Sarant's father-in-law
Rossetti, Clemens – Abwehr officer
Ruhel, Josefine – Arnold Deutsch's wife and NKVD radio operator
Rumrich, Gunther – US Army soldier and Abwehr spy, convicted
    1938
Rumrich, Gustav – Abwehr spy in Czechoslovakia
Sadat, Anwar – President of Egypt, 1970–1981
Sarant, Al – Soviet spy codenamed HUGHES, alias Philip Saros
Saros, Philip – Alias of Al Sarant
Sax, Saville – NKVD spy codenamed OLD
Schallburg, Vera von – Abwehr spy imprisoned in England, 1940
Scharr, Rosa – Percy Glading's Austrian wife
Scheutz, Theodor – Abwehr courier on SS *New York*

Stewart, Bob – Head of CPGB Control Commission
Stilwell, Richard – Chairman of Walker damage assessment panel
Straight, Michael – NKVD spy codenamed NIGEL
STRELA – Unidentified NKVD spy
Stuart, Charles – SIS officer
Studeman, William – US Director of Naval Intelligence
Sulick, Michael – CIA officer
Suschitsky, Edith – Comintern agent codenamed EDITH
Suschitsky, Ilona – Suspected Soviet agent and wife of Wolfgang
  Suschitsky
Suschitsky, Wolfgang – Suspected Soviet agent
Sussman, Nathan – NKVD spy codenamed NIL
Sutyagin, Oleg – Russian academic included in 2010 spy-swap
Sykes, Claud – MI5 agent M/S
Szabo, Zoltan – Hungarian intelligence officer, convicted 1989
Tartakow, Eugene – CPUSA member and FBI informant
Thost, Hans – Nazi newspaper correspondent in London
Thwaites, William – Director of Military Intelligence
Tiltman, John – GC&CS cryptographer
TIMUR – KGB codename for unidentified illegal
Tinsley, Richard – SIS officer in Rotterdam
Tkachenko, Alexei – KGB officer in Washington DC
Tokaev, Grigori – GRU defector, 1947
TOPHAT – CIA codename for Dmitri Polyakov
de Trairup, Kristian – Danish arms dealer
Travaglio, Hans – Abwehr officer
Tudor Hart, Alex – Physician and CPGB member married to Edith
  Suschitsky
Tudor Hart, Edith – Edith Suschitsky's married name
TWAIN – NKVD codename for Semyon Semyonov
U.35 – MI5 agent Klop Ustinov
Ustinov, Dmitri – NKVD officer
Ustinov, Klop – MI5 agent U.35
Vasilenko, Gennadi – CIA agent codenamed AE/MONOLIGHT
Vasiliev, Vladimir – GRU officer and CIA asset codenamed
  GT/ACCORD
Vassiliev, Alexander – KGB officer
Vavilova, Elena – SVR illegal, alias Tracey Foley
Venednikov, Evgeni – KGB officer

Dramatis Personae

Yurchenko, Vitali – KGB defector and redefector 1985
Zabotin, Nikolai – GRU *rezident* in Ottawa
Zahringer, Kurt – Abwehr officer
Zaporozhsky, Alexander – KGB officer and CIA agent, arrested in Moscow 2003
Zaporozhsky, Galina – Alexander Zaporozhsky's wife
Zaporozhsky, Maxim – Alexander Zaporozhsky's son
Zaporozhsky, Pavel – Alexander Zaporozhsky's son
Zamir, Zvi – Director of Mossad, 1968–1974
Zeira, Eliyahu – Israeli Director of Military Intelligence
ZORA – NKVD codename for Flora Wovschin
Zubilin, Vasili – NKVD *rezident* in Washington DC

Introduction

The spy can achieve something great by acquiring some
vital information that may change the course of a battle,
or even the history of a nation.

[Allen Dulles, Director of Central Intelligence, 1953–1961,
Great True Spy Stories[1]]

Spies have made an extraordinary impact on the history of the twentieth century, but fourteen in particular can be said to have been demonstrably important. As one might expect, few are household names, and it is only with the benefit of recently declassified files that we can now fully appreciate the nature of their contribution. The criteria for selection has been the degree to which each can now be seen to have had a very definite influence on the course of events, either directly, by passing vital classified material, or indirectly, by organizing or managing a group of spies.

Some of the names included will be unexpected, and it would have been too easy to list 'the usual suspects', a collection that might arguably include Richard Sorge[2], Fritz Kolbe[3], Ronnie Seth[4], Klaus Fuchs[5], Ursula Kuczinsky[6], Erich Vermehren[7], one or all of TATE[8], BRUTUS[9] and GARBO[10], Alan Foote[11], Igor Gouzenko[12], Julius Rosenberg[13], Anatoli Golitsyn[14], Oleg Penkovsky[15], John Vassall[16], George Blake[17], Kim Philby[18], Anthony Blunt[19], Stig Wennerstrom[20], George Paques[21], Vladimir Petrov[22], Ryszard Kuklinski[23], Larry Wu-Tai Chin[24], Adolf Tolkachev[25], Oleg Gordievsky[26] and Vasili Mitrokhin[27]. However, much has been written about all of these and a dozen other potential candidates, and little has emerged from recently declassified files to radically alter what is already known about them. This is certainly not to belittle their significance or considerable achievements, but to rather to focus on cases on which new light can be shed.

Some intelligence agencies seek to recruit new staff by promising them the opportunity 'to make a difference', the implication being that there is a likelihood that their profession will offer the chance of making a lasting impact on world events and, as we shall see, this can happen, perhaps more often than many people think, especially those historians, journalists and commentators who can be so quick to denigrate the profession and portray the intelligence community as a self-perpetuating, unnecessary distraction or aberration from ethical statecraft.

Those selected for inclusion were active in the First World War, the inter-war period, the Second World War, the Cold War and even the post-Cold War era. The fourteen are: Walther Dewé, who pioneered the technique of train-watching, the source of fast, accurate intelligence for the Allies during the First World War; Christopher Draper, the air-ace and MI5 asset whose recruitment by the Abwehr in 1933 demonstrated the potential for manipulating double agents to undermine an adversary; Olga Gray, the MI5 agent insinuated into the Communist Party of Great Britain who exposed a major Soviet spy-ring; Arnold Deutsch, the NKVD illegal *rezident* in London who recruited some nineteen spies that penetrated almost every corner of Whitehall; Renato Levi, the SIS double agent whose activities across the Middle East developed the concept of strategic deception; Richard Wurmann, the reluctant Nazi defector who then changed his mind; Al Sarant, the key member of the Rosenberg network responsible for managing the document copying studio; Engelbert Broda, the Austrian physicist who masterminded wartime atomic espionage in England; William Whalen, the Soviet source well–placed in the Pentagon at a critical moment in the Cold War; John Walker, the venal traitor who altered the East-West balance of power; Clyde Conrad, who betrayed NATO's defence strategy for Europe; Vladimir Kuzichkin, the KGB officer who single-handedly prevented a Kremlin-inspired coup in Iran; Ashraf Marwan, the Mossad walk-in who alerted Israel to the Arab surprise attack on the Yom Kippur holiday; and Gennadi Vasilenko, the CIA mole inside the KGB who facilitated the detection of Aldrich Ames and Robert Hanssen.

These may not be particularly well-known names outside the intelligence community, but with the benefit of declassified files, including hitherto secret damage assessments, we can make a better-informed judgement about the relative significance of spies who were active in the last century.

Chapter 1

Walther Dewé

The information they sent us was of priceless value to
the Allies.

[Henry Landau, *The Spy Net*[1]]

Modern warfare conducted during the First World War brought many
innovations to the intelligence field, including aerial reconnaissance conducted by aircraft, and the analysis of overhead photographic imagery.
However, in the realm of human intelligence, the lasting technique has
been the discipline of train-watching.

Prior to the outbreak of that great conflict the observation of bridges
and the reporting of enemy movements had become an accepted method
of collecting information, and this had been especially true during the
Peninsular campaign during the Napoleonic Wars when choke-points
such as bridges and road junctions were kept under observation by scouts
so as to monitor an adversary's troop concentrations. However, the railway era brought new opportunities for armies to move large quantities of
troops, armour, horses and materiel swiftly over long distances, thereby
increasing the chances of surprise attacks and unexpected withdrawals.
In intelligence terms, the existence of a quite comprehensive railway
system created a military environment in which rapid transport could be
exploited for offensive and defensive purposes. Accordingly, a new dimension to intelligence collection was developed by the Allies to take advantage of the German occupation of French and Belgian territory where the
local population was hostile to their conquerors, who, in a largely static
battlefront, came to rely on a sophisticated rail network in preference to
horse-drawn transport and poorly maintained roads choked with slow-
moving vehicles.

These were the circumstances in which a group of Belgian patriots,
mainly railway workers, was recruited by the British Secret Intelligence
Service (SIS) to log their observations of enemy troop movements and

1

send their reports over the frontier to Rotterdam. At the time, in 1915, Allied intelligence collection from behind enemy lines consisted of the screening of refugees at Folkestone, where arriving passengers were interviewed about their observations, many of which were inevitably out-of-date or imprecise. Additionally, there were individual agents, organized into networks, which passed reports into neutral Holland, where, following the capture of Brussels and the sudden evacuation of the recently established SIS station, a new site was established in Rotterdam, headed by controversial figure Richard Tinsley, a 38-year-old former Cunard seaman from Bootle. Also a Royal Naval Reservist since 1903, and the proprietor of the Uranium Steamship Company and the Uranium Hotel in Rotterdam, he had been recruited originally by the local British consul-general, Ernest Maxse, because of the depth of his local knowledge. Maxse had been entrusted with the task of building an intelligence headquarters staff from scratch, and he had been assisted by the recently withdrawn British naval attaché in Berlin, Captain Wilfred Henderson. Neither he nor Maxse was deterred by Tinsley's reputation, which had been somewhat tarnished in October 1913 when one of his ships, SS *Volturno*, carrying 647 passengers, mainly Jewish immigrants to the United States, plus a crew of 93, caught fire in the Atlantic a week into the voyage, leading to the death of 168 people. On another occasion, in 1911, Tinsley had been deported from Holland after he had been found to have breached Dutch immigration rules by allowing some Russian emigrants to land illegally.

By April 1915 Tinsley's organization, known within Whitehall as the 'T Service' was operating on a budget of £3,000 per month, a figure that would rise within seven months to £5,000. It consisted initially of a small administration of two women and a typist, and subordinates assigned to deal with contraband and mainly naval questionnaires. Among his first agents were a Russian, a Hungarian, a Ruthenian, nine Belgians (with one in Germany) and four Germans, one of them being a Krupp employee, and one each in Cologne and Augsburg. Tinsley ran his SIS bureau under commercial cover from his shipping office at 76 Boompjes, which grew by November 1916 to house a staff of twenty-seven divided into four sections dealing with military intelligence, counter-espionage, naval intelligence and newspaper monitoring. Tinsley's organization, which at its height numbered nearly 300, also invested heavily in his neighbour, Francois van t'Sant, Rotterdam's police chief, who would later be appointed police commissioner and, ultimately, director of Holland's intelligence agency. Placing van t'Sant on the SIS payroll gave Tinsley an element of protection from the local authorities, which were nervous about his activities. Indeed, two of his principal agents, Willem Both and J.M. van Gelderen, had only recently completed prison sentences in the Netherlands, having been convicted of espionage, and in May 1916 *De Telegraff* had published a German-inspired article describing Tinsley's true role. Tinsley was also widely suspected of running several waterfront rackets, including the extortion of shippers anxious to avoid being placed on the Ministry of Blockade's blacklist, which effectively would put them out of business. Evidently an element of corruption was tolerated by SIS as the London management became increasingly reliant on the T Service. One officer, Sigismund Payne Best, who was assigned to Rotterdam by a competing War Office intelligence directorate, dared in 1917 to complain about Tinsley's behaviour and found himself posted elsewhere.

Tinsley, however, was undeterred by his exposure, and appears to have benefited from the publicity by making it act as a magnet for people with information to sell or pass on. The T Service conducted much of its business at the Uranium Hotel, which was managed for Tinsley by a German couple, Gottfried and Thérèse Huber.

Ultimately Tinsley's success as a spymaster rested on his recruitment of a 'walk-in', Karl Krüger, a disaffected Kaisermarine officer who supplied valuable naval information, and the FRANKIGNOUL organization, which pioneered the new technique of train-watching.

Established during 1915 by Charles Frankignoul, the FRANKIGNOUL network began by providing Tinsley with accurate, timely reports of German troop movements in enemy-occupied France and Belgium, through a train route across the Dutch frontier at Maastricht. At its peak, the organization consisted of some two hundred agents who manned up to forty individual observation posts. Ultimately it was the capture in June of *Brussels*, a cross-channel steamer operating for the Great Eastern Railway Company between Tilbury and the Hook of Holland, which led to FRANKIGNOUL's collapse. Among the mailbags retrieved by the Germans was a pouch containing messages compromising a batch of reports addressed to Tinsley and relayed by the military attaché in The Hague, Colonel Laurie Oppenheim, to London. Consequently, FRANKIGNOUL became the subject of a German counter-espionage penetration operation in Maastricht which wound up the organization, and in December eleven of its members were executed for espionage. A new network, led by Tinsley's deputy Henry Landau, started afresh in July 1916 and proved successful; it developed into the WHITE LADY ring, named after the legendary apparition whose appearance would herald the fall of the Hohenzollerns.[2]

Led by an engineer, Walther Dewé, WHITE LADY was able to warn the Allies of imminent offensives, monitor the deployment of German troops and indicate weaknesses in the defences. Dewé had been inspired by the execution in April 1916 of his cousin, Dieudonné Lambrecht, who had himself founded a train-watching network in contact with the British. Lambrecht scored a considerable coup in May 1915 prior to the battle for Verdun when he supplied his handlers with detailed reports from Jemelle and Namur plotting the progress of reinforcements from Serbia destined for Flanders. Lambrecht himself was finally caught at home in Liege when one of his subordinates unwisely recruited a German agent who penetrated the organization and in March 1916 enabled the very extensive security apparatus in Maastricht to round up much of the membership. Dewé's principal assistant was an academic, Professor Herman Chauvin.[3]

Because Dewé's agents had no formal training in the recognition of enemy formations and uniforms, and only a relative few were railway employees, manuals were compiled to assist in the identification of units and to help distinguish between cavalry and artillery uniforms. These handbooks included details of the composition of particular trains, highlighting the difference between livestock cars, flatbeds for artillery pieces, and passenger carriages for infantry. Gradually, the agents became expert in matching their observations to silhouettes prepared by SIS to indicate what a train of a particular length and composition was likely to be carrying. Some trains, known as 'constituted units', took several hours to rumble slowly through heavily congested switching-points, and it was estimated that the transfer of a division from the Eastern Front to the west could take up to six days. Agents were encouraged to employ standardized formats for their reports so the data could be retrieved without unnecessary, time-consuming interpretation, thus allowing the intelligence to be acted upon without delay. Analysis at headquarters allowed the development of a comprehensive order-of-battle, with the ability to monitor the movement of a particular regiment or battalion as it passed from one railway junction to the next. By 1916 it was estimated in London that up to 70 per cent of GHQ's strategic intelligence was derived from train-watching. Accuracy of observation was at a premium, and the SIS staff in Folkestone kept a keen eye out for refugees who might be willing to return to occupied territory on long-term missions, having undergone a period of training.

The collection process was but one part of WHITE LADY's work, as the intelligence then had to be delivered across the electrified border fence that had been erected during the spring of 1915. This was a formidable obstacle and *passeurs*, or professional smugglers, became adept at circumventing the German security measures.[4]

WHITE LADY's value lay in its ability to make observations very close to the front line, and to cover areas previously considered too dangerous, such as the Hison-Mezieres line. Much of this information was reaching GHQ within forty-eight hours, and SIS was soon paying £10,000 a month to maintain the organization, with additional sums going to the *tuyaux*, who acted as couriers across the Dutch frontier. To reduce the pressure on carrying incriminating material over the border, Landau took it upon himself to borrow £30,000 from one of the membership, who was a banker, on the promise of repayment after the war.

By the time of the final big German offensive in March 1918, WHITE LADY was running fifty static posts and received reports from hundreds of *promeneurs* who fed their observations, made from Fabry and the sector around Avesnes, into the communication chain to Holland. Plans were also under way to speed up the most dangerous link, at the frontier, by building a ground induction transmitter that could signal the messages across the border without the need of a landline connection. This innovation was under construction when the Armistice was declared, making it redundant.

Under Dewé's direction, the organization expanded by reviving older networks, such as the circuit around Valenciennes, until it grew to a membership of 1,300 agents, a high proportion of whom were women employed in pharmacies which, for historical reasons, were often located near railway stations and enjoyed good views over the tracks and marshalling yards. Dewé, who had once worked as a telephone engineer in Brussels, exercised rigorous security and eventually absorbed an existing spy-ring in Luxembourg headed by Louise de Bettignies. Born in July 1880 in Valenciennes, she was educated there by nuns at a convent before moving with her family to Lille in 1895. The following year she travelled to England to study with the Ursulines at Upton, Wimbledon and finally Oxford. She was then employed by various noble families in Italy and Germany as a tutor, but returned to Lille in France in 1914, and then went to live with her brother Albert in Bully-les-Mines. When the Germans occupied Lille in October 1914 de Bettignies volunteered to help the Allies in January 1915 and, having adopted the alias of Alice Dubois, ran

an escape-line for evading British troops trapped in the region. Her organization also collected information about enemy activity on the railways
and reportedly passed on details of an imminent visit to the front by the
Kaiser's imperial train, prompting an unsuccessful air raid on the
carriages. She was arrested near Tournai in October 1915 and sentenced
in March 1916 to life imprisonment, but died in September 1918.

By the end of hostilities two members, Louis and Anthony Collard, had
been executed and a further forty-three arrested. There was, of course, no
disguising WHITE LADY's huge success, and despite opposition from
SIS the War Office succumbed to pressure from the membership for postwar recognition of their remarkable contribution. Honours were distributed to the survivors, including Dewé and Chauvin, who were appointed
CBE, and these decorations were duly acknowledged in the *London
Gazette*. So keen were Dewé and Chauvin to be considered soldiers, rather
than common spies, that a special unit, the Corps d'Observation Anglais,
was invented to mollify the leadership. Altogether 727 Belgians, among
them 210 women, were 'mentioned in despatches' and in January 1920 the
Director of Military Intelligence, General Sir William Thwaites, with
Landau at his side, undertook a series of very public investitures in Lille,
Liege, Ghent and Brussels to distribute the medals. Unfortunately the
Germans took note of the names so listed, and wreaked their retribution
in 1940 when Belgium and Luxembourg were again invaded and occupied. Dewé also attempted to repeat his espionage experiences by forming
the CLARENCE resistance group, which survived until January 1944
when Dewé was shot dead by a Luftwaffe officer while attempting to
avoid arrest.

WHITE LADY achieved further notoriety in 1935 when a disaffected
Landau, who had resigned his post as SIS's representative in Berlin, under
Passport Control Officer cover, released *Secrets of the White Lady*[5] from the
safety of the United States, where he was out of reach of the British courts.
No action was taken against his memoir *All's Fair*, which had been
published in 1934, but on that occasion the government apparently had
threatened a ban on the distribution of the sequel. In it, he admitted that
he had 'not attempted to disguise the names of Allied agents. My friends in
Belgium and France assure me that if damage could be done by divulging
them, it was done years ago when a complete list of agents' names was
published in the various decoration lists.' SIS's embarrassment at the
publication of *Secrets of the White Lady* was enhanced considerably by the
author's assurance that the documents quoted in the text 'have been taken

from secret service records which have hitherto been unavailable for publication'.

Landau claimed that Allied intelligence services had run approximately 2,000 agents behind enemy lines in France and Belgium, mostly working for train-watching organizations, of whom about 100 were executed, with a further 220 shot on suspicion of espionage. He also opined that 75 per cent of reliable intelligence reaching GHQ had come through neutral countries, and of that figure some 95 per cent had originated in enemy-occupied territory.

Chapter 2

Christopher Draper

Better the devil you know, than you don't.

[Guy Liddell, 22 January 1935[1]]

In July 1933, soon after having attended the Munich air show in the previous May, Major Christopher Draper, a well-known pilot and former Royal Flying Corps ace, was cultivated by Dr Hans Thost, the London correspondent of the Nazi newspaper *Volkischer Beabacher*. Short of money, single and 41 years old, Draper had been flying since 1913, and had joined the Royal Naval Air Service the following year. He saw action in France and in December 1917 was promoted commander of 8 Naval Squadron. After the war, decorated with the Distinguished Flying Cross, Draper was unsuccessful in his second-hand car business and in 1920 rejoined the Royal Air Force, but soon left again to pursue work as a stunt pilot with an aerobatic team. In September 1931 he acquired a degree of notoriety by flying a de Havilland Puss Moth monoplane under two of London's fourteen bridges as a protest at the government's treatment of war veterans. This demonstration led to an invitation to Germany, where he was introduced to Adolf Hitler.

Although disaffected with Whitehall, Draper was no traitor, and he reported his contact with Thost to MI5, where a case officer was assigned the delicate task of persuading him to give mild encouragement to Thost without actually compromising any sensitive information. On 3 August 1933 MI5's Director-General, Vernon Kell (DSS), and his Director, B Division, Jasper Harker, held a meeting with Draper, as was minuted in his personal file:

DSS and I had a long interview last night with Major Christopher Draper, and though we did not have any opportunity of taking notes at the time, I think the following roughly represents the salient facts of the case.

For some months past Major Draper has been in touch with certain Germans who represent the Hitler interests. He took part in a lecture tour in which two German war aviators came over to this country, and visited Munich where he met various German aviators and associates of Hitler's.

Amongst other persons in this country with whom he has become very familiar is Thost, and to come straight to the point, a comparatively short time ago Thost suggested to him that, if Draper could furnish certain friends of Thost with details of military information, Thost was of opinion that there was plenty of money to be made. It is to be noted that, at this time, Draper was out of a job and on his own admission practically on his beam ends.

Draper expressed his willingness to get in touch with Thost's friends and it was eventually, after a great deal of discussion, decided that he should go to Hamburg where he was told to meet a certain Degenhardt.

After a good deal of unseemly wrangling on the subject of expenses, Thost eventually provided Draper with a ticket on the Hanslufte line to Hamburg; he was given no other money for expenses nor for his return journey.

When he took his seat in the airliner, he found that he was sitting next to a German, one Dr [Ernst] Hanfstengel [*sic*], who is an intimate friend of Hitler, and believed by Draper to be one of his right-hand men.

Dr Hanfstengel expressed considerable surprise at meeting Draper and cross-questioned him pretty thoroughly as to what he was doing. Somewhat indiscreetly, I think, Draper more or less told him what he was up to and though pressed by Dr Hanfstengel to accompany him to Berlin, Draper decided to keep to his original plan and go to Hamburg.

He put up at an hotel in Hamburg and was visited by a young German student, who spoke English extremely well, and said he had been sent to take him to meet Degenhardt. This young gentleman walked Draper about Hamburg for an hour and a half, and eventually he was brought to meet Degenhardt, whom he described as a German, aged about 55, rather Jewish, and obviously – according to Draper – not a man who had served as an officer in the Forces.

After a good deal of discussion this individual (who by the way could not speak English very well and depended a certain amount on the young student as interpreter) handed over to Draper the sum of 250 marks to pay his expenses back and out of pocket expenses in Hamburg, and obtained from him a receipt which Draper himself wrote, signing it with an illegible scrawl.

What Degenhardt explained they wanted was confidential or secret information, documents or books. The suggestion made by [Kristian] de Trairup in his original report to DSS, that there was someone in the War Office supplying them with the names and numbers of confidential military books, is incorrect. No such suggestion was made, but what was said was that, if he gave them the titles of the books, they would know what value to give to them.

According to his own account Draper gave them to understand that he had the entrée, by reason of his present employment in the Inca Aviation Company, to various Government establishments, and while it would be difficult for him to fix matters with his Company, he did not think he would have any very great difficulty in getting them the kind of stuff required.

There was a certain amount of discussion on the subject of funds, and it was evident that Degenhardt was not paying for anything until he had seen it.

Methods of communication were then discussed, and on this subject Degenhardt was insistent that the utmost precaution should be taken. He gave to Draper two cover addresses (see attached note) and advised him to write to him at one or other address, giving him (Degenhardt) the address of a woman in this country with whom Degenhardt could communicate as a cover for Draper.

It was further suggested that Draper should arrange that his letters to these cover addresses should not be posted in England, but should be given to some friend who could post them from Calais or Ostende. In the same way Degenhardt said he would arrange that letters he sent to the cover address which Draper was to provide, would be sent to this country by a sure hand and posted here.

As an alternative it was suggested that Draper might give communications to Thost, who could arrange to send them by one of the pilots of the Hanslufte Line, but as at a subsequent stage in their conversation it was decided that Thost was not to be brought into the matter, there appears to be some confusion of thought either on the part of Draper or Degenhardt.

This visit to Hamburg took place on Monday (14 July 1933) and Draper had returned to this country by Wednesday (16th).

As we already know, he discussed matters with de Trairup and asked him to get in touch with the proper authorities.

When Major Draper left, it was arranged that we would communicate with him during the course of today, would furnish him with the necessary female cover address, and draft the necessary letter to be sent to the cover address, and duly arrange for its posting abroad.

DSS is of opinion, and I am in agreement, that there is a reasonable ground for believing that, at one time when he was very much up against it, Draper was seriously considering Thost's proposal, but the fact of his having obtained a job and probably realising the extraordinary danger of what he was doing, seems to have made him change his mind, and there is no doubt now that he is prepared to play.

It is also obvious that he is anxious to sting the Germans for any money he can, as he was insistent in his enquiries as to what might happen to any money that might come over.

Three days later Harker entered a further note on Draper's dossier:

Major Draper asked if he might come and see me and I accordingly saw him this morning.

He informed me that on Wednesday he had had an interview with Thost. Judging from Major Draper's statements, it seems fairly clear that Thost is still anxious to take a hand in Major Draper's activities, but in accordance with instructions Major Draper told him that in no circumstances would it be possible for him to have any dealings with him over this matter and that in view of Major Draper's rather delicate situation he must absolutely decline to have any dealings with Thost. Eventually Thost agreed to this.

In the course of conversation Major Draper reminded Thost that he had given him (Draper) an address with which he could communicate if he went to Berlin. Draper stated that he had handed over this address to Degenhardt when he had met him in Berlin and he had retained it. Thost made no difficulty about this and wrote the accompanying address for Major Draper.

I impressed upon Major Draper the necessity of having no further dealings with Thost and generally remaining absolutely quiet until

12

such time as we heard from Degenhardt. This he promised he would do.

I do not think Major Draper is very discreet as in the course of conversation he told me that he had seen [Major H.H.] Prince de Mahe and had mentioned to him his interview with Colonel Kell, though Major Draper assures me that he did not tell him anything regarding the arrangements we have made.

It was thus through Draper's visit to Germany that he met 'Degenhardt', who supplied him with two cover-addresses, one in Hamburg, the other in Hillegersberg in the Netherlands. The first was Postbox 629, and the other was traced to Ludwig Fischer, an employee of Damco, a Dutch company engaged in the river trade between Holland and Germany. A third option, of passing his letters to HansLuft pilots at Croydon Airport, was also suggested.

Accordingly, MI5 imposed a Home Office mail intercept warrant on any letters posted to the Hamburg postbox, and this measure would yield extraordinary dividends. Thus, in June 1933 Draper accepted an offer to visit Hamburg, where he met his Abwehr handler, and thereby became MI5's first double agent run against the Germans since the end of the First World War. Over the next three years he stayed in contact with the Germans, but the relationship became strained because MI5 could not authorize the disclosure of any information that the Germans were interested in.

The likely candidate for '*Korvettenkapitan* Degenhardt' was veteran German intelligence professional Hilmar Dierks, who had joined the Abwehr in 1932 after having tried his hand, unsuccessfully, in the second-hand car trade. During the First World War he had worked in Rotterdam for the Admiralstab's Nachirchtenabteilung and learned his trade by establishing commercial cover companies and at least two of his agents would be arrested while on missions to England. In October 1915, under pressure from the British, Dierks had been arrested by the Dutch police on charges of espionage, and sentenced to a year's imprisonment.

In March 1946 Thost was interrogated by the US Army and completed a long statement, which included a version of his dealings with Draper:

In autumn 1932 I moved from Wimbledon to Swan Court, Chelsea, to a more expensive furnished flat. I wanted to take that flat for the cold winter as I thought of getting married. I think it was during that time that I got a letter from Alfred Rosenberg with a photo, showing

13

Major Draper on the Munich aerodrome together with Hitler and a lot of SA people. The letter said that Major Draper was one of the most honoured British fighter pilots with a DSO and other decorations, that he is a friend of Germany and Hitler and that he is prepared to convince his fellow-Britishers in favour of Hitler. I was ordered to receive Major Draper well but the letter said nothing about me giving him money or such things.

I cannot remember whether Major Draper came to see me before or after the *Llachtuebernalime*, before or after Hitler took power.

It must have been in the same winter when I lived in Swan Court, Chelsea. Major Draper arrived together with the German fighter-pilot ace Major Ritter von Schleich (or similar name) who became later during the war a well known Luftwaffen-general. Major Draper and Major Ritter von Schleich (or similar) hired the Plaza Cinema in Lower Regent Street, London for one afternoon and addressed a meeting of British airmen and the general public on Germany and Hitler. He said that the enemies of 1914/19 should join in friendship and that especially the brave fighters of the air on both sides ought to lead their compatriots to a common mutual understanding and friendship of Britain and Germany. The German air ace said practically the same from the German point of view.

I was not present myself at that meeting but invited both Major Draper and Ritter von Schleich to lunch in Oddenino's Restaurant and my impression of Major Schleich was that he was a keen realist ready to work for Anglo-German cooperation as much as he could. I asked him to visit me and to have tea with my wife and me.

Major Draper was then several times in my flat, either for tea or for dinner. Casually I knew the editor of the British periodical *Flight* and when once I visited him in his office I mentioned Major Draper as an acquaintance of mine. The editor asked me in very careful words to avoid him because he was considered as 'immoral'. I did not know what he meant by that word but watched Draper's behaviour during his visits in my flat more carefully. The only thing I realized was that his compliments to my wife were rather a bit overrated but I had no reason to be jealous.

Major Draper visited my wife and me about 5–6 times and we spoke mostly of the activity of the anti-Hitler press in London with their reports on Germany which I always took as evil-meant propaganda similar to that conducted during the war of 1914/19. I asked

14

him to reply to several newspapers by way of the 'Letters to the Editor' and told him that to my mind his words as that of a well known war-time air ace would carry weight with the general public.

It was much later, I think in the late summer of 1933 or 1934, that Major Draper invited my wife and me to an air-display. He introduced to both of us a certain Danish count of whom he said that he was his manager and financier. This Danish count had as far as Draper told me property in London and Spain and was prepared to finance a project for transporting gold in Africa from the digging grounds to the main cities. Draper and his air circus would do that job, the main thing about which was the possibility to take off and land on small aerodromes or in open country. Draper asked me whether I would be prepared to invest money in that business, but I had to reply that it was an impossibility to get my money out of Germany, and that furthermore my money is tied up in real-estate. Major Draper then took me up in the air in his plane, which was a converted British war-time fighter.

After that air display Major Draper did not visit me again for a long time until – I think it was 1934 or 1935 – he suddenly rang me up and asked for a private conversation. He told me in very careful words that he was prepared to work on behalf of Germany, that he was very short of money and that he would like to assist the German Luftwaffe which was just refounded by Goering. To my question 'In what way?', he replied that in his opinion a war between Britain and Germany is an impossibility and if there would come a war the things with which he would assist Germany would be obsolete a long time. He could furnish the German Luftwaffe with the newest type of British air engines, but he knew that these engines are obsolete at least after two years and within that time there would certainly be no Anglo-German war. He (Draper) was of the opinion that as the big business men did such jobs, why should it be considered as betrayal if a small man like himself did such a job. I replied that as a newspaper correspondent I could not mix up in business of that kind and that all he had to do if he wanted to step into business of that sort was to travel to Berlin and look up the telephone directory for the Reichswehr Ministry or the newly founded Air Ministry. Draper then told me that he had not the money to travel to Berlin, so after certain hesitation I gave him about £6 to buy a ticket to the German capital. Rather a long time later I heard from Mr [Otto] Bene, then chief of the Nazi Party in Great Britain (the German Nazi Party having only Germans as members), that the German military authorities received [Draper] but also watched him and found out that he was a homosexual. In all my dealings with that man I never realized that, on the contrary I thought he paid rather too much attention to my wife. Then I never heard of Major Draper any more.

Very much later, in the spring of 1938, just after the *Anschluss* of Austria, I was called up by telephone in my flat in Berlin by that Danish Count, who told me that he was staying in the Hotel Bristol (or Adlon) and wanted to see me the same night. We had dinner together in that hotel and later went into the Wintergarten Music Hall. The Danish Count did not mention the reason why he wanted to see me until we had drinks somewhere in a night club at about one o'clock. He then told me that in his opinion I was not only a newspaper correspondent but also a businessman. I asked what he meant by saying that. He said that I could earn a lot of money if I could bring him into contact with German air-bomb manufacturers, to which he would be prepared to sell a brand-new type of British air-bomb fuses which were manufactured in Woolwich Arsenal. He said he is the owner of a yacht and had connections in Woolwich who would bring a whole bomb with fuses into his yacht and then he would sail towards Germany. I replied that I was not prepared to do business with him, but I would advise him to go to the Reichswehr or to the Air Ministry next morning and ask these people about it. After saying goodbye to him I drove with my own car to the *Reichswehrministerium*. I told the officer on duty that night what the Danish Count had proposed to me and he telephoned though it was only three o'clock in the morning to one or two *Abwehr Offiziers* one of whom received me at once. I told the officer again what the Count wanted to do and the Abwehr officer was very pleased that I reported the matter at once. He asked me to telephone the count early next morning and to tell him that I changed my mind and knew a German industrialist who would be prepared to talk the matter over with him. The officer and I met next morning in a restaurant in Berlin and I telephoned the count, saying I would like to meet him for lunch and introduce him to a German manufacturer. So we all three had lunch together – again in the Bristol (or Adlon?) – and I introduced the officer as a 'bomb-industrialist'. After that lunch the officer took me aside and asked me to retire from the whole matter, as he would take it over officially and the less I knew about it the better for all of us. I gladly obliged because I did not want to be mixed up in spy-affairs, but on the other hand did not want to miss an opportunity to serve my country. The count had formerly told me that if I could not find a bomb-manufacturer suitable for his business he would go to Prague, Rome and Paris and sell his secret there. This is why I was in a hurry to get the German Intelligence Service in as quickly as possible. But being a man of independent means and decent thinking, I would never have been prepared to earn money out of such a type of business. I never heard of the Danish Count again and never knew what resulted out of his proposals but I have got to add that of course I asked him about Major Draper and was told that Draper worked for the German Intelligence.

This version of Draper's recruitment by the Abwehr may have been some-what sanitized by Thost who may, given his role as an interpreter at Oranienberg concentration camp from October 1944, have thought he had much to lose by admitting his past intelligence links. Certainly Thost's account is somewhat vague about the role of 'the Danish Count', who was Baron [Kristian] de Trairup, an emigré Danish nobleman who was known to MI5 as an arms dealer.

Thost's activities in London were terminated in November 1935 when his visa was not renewed by the Home Office, which had been pressured by Sir Robert Vansittart of the Foreign Office to expel the spy because of his espionage. The irony, of course, is that MI5 was not consulted on the decision to get rid of Thost and, given the opportunity, probably would have argued in his favour, preferably without the necessity to compromise Draper. Almost comically, it was alleged by the Home Office in justi-fication of its expulsion decision that 'information from MI5 indicates that he may be dangerous'. Indeed, the MI5 brief circulated in September 1935 avoided spelling out Draper's role as a double agent:

Since 1933 it has been definitely established that he [Thost] has been in touch with a German espionage organisation, which operates against this country from Hamburg. At that time he enlisted the services of a British ex-officer whom he sent to Hamburg to be inter-viewed, he (Thost) paying his passage money. This officer was sub-sequently supplied with cover addresses in a 'neutral' country and supplied certain information relating to the Royal Air Force, for which he received payment from Germany.

The interception of mail to the Hamburg address revealed that the same postbox was the recipient of correspondence from Jessie Jordan, a 51-year-old hairdresser of Kinloch Street, Dundee. The widow of a German soldier killed during the First World War, Jordan had spent most of her adult life in Germany and had returned to Scotland to open a small business. By the end of 1936 MI5 had established that not only was the hairdresser receiving an unusual amount of mail, but she was posting a great deal too; the bulk of it went to America but she received letters from Holland, France, Germany, Sweden and South America.

Jordan's intercepted mail showed that she was acting as a postbox for the Abwehr so at the end of January 1938 the Deputy Director of MI5's B Division, Guy Liddell, went to Washington DC and explained to the Director of the FBI, J. Edgar Hoover, that Mrs Jordan had been in communication with a 'Mr Kron' in New York. Hoover checked the address and established that 'Herr Kron' was Günther Rumrich, a Sudeten German who had become a naturalized American. His record showed that he had served seven years in the US Army and had been sentenced for desertion and embezzlement of mess funds from Fort Missoula in Montana. The FBI kept Rumrich under surveillance so the Jordan postbox could be monitored but on 16 February 1938 he was arrested by detectives from the Aliens Squad after a tip-off from the State Department. Rumrich had been taken into custody after a bizarre attempt to obtain a quantity of blank American passports. This unexpected development resulted in an admission from Rumrich that he had been directed by Karl Schleuter, a steward aboard SS *Europa*, to obtain fifty passports for the Abwehr.[2]

After his arrest Rumrich confessed that he had been active as a spy for the past twenty months, between May 1936 and February 1938, and had succeeded in passing a considerable amount of intelligence back to Hamburg via Dundee.

Under interrogation Rumrich also implicated Schleuter's girlfriend, Johanna Hofmann, an American from Queens but born in Dresden, who was working on the same liner as a hairdresser. Accordingly, Hofmann was promptly arrested by the FBI and she compromised a dozen other members of the spy-ring, among them Erich Glaser, a soldier based at Mitchell Field, Long Island, with the 18th Reconnaissance Squadron; William Lonkowski, an aircraft mechanic from Silesia; Eleanor Boehme, apparently an occasional courier, resident on Long Island; Werner Gudenberg, a young engineering draughtsman, and Otto Voss, who worked for the

Sikorsky factory at Farmingdale, Long Island; Johann Steuer, an inspector at the Sperry gyroscope bombsight factory in Brooklyn; Johann Koechel, of the Kollmorgan Optical Corporation, engaged in the manufacture of submarine periscopes; Dr Ignatz Giebl, a First World War artillery officer, graduate of Fordham University and a US Army Reserve physician in the Medical Corps; and Theodor Scheutz, a steward on SS *New York*, who disembarked in Havana as soon as the arrests were announced. Also indicted was Erich Phieffer, the network's chief, who allegedly had been based in Wilhelmshaven.

The FBI round-up triggered the arrest in Scotland of Mrs Jordan on 2 March 1938 and she quickly admitted her espionage and confirmed she had received various small sums for her service to the Abwehr. These well-publicized events suggested that Jordan's postbox in Hamburg had been compromised, which in turn appeared to contaminate Draper, so to protect his source Liddell prevailed upon Hoover to exercise discretion over references to the Hamburg postbox and avoid alerting the Germans to the double role played by Draper, who was described in MI5's pleas to the FBI as a patriotic Englishman who should not be compromised. MI5 also engaged in some deliberate distraction by briefing the press that Jordan's unusually heavy foreign mail had alerted her local postman, who had reported his suspicions to the authorities. In reality, of course, she had fallen victim to the domino effect of related cases.[3]

Furthermore, although there was a theoretical need to protect Draper, his utility was long over because of MI5's inability to keep him supplied with information that had any value to the Germans. In short, it simply had not been possible to continue fobbing them off with worthless material, a fundamental flaw in the organization's ability to manage double agents.

When Rumrich's brother Gustav, then a student at Teplice in Czechoslovakia, was arrested, he was found to be in possession of the address of Mrs Gertrud Brandy at 14 Willow Terrace, Dublin; this was the second mail-drop. Clandestine examination of her correspondence showed that she was receiving accurate and therefore dangerous intelligence messages from a French merchant navy officer, Ensign Marc Aubert, who was arrested at the end of 1938 and shot by firing-squad in January 1939. When news of the execution reached Ireland, Mrs Brandy fled to Germany, unhindered by the Irish G-2, which had kept her under surveillance at MI5's request.[4]

The third Abwehr mail-drop to be identified by MI5, inadvertently compromised by Gustav Rumrich, was Mrs Duncombe of 90 Broadhurst Gardens in north London. She became the subject of a Home Office warrant in July 1937 to intercept her mail, an expedient which revealed her instructions the following month to pay a German visitor, Walter Simon, the sum of £5 upon application. He turned out to have visited England three times in recent months and he was arrested in February 1938 on a charge of having failed to register as an alien, which resulted in a prison sentence of five months.[5] Under interrogation, Simon gave an account of his recruitment and mission, and identified his London contact as Mrs Duncombe, a 49-year-old widow of German origin, whose real name was Else Schmidt. She took her own life on 3 March with an overdose of aspirin, three weeks after Simon was arrested. Simon had also been in touch in January 1938 with My Eriksson, a woman who had arrived in Southampton in February 1930 to be employed as a cook and housekeeper in Roehampton, and in a succession of large homes. She was arrested in December 1939 and convicted the next month of various immigration offences, served three months' imprisonment, and then was interned at Holloway and on the Isle of Man.[6]

MI5's investigation of Eriksson confirmed that as well as Simon, she had been in contact with two other agents, one of whom, the Duchesse de Chateau-Thierry, she had introduced to a mysterious Hamburg spymaster, Dr Rantzau. The other, Vera von Schallburg, was a spy who would land in Scotland in September 1940 accompanied by two other Abwehr agents.[7]

The domino effect traceable to Draper was remarkable, and an illustration of what benefits might accrue from a well-managed double agent programme. As well as the ten spies caught in the US, the Hamburg postbox had compromised two other 'live' letter-boxes managed by Jordan, Brandy and Duncombe, who, in turn, had contaminated their correspondents. Perhaps best of all, monitoring of the Hamburg postal address would lead MI5 to Arthur Owens, a supposed SIS asset who was actually working for the Abwehr.[8] As soon as he was arrested, on the first day of hostilities, he volunteered to establish a radio link to Germany, and this not only became the foundation of what would develop into the famous XX system, but also enabled the daily key to the Abwehr's hand cipher, and then the machine cipher, to be solved by cryptanalysts working for MI5's subordinate Radio Security Service at Barnet.

Draper himself was never aware of the full ramifications of his three-year role as a double agent, and during the Second World War he joined the Royal Naval Reserve to serve as a pilot on anti-submarine maritime patrols in Trinidad, Evanton and Machrihanish in Scotland, and on HMS *Wara*, a naval air station in Sierra Leone, where he was promoted to command 777 Squadron.

Eight years after the war Draper repeated his low-flying stunt under London's bridges, and in 1962 published his memoirs, *The Mad Major*[9], in which he provided a fascinating account of his prewar involvement with the Abwehr in a chapter unequivocally entitled *Espionage*, in which he recalled that, having been approached by Dr Thost, he had little idea about how to proceed: 'And so it began. I became a fully-fledged German spy – anyhow in German eyes – though I still had not the faintest notion of what I had to do!' Eventually, Draper decided to confide in his acquaintance, 'Baron K. de Trirop':

> I never knew his occupation but someone hinted that he had been closely connected with the British intelligence service, so I now took him into my confidence.
>
> Like all intelligence people he admitted nothing and told me nothing. In all my dealing with such folk, in England and in Germany, I never learned much from them, and it is only an assumption on my part that the 'Herr Barone', as I called him, had anything to do with MI5. All he would say was 'Do nothing, say nothing. Leave it to me.'
>
> Within 24 hours I received a telephone call asking me to go to one of the best known Service Clubs in London at a certain time, there to ask for Major X (I've forgotten his name). Meantime, at the end of two days as promised, I had telephoned Thost and said: 'Go ahead, I'm your man!'
>
> At the meeting with Major X I was both flattered and honoured to be introduced to no less a person than Sir Percy Sillitoe, the head of MI5. It was all very friendly and informal. In fact, I think they were pleased at the possibility of opening up a new line in counter-espionage. They told me to do whatever Thost requested and keep them informed of everything.

Draper's memory let him down regarding his meeting with Vernon Kell, mistakenly identified as Sillitoe (who did not join MI5 until 1946), but the rest of his version is largely accurate and amounts to the very first personal account given by any MI5 double agent deployed against the Abwehr. Certainly Draper fully understood the nature of his role and reproduced

21

a questionnaire received in July 1937 to which he supplied a detailed answer.

> I know nothing of the actual report prepared by MI5. I just signed, as usual, on the dotted line, and there were no further communications on either side for many weeks.

Draper also recalled his visit to Germany when he had been entertained by Dr Hanfstangl and was briefed in Hamburg about the Abwehr's intelligence requirements concerning information about aircraft performance, armaments, production figures and the composition and size of RAF squadrons.

> On my return to London I reported full details to MI5, handed over the two addresses and thereafter acted entirely on instructions from British Intelligence.
> In one of my files there are copies of most of the letters sent by me to 'L. Saunders. Post Box 629, Hamburg.' Unfortunately there is only one reply from Germany. The rest were duly handed over as they came in.

Significantly, Draper says 'MI5 had agreed that any money "Mr Saunders" sent should be mine', and these payments arrived in the form of £5 notes mailed in envelopes bearing English postmarks, an indication that the Abwehr had established an as yet undetected paymaster somewhere in the country. However, despite two letters sent in December 1937, there was no acknowledgement from Hamburg.

> Had they tumbled to the double-crosser and were they planning some trap? Nearly a year passed. It was most distressing to find that my little private income had ceased; nor would MI5 allow me to write again.

Draper's double game came to an abrupt conclusion in October 1938 when, at the trial of Gunther Rumrich in Manhattan, the defendant had testified that he had 'received instructions to say that he was working for England. In case of apprehension I was not to make any reference to Germany ... I was to say I was working for Major Christopher Draper of London.'

This unexpected and unwelcome disclosure was also a surprise to Draper, who acknowledged 'I had never heard of Rumrich or Mrs Jessie Jordan, neither of whom had anything to do with me.'

There was I, branded a Nazi spy. The first action I took was to get in touch with my contact in MI5. My only comfort was that they knew the truth, but they instructed me to say nothing.

Having reluctantly accepted that its first double-cross operation was well and truly blown, ironically by the Abwehr and the FBI, it was agreed that Draper's reputation, tarnished by press speculation, should be restored. Accordingly, arrangements were made for the Air Ministry to announce formally that 'it is officially stated that the loyalty and integrity of Major Christopher Draper DSC, late of the Royal Air Force, is not in any way called into question'.

Until the publication of his memoirs, Draper himself remained silent about his remarkable espionage experience, and never knew that he had pioneered the famous double-cross system which played such an important role in deceiving the Axis in the second German war. Draper died in London in January 1979, aged 96, but there is nothing to suggest in the files that he was ever told that his covert activities as a double agent had been responsible for one of the great triumphs of wartime espionage.

Chapter 3

Olga Gray

She has done a great service to her country.

[Mr Justice Hawke, March 1938]

Employed as a shorthand typist by the Communist Party of Great Britain (CPGB), Olga Gray was the 27-year-old daughter of a *Daily Mail* sub-editor, who in 1931 undertook a mission for MI5 to penetrate the organization and discover its secret channel of communication with Moscow. Her target was 46-year-old Percy Glading, the Party's National Organizer, who had been a founder member and activist since he was 17 years old. In April 1925 he had travelled to India under several false names, and had not returned until June the following year, when he became active in the Workers Welfare League of India and other cover organizations. A police raid on the King Street headquarters in September 1925 provided more evidence that his radical politics had crossed the line and encroached on subversion and espionage.

Olga's background was quite ordinary, apart from the loss of her father during the First World War. She was born in November 1906 at Chorlton-cum-Hardy, a Manchester suburb, and was the second eldest of the seven children of Charles Gray and his wife Ada. Her older brother Edward died in 1911 at the age of 5 and her five surviving siblings were Marjory, Victor, Lily, Frederick and Charles James. Their father had enlisted with the 11th Battalion, the Royal Warwicks, as a private soldier but was promoted to corporal and then commissioned as a subaltern. He died in December 1917 from wounds suffered during the battle of Ypres, when Olga was just 11.[1]

Olga's testimony, initially set out in a formal witness statement dated 28 January 1938 and presented at the Old Bailey trial, came as a shock to Glading and his fellow defendants, who were charged with stealing secrets from the Woolwich Arsenal and had not anticipated the appearance of the prosecution's surprise witness. Although Glading had been dismissed from his post at the Arsenal in October 1928, he had remained in contact with other members of the staff, and enrolled them in his Soviet-sponsored spy-ring.[2]

My name is 'Miss X'. I was born in Manchester but lived in Birmingham and worked as a secretary there until 1931, when I met an officer of the Intelligence Department, War Office, and agreed to work under instructions. Under instructions I came to London and joined the Friends of the Soviet Union. I worked there voluntarily until 1932 and as a matter of course was required to join the Communist Party of Great Britain.

In August 1932 Isobel Brown of the Communist Anti-War Movement asked me to do a part-time paid job as typist in the Anti-War Movement.

In May 1934, when I was still working there, Harry Pollitt, then Secretary and Leader of the British Communist Party, asked me to undertake a special mission 'carrying messages from here to other countries'. Glading interviewed me on the same subject. I left England on 11 June 1934 for Paris where I met Glading, was given certain instructions and proceeded to India where I handed over money and messages to certain Communist leaders. I arrived back in London on 28 July 1934.

I then took temporary employment until February 1935 when I was approached by Glading and asked to take on a paid job as Secretary to Harry Pollitt at Communist Party Headquarters, 16 King Street, London WC. The work was very hard and after three or four months I informed the officer of the Intelligence Department that I found the work too great a strain and would prefer to drop my connection with the Communist Party and return to ordinary life. About July 1935, on the grounds of ill health, I resigned my position as Harry Pollitt's secretary. I started work with a private advertising firm on 11 November 1935. On instructions I continued to maintain purely friendly contact with Pollitt and Glading. I saw Henry Pollitt and Percy Glading from time to time, and on 17 February 1937 I lunched with Percy Glading and he asked me if I would like to live away from home and be willing to find a flat where I could live, of which I should be the nominal tenant. He told me I could continue with my present ordinary employment and all that was required was that I should live at the flat, and make it available for two men and himself to meet and talk when they wished. He said that he would be responsible for the rent of the flat, telephone and any other incidental expenses. He did not give me any indication of what he and the other men wanted to talk about. I thought it was probably something to do with Glading's work in the colonial section of the League Against Imperialism. I telephoned the Officer for whom I had worked in the Intelligence Department and he asked me to agree to the scheme if I had no serious objection.

After a while I accordingly agreed to Glading's plan, and he gave me the following instructions in regard to the flat: Firstly, it must not be in a block because there must be no porter; and secondly, it was not to be in the Notting Hill Gate district.

In due course I found, and Glading approved, a suitable flat at 82 Holland Road which I leased as from 1st April 1937 from Sladden, Stewart & Powell, House Agents of Holland Park Avenue, at an agreed rent of £100 per annum.

Glading gave me the money monthly in cash and I paid the rent. He also agreed to the purchase of £60 worth of furniture on hire purchase and gave me monthly instalments to pay.

Glading told me to have made three sets of keys of the flat and to give him two sets. He also undertook to warn me before visiting the flat.

On the night of 21 April 1937 Glading came to the flat with a man he called 'Mr Peters'. They stopped about three quarters of an hour. Nothing was discussed in front of me and I gathered they had merely come so that 'Mr Peters' could meet me. He was obviously a foreigner, but I cannot say what nationality.

At various times later Glading told me scraps of information about this man. He said he was an Austrian and had been in a monastery in Austria at the beginning of the war, that he had fought in the Russian cavalry, and rose to be a captain.

On 19 April 1937 Glading called on me and in the course of conversation mentioned another man to me in connection with the work, He said he was 'a small man and rather bumptious in manner', that he disliked him personally, but had to tolerate him for business reasons.

On the night of 20 May 1937, Glading called on me at 82 Holland Road and suggested I should take a new job with shorter hours, but that I should first take a fortnight's holiday for which he would pay. He told me that on my return I should learn from another comrade something about photography so that I could do work for him. He suggested I should get a part-time job and he would make up my money to £5 a week. At that time Glading inferred there would be photographic work to do about once a week.

Glading pointed out that this work would be very secret and there would also be drawings. I duly left the firm for which I was working and went on a holiday in June 1937.

On 4 August 1937 Glading called on me and warned me that in about a week's time some definite last instructions would be given regarding the work I was required to do. I had in the meantime returned from my holiday, but had not yet started work.

On 18 August 1937 Glading called at my flat accompanied by an individual whom he introduced to me as 'Mr Stevens'. He told me that Stevens' wife would come to the flat about twice a month to do the necessary photographic work and that I was to help. He then said that the work would start in October.

On 11 October 1937 Glading told me to get a long refectory table as soon as possible as the gate-legged table already there would not be steady enough for photography. Actually four days later, he told me he had already bought the table from Maples and he would be at the flat the next morning, 16 October 1937, to take it in.

On 13 October 1937 Glading arrived at the flat in a taxi with Mr Stevens and a woman he introduced as his wife. (I am not certain the name was Stevens but it sounded like that.) They brought a case which contained the camera and complete apparatus. Mr and Mrs Stevens were obviously foreigners. Mrs Stevens, whose Christian name seemed to be Mary, spoke to her husband in French.

A further meeting was arranged for Monday 18th October at 7.00pm to test the photographic apparatus preliminary to carrying out the first 'job' on Thursday, 21 October at 7.00pm.

On 18 October Mr and Mrs Stevens called at the flat without Glading where for 3½ hours they carried out elaborate experiments, photographing maps of London Underground railways, and after the photography had been done and the films developed they told me to give the films to Glading the following day at lunchtime.

On 21 October 1937 Mrs Stevens entered the flat with a large plan she said had to 'be photographed in sections' and that forty-two exposures would be necessary. The films were developed and left in the bathroom to dry. Mrs Stevens left the flat at 10.35pm taking the plans in a bundle of rolled newspapers. After she had left the flat I copied the name and number of the plan from the negative. I was not in the room while the whole of the actual photography was taking place; I was making tea. Mrs Stevens was very nervous and fidgety and asked me to have my tea in the bedroom.

On 28 October 1937 Glading and I went to the Ford Exhibition. He returned to 82 Holland Road at about 9.45pm. At 11 o'clock Glading left the flat, taking the negatives with him.

On the 2nd November 1937 Glading told me that Mr Stevens and his wife were going back to Moscow almost at once owing to the illness of Mr Stevens' daughter. He said he did not think there would be any more work this side of Christmas, but the apparatus would stay, and he and I would practise so that we could do the photographic side of the work later, by ourselves.

Some while afterwards Glading came and took away the stand for the camera as he said he wanted to do some work at home and could not get the right stand. He said that he had a 'rush job' of copying and it had been difficult because he had to balance his own camera on a pile of books. Glading told me during this visit that he did not think Mrs Stevens would ever return to this country, and that Stevens would only return for a week. He inferred that some other man would take over Stevens' job here.

On 12 January 1938 Glading told me that he had a special job to do at his house at the week-end of 15–16 January. He said he thought it would be a book of about 200 pages.

On the 20th January 1938, Glading telephoned me at my office to say that he wanted to lunch with me the next day and he asked me to have my flat free for something important in the evening. I telephoned the Intelligence Department and warned them of this.

On the 21st January 1938, I lunched with Glading at the Windsor Castle Bar and he told me to get back to my flat at 6.00pm as there was some urgent photography to be done. I thought he said that he had to return the thing photographed by 8.15pm at Charing Cross. Later at my flat I learned that he had gone there early to set up the apparatus and was intending to fetch the object to be photographed at 8.15pm. The hurry was that he had to get it photographed and return the original the same evening.

All this information I telephoned as soon as I was able to the Intelligence Department.

While Glading was fixing up the apparatus in my flat at 6 o'clock on the evening of 21st January, he told me that he was very worried that neither Mr Stevens nor the other man he was expecting had turned up. He was running short of money and moreover had 'stuff' parked all over London waiting to be collected.

This eyewitness evidence, combined with additional damning proof of espionage obtained at their arrest, ensured the conviction of Glading and two of his co-conspirators, who were sentenced to terms of imprisonment. While the jury learned how Soviet spies had manipulated Glading and his colleagues, it was not given the full picture, nor even a hint of the elaborate operation conducted over several years to monitor the CPGB, both with technical surveillance equipment, telephone and mail intercepts, and with the deployment of deep-cover agents, like Olga Gray, to penetrate every level of the organization. By the time Olga had been recruited in 1931, the CPGB had been under scrutiny for several years, and Glading had been watched intermittently since 1925, when he visited India to make contact with subversive nationalists. To complete his credentials as a national security threat, Glading had attended the Lenin School in Moscow under an alias from October 1929 to March 1930.

One of the first of the Security Service agents directed against the CPGB had been the novelist Jimmy Grierson Dickson, an Air Ministry civil servant and former RAF officer who posed as a Communist sympathizer and had deliberately cultivated Glading. Born in August 1900, Dickson would become well-known as a criminologist, the author of *Soho Racket* and *Cain Business* in 1935, *Traitors' Market* in 1936, and *Devil's Torch* and *Design for Treason* in 1937, followed by *Knight's Gambit* and *Seven Screens* in 1950. His 1958 study of serial killers, *Murder by Numbers*, remains a classic in the field of forensic analysis.[3]

Dickson's MI5 case officer was the legendary Maxwell Knight, a brilliantly intuitive intelligence officer who exercised a remarkable talent for identifying and recruiting agents to insinuate themselves into extremist political groups. He was also a novelist, and the author of several 'penny-dreadfuls', such as *Crime Cargo*.[4] Curiously Knight, who designated Dickson his source M/3, employed other writers on his staff: his deputy Jack Bingham would publish several thrillers, including *Night's Black Agent*[5], and his colleague Bill Younger wrote spy stories under the *nom-de-plume* William Mole.[6] In 1930 Claud Sykes, while acting as one of Max Knight's agents codenamed M/S, had penned *The Secrets of Modern Spying* under the pen-name Vigilant.[7] This was followed in 1933 by *Richthofen: The Red Knight of the Air*.[8] Another agent, *Daily Express* gossip columnist Tom Driberg, was M/8.[9] Finally, Knight's subordinate Norman Himsworth had spent his early career as a provincial newspaper journalist on the *Lancashire Evening Post* in Preston.

Knight's problem as an intelligence professional was the age-old challenge of retaining the interest of the target organization while running a double agent 'dangle'. Glading was strongly suspected of espionage but how could he be entrapped without endangering authentic secrets? In July 1936 an internal MI5 report highlighted the obstacle:

> M/3 had an interview with Percy Glading on the evening of Wednesday, 10 June. The meeting was at Glading's request. He was anxious to know if M/3 could ascertain from his 'friend at the Air Ministry' whether there had been any further incidents involving Communists employed there. Glading was very frank with M/3 and confessed that he was dissatisfied with his information about the Air Ministry. He said: 'There are too many freelance comrades doing illegal work.'
>
> M/3 said that Glading definitely appeared to be worried and he formed the impression that Glading has got so much to do that he is in danger of losing touch.
>
> M/3 pointed out to Glading that this enquiry was a very tricky one, but that in due course, when an opportunity presented itself, he would do what he could.

In September 1936 Dickson was able to implicate Glading in an Official Secrets case, that of Eric Camp, a draughtsman employed by the Gloster Aircraft Company, who had been arrested for passing information to M. Sokoloff, a Soviet employee of ARCOS.[10] According to Knight's report, M/3

> this day had a conversation with Glading, during which the case of Eric Joseph Gardner Camp[11] Camp is accused of making notes while employed at the Gloster Aircraft Co. Ltd, calculated to be useful to an enemy; he is at the same time known to have had contact with M. Sokoloff of the Engineering Dept of ARCOS Ltd. With regard to Camp, Glading is stated to have said: 'they are trying to make him out to be a communist and Harry has been in an awful state about it, he has had an enquiry and Camp is definitely not a Party member'.

31

Glading went on to say that he had heard from a reliable source that the man had bragged to his wife that he was a communist and working for the Soviets; he had heard that Camp had been 'given away', and that 'the Dicks knew just what they wanted to find and where to find it'. He got quite excited here, but then suddenly had an attack of caution and pointed out with emphasis the reasons why Camp should not have been spying for the Soviets; it appeared that Glading knew a great deal more about the case than he should, and was desperately anxious not to let the informant think that the party as such had any connection. He said at one point 'till all this happened I did not even know he was at Handley Page's or De Havilland's'.

A few weeks later, in November 1936, the situation remained unchanged, with Glading expressing dissatisfaction with Dickson's failure to develop his supposed colleague at the Air Ministry:

Percy Glading sent for M/3 recently and an interview took place on 10 November 1936. Glading was anxious to know whether M/3 had heard anything about the RAF experiencing trouble with certain metal parts in our new fast fighting machines. It appears that Glading had heard that certain metal parts had been found to be unable to stand up to the stress of the acute angle that these machines leave the ground. M/3 said that he had no precise knowledge and that he was not inclined to think that this was the case as he understood that finished machines went to the Experimental Station at Martlesham Heath before being taken over by the RAF, and that the tests at the Experimental Station were very rigorous. However, he promised to try to ascertain if these facts were true.

M/3 was but one of Knight's assets, and these encounters, when Glading the spy posed very specific questions, illustrated the inherent counter-intelligence dilemma. If questionnaires remained unanswered, the spies would probably seek the information elsewhere by recruiting sources as yet unknown. On the other hand, to give accurate answers to every query could jeopardize real secrets. The difficult balance to strike was to supply enough 'chickenfeed' to keep the target hooked, while simultaneously shielding important classified material.

Other assets included M/1, Graham Pollard, proprietor of the Soho bookshop Birrell & Garnett, and a part-time journalist, whose wife Kay Beauchamp was also employed by the *Daily Worker*. He was the son of the respected Oxford historian Albert Pollard, and was an active member of the CPGB's St Pancras branch and submitted regular reports to Knight, who was known to his subordinates as 'Captain King'.

Another asset, M/2, was Mona Maund, a well-known union activist in the Association of Women Clerks and Secretaries. Aged 37 and unmarried in 1932 when she began her life as a mole, it would be six years before she was invited to work at King Street, always unaware that there were others working in parallel.

As well as engaging in conventional counter-intelligence, seeking to identify the CPGB's senior management and the precise roles played by particular individuals, such as the mysterious Scotsman Bob Stewart, who was a key member of the all-powerful Control Commission and was thought to be the Party's clandestine link between the underground cadres of uncarded Party members and the embassy *rezidentura*.[12] Knight's task was to gain access to the branch membership lists and find out the true identities of those members who operated under aliases or had been granted 'Party names' to protect them.

M/4 was a CPGB member based in Liverpool, and M/5 was another Party insider, based in Glasgow. M/7 was a barrister, Vivian Hancock-Nunn, who acted for the CPGB and was the Party's unofficial legal adviser.

One of the hurdles encountered by Knight was the CPGB's policy of referring all membership applications to Moscow for screening. This was a mysterious process because, as a security measure, it was intended to prevent hostile penetration, and the only people to avoid the vetting procedure were well-established members of the Young Communist League (YCL), who were automatically promoted at the age of 18. Seeking to exploit this potential loophole, Knight adopted the expedient of recruiting teenagers, such as Graham Pollard, to volunteer for the YCL. Another example was Tom Driberg, the future Member of Parliament and chairman of the Labour Party, who much later would be elevated to the peerage as Lord Bradwell.

The concealment of Gray's identity in court as 'Miss X' caused a public sensation, but of course she was well known within the Party, and the trial terminated her usefulness as a source. Although the CPGB leadership realized it had been duped, there was continuing uncertainty about the extent of the damage she had inflicted. Clearly she had compromised the Party's connections in India, and had been of immense value to the

British-managed Delhi Intelligence Bureau, as well as the Indian Political Intelligence office in London, but what of the other information with which she had been entrusted as a courier? One such item that would be of lasting value to the British authorities was her disclosure that the Party's secret wireless transmitter, based in south London and used to communicate with Moscow in a hitherto unbroken cipher, was dependent on a book system based on *Treasure Island*. This breakthrough enabled the Party's messages to be read by Whitehall cryptographers, an invaluable source codenamed MASK. This traffic was read successfully by GC&CS cryptanalysts led by John Tiltman, who between 1935 and 1937 provided MI5 with access to the Party's most secret communications, including the messages sent by Bob Stewart. The two main CPGB radio operators, Stephen Wheeton and William Morrison, were placed under MI5 surveillance, and study of the messages proved once and for all that the CPGB was not a legitimate, independent political party, but was a wholly controlled instrument of the Kremlin, regarded in Moscow as a branch of the NKVD.

The imprisonment of Percy Glading would have lasting consequences, especially for Glading personally. He was already separated from his Spanish wife Elizabeth at the time of his arrest, and living with Rosa Scharr, who had a husband named York. She changed her name by deed poll to live with Glading and bore him a daughter, Jane, but York did not divorce her until Glading's conviction.

Olga's remarkable mission to penetrate the CPGB, which paid off so handsomely for MI5, would not end well for her. Although her true name was protected during Glading's trial, his CPGB colleagues were well aware of who she was, and she feared for her life. Of no further use to MI5, she was rewarded with a severance payment of £500, and left to herself to find work. In September 1939 she was employed as a shorthand typist, lodging with a chartered mechanical engineer, Raymond Billingshurst, and his wife Edith at The Hyde in Maidensgrove, a hamlet 5 miles northwest of Henley-on-Thames. During the war Olga became an ambulance driver, and in 1944 she met Stanley Simons, a Royal Canadian Air Force officer, on the London tube and they married in Chelsea in May 1945.

Three years younger than Olga, Simons had no connection to the world of espionage. He had been born in Chatham, Ontario, and had emigrated to Buffalo in the United States in 1926. He then moved to Detroit to work as a salesman but returned to Canada on the outbreak of war.

After their marriage Olga and Stanley lived for several years in Surrey, where both their children, Valerie in 1946 and Shane Stanley David in March 1953, were born. They all travelled to Canada and the United States at least twice, in December 1947 and March 1948, before they emigrated permanently, and in 1958 they were living with his parents at Lindsay Street South in Victoria County, Ontario. By 1963 Stanley was working as a civil servant, and Olga was a public school secretary and part-time journalist on the local newspaper, and they were living at Dixon Road in the York district of Toronto.

In 1986 Max Knight's biographer, Tony Masters, the author of *The Man Who Was M*[13], tracked her down and interviewed her for the *Mail on Sunday*. Alarmed by the unexpected publicity, Olga took to her bed and had a breakdown. She died in July 1990, in the Etobicoke district of Toronto, always anxious that she might be traced by the Soviets. Her husband died the following year.

Although Olga of course knew what she had accomplished in terms of securing the conviction of Glading and two of his accomplices, she was never indoctrinated into MASK and therefore never fully understood the profound impact of her own espionage. Not only did the MASK traffic provide an invaluable insight into the CPGB's most confidential deliberations and decisions, but it proved beyond all doubt that the party was not a legitimate political movement, but the instrument of a foreign power. When the CPGB's illicit wireless operator William Morrison[14] was interviewed by MI5's Max Knight and Jane Sissmore in August 1939, a note was placed on his personal file, setting out what the MASK operation had accomplished:

From 1934 onwards, SIS and MI5 were aware that there was constant illicit wireless transmission between London and Moscow. The station was located in January 1935 and from that time MI5 were able to obtain every message that was transmitted from the Comintern to this country and the replies. By this means were found out the exact amounts of the subsidies to various subversive organizations here – the Communist Party of course and the *Daily Worker* – the identity of Soviet couriers and the policy pursued by the Comintern in connection with the general election here, the civil war in Spain and other political events.

During the period January 1935 to October 1937 there were three different locations for the illegal transmission centre and a number of changes in the technical personnel. By careful watching we were able to establish the identity of the personnel and the very few members of the Communist Party here who were allowed to deal with them.

Although Olga will be remembered for her role as the peroxide blonde who gave sensational evidence at Percy Glading's trial at the Old Bailey, and received praise from the judge for her conduct, few were ever allowed to know the real importance of what she accomplished.

Chapter 4

Arnold Deutsch

Arrived in the UK on a genuine passport under his own
name in 1933/34. He was still sending important naval
information to Moscow in April 1937. Highly successful
agent for naval and RAF material.

[Walter Krivitsky, January 1940[1]]

According to his personal file, lodged in the KGB headquarters and
partially declassified in Moscow in 1987, Arnold Deutsch was an Austrian
psychologist, and one of the most successful spies of all time, responsible
for the recruitment of seventeen agents in England during the period
between April 1934 and November 1937 when he acted as the NKVD's
illegal *rezident* in London. Ostensibly a 27-year-old post-graduate student
at London University, and renting a small apartment at 7 Lawn Road
Flats, Hampstead, he lived under his own name with his wife Josefine
Ruhel and baby daughter Ninette Elisabeth, but was known to his covert
contacts only as OTTO. To their casual acquaintances, Deutsch was an
adherent of the controversial psychologist Wilhelm Reich, ran a small
publishing business, Münster Verlag, which published his research, and
had studied Chemistry, Physics and Philosophy under Professor Alfred
Adler. He was devoted to his wife, who looked after their baby, born in
London in May 1935, although Josefine was also a Soviet intelligence
officer and qualified radio operator. She was three years older than her
husband, and they had married in Vienna in March 1929.

In contrast to the voluminous NKVD file, the dossier on Deutsch
compiled by MI5 is very thin, and opens with a reference to him made in
January 1940 by the GRU (or 4th Department) defector Walter Krivitsky,
who was interviewed in London by several MI5 officers, among them Jane
Sissmore, who wrote a short report dated 25 January about Deutsch:

Information regarding Naval and RAF matters were obtained through
an independent source (Alfred Deutsch) – nickname STEFAN,

an Austrian D.sc (Chemistry). This was a man who came to this country with his wife and had many connections in University circles – about 1935.[2]

Evidently Krivitsky was not impressed by Deutsch, who was apparently thought 'bumptious' by both Mally *and* Glading, but by linking him to the famous Woolwich Arsenal case, in which the CPGB National Organizer Percy Glading had been convicted of espionage in 1938, he identified at least one spy-ring which had been directed by Deutsch.[3]

Alfred Deutsch (Austrian doctor of Chemistry) arrived in the UK in 1933/34. He was bumptious, and Percy Glading did not like him. [Paul] Hardt complained about his manner and said he was difficult to deal with. Records regarding Deutsch should be procurable from the police as he travelled on his own passport with his wife who had a child in the UK. (Deutsch's nickname is 'Stefan'.) His wife was a radio operator. 'Stefan' arrived here alone in 1933/34. His wife at that time was being trained at Abramoff's radio school. Later, in 1934, she came to the UK and worked on OGPU staff. 'Stefan' brought his mother-in-law to the UK. He first came to the UK with [Ignaty] Reiff, his chief, when the 4th Department was waiting for important material which was received from UK on 12 May 1935. Orloff Head of Fleet OGPU refused to hand this to 4th Department.

Evidently the OGPU had been reluctant to share its London report-ing with the GRU. Krivitsky explained that 'Reiff was representative of OGPU in the UK in 1931–34. His very able assistant was Deutsch. On his return to Moscow they made him chief of a section dealing only with Deutsch's material.'

In a further summary, dated the same day, Krivitsky indicated the quality and importance of the intelligence coming from the London *rezidentura*, and described the sensitivity with which it was handled, recalling that

In April 1937, when [Krivitsky] was in Moscow he was in the 4th Department waiting with Orloff, who was the head of the Russian Navy, to see some material obtained by Deutsch which was in the OGPU offices. They waited a long time but the material was not sent over. [Krivitsky] said that it was an unheard-of thing to keep Orloff waiting and still more surprising that the OGPU office decided not to send the material over, but that Orloff must go over to the OGPU office and see it, which Orloff did.

The head of the English Department of the OGPU at this time was a man named Reif or similar spelling, who was the OGPU representative in England between 1931 and 1936. Then he was recalled to Moscow and made head of the English Department there. Reif received this information from Dr Alfred Deutsch who was his assistant in London. On this occasion [Krivitsky] stated quite definitely that Deutsch was an agent of Hardt.

On 30 January 1940 Sissmore clarified more details about Deutsch:

I gave [Krivitsky] more details of Arnold Deutsch yesterday, and he said that this was the man to whom he had previously referred to as Alfred Deutsch. He will be able to be absolutely sure when he sees the photograph.

He says that he now remembers that Arnold Deutsch came over through the good offices of a relative.

I showed him a photograph of David Biering who he says was definitely an OGPU agent and had done a great deal of OGPU work in Austria.

I showed him a photograph of Paul Eisler. He said he had seen this man before, but he could not remember anything about him.

It is interesting that Paul Eisler came over here and gave as a reference Oscar Deutsch and that David Biering was a friend of Paul Eisler. Now we find that a highly important Soviet agent is a cousin of Oscar Deutsch and through Oscar Deutsch obtained permission to remain here.

Krivitsky also explained how the illegal *rezident* was likely to be in occasional, discreet contact with the legal *rezident* at the embassy, who at that time had been Anton Schuster, operating under his own name. In mentioning Deutsch, MI5 noted that after Schuster, Deutsch had worked under Theodore Mally (alias Paul Hardt):

In June 1937 he went abroad to report to Krivitsky that a woman OGPU agent in London had lost her diary and it was feared the whole organization might be compromised. Krivitsky cannot remember anything about the woman except that her hair was always untidy and she was apt to get very agitated and nervous. If this description fits Edith Tudor-Hart he thought it might be she.

As MI5 attempted to forensically reconstruct Deutsch's activities in London, it acquired a copy of his Home Office file which revealed that he had been abroad twice, apparently to make visits to Vienna, once in 1935, returning in November, and again the following year, landing in June 1936. He made a third journey abroad in September 1937, accompanied by his wife and daughter, and came back in November.

The Home Office recorded his various addresses as Ormonde Court, the Vandyke Hotel in the Cromwell Road, and the Strand Palace Hotel. His file also detailed his connection with his uncle Oscar, a Hungarian immigrant, which dated back to October 1936. An immensely wealthy businessman, Oscar ran a chain of a hundred cinemas across the country, and had plans to expand by building another seventy:

> Oscar Deutsch, Governing Director of Odeon Theatres Ltd, of 22 Bennets Hill, Birmingham, applied for permission to employ Dr Arnold Deutsch of 85 Ormonde Court, Upper Richmond Road, SW15 as an Industrial Psychologist at a salary of £250 a year. Oscar Deutsch stated that he had not employed Arnold previously and that his offer of services was obtained through a friend. Oscar wished to employ Arnold permanently and stated that Dr Arnold Deutsch was responsible for the idea and also for working out the necessary plans in connection with the Industrial Psychology Dept, and he had made an intensive study of Psychology in relation to the Cinema. From the applications received, Dr Deutsch was the most suitable candidate, although others would be employed in the Department.

Deutsch's formal application was submitted a fortnight later, supported by Otto Schiff of the Association of Jewish Refugees. In December the Ministry of Labour minuted that Deutsch's confidential secretary had been interviewed, and had revealed that Arnold was distantly related to Oscar, and that they had never actually met prior to his arrival in England.

> Oscar had consulted the Institute of Industrial Psychology which was prepared to act for him as consultants at a fee of 600 guineas. He thought he would get better results by having his own psychologist, who would be required to investigate the suitability of sites for cinemas, popularity of certain types of films, lighting, colour schemes, etc. The post would be a full-time one and it was planned to have a department which would eventually employ others in this study. Arnold proposed to give up his studies if employed by Oscar.

It appeared that no effort had been made to obtain a suitable British subject, although when the vacancy became known in circles interested in Industrial Psychology, applications were received by post and Oscar interviewed the applicants. A representative of the Birmingham University Appointments Board had expressed the opinion that there should be no difficulty in obtaining a qualified British psychologist for this post and therefore it was not considered that the employment of the alien should be recommended.

Accordingly, Deutsch's application was rejected, but this prompted an appeal submitted by the eminent barrister Neville Laski QC, who claimed that Oscar had offered to spend a minimum of £1,000 a year on his psychology department, and would undertake to employ an additional two British psychologists. This extravagant suggestion was also rejected. The latest proposal was for Dr Deutsch to set up a consultancy business, Cinema Research & Development Ltd, with Mr S.C. Joseph of Motor Components Ltd, which would study the cinema industry and be contracted by Odeon for an annual fee of £1,000. The private company would, according to the scheme submitted,

1. Research statistics in relation to the industry;
2. Research regarding the 'likes and dislikes' of the population in different places in regard to particular types of films;
3. Research in connection with programmes, etc.;
4. Research in connection with the influence of film on children and composition of educational films;
5. Research in connection with light and sound; and
6. The acquisition and development of inventions in connection with technical problems.

The new company would have a capital of £2,000, with Arnold owning a share worth £300. He also had plans 'to rent a West End Office and to employ two scientific collaborators, graduates of London University and a typist'.

Dr Deutsch possessed about £1,000 in this country, partly deposited with Barclays Bank at the High Street Kensington branch, and partly with the National Provincial Bank Head Office. Dr Deutsch had as referees Professor Cyril Burt, head of the Psychological Department of the University of London, London University College, and Mr Walter Mutch, chief film critic of the *Daily Mail* and *Sunday Pictorial* of 27 Ranelagh Gardens, Barnes, W13.

It was also stated that Dr Deutsch 'was also interested in the technical development of the Cinema Industry and had invented a Port device designed to increase the volume of light thrown on to the screen when projecting films, an improved means of indicating vacant seats in darkened theatres, more practical ash-trays for cinemas, etc. It was intended to grant non-exclusive licences in regard to these inventions.'

This proposal, described as 'an ingenious wangle', was rejected by the Home Office in April 1937, and a further plea to the Ministry of Labour was declined in June when the police were instructed 'to ascertain what he is doing, how he is being maintained, and what are his plans'. In September 1937 the police visited Deutsch at his flat in Putney and on that occasion he declared his intention to leave for Paris from Victoria within a fortnight, with no intention of returning. However, he was back on 3 November, carrying a letter from Oscar:

> I do not think that in the circumstances the Home Office will refuse to grant you a permit to live in this country and continue your research studies and I may say I am prepared personally to make you a monthly allowance of £30 which, with your own funds, should be ample ...

Deutsch was granted permission to stay for a month, but left a week later from Folkestone, never to be seen again by the British authorities. When Krivitsky identified Deutsch as having been the NKVD's illegal *rezident* in London an all-ports bulletin was issued to alert MI5 to his return, and MI5's Kenneth Younger discouraged the Ministry of Information in November 1940 when Oscar Deutsch and his cinema managers were enrolled in a project to monitor the morale of Odeon audiences. This clearly was a topic of interest to an enemy, and Younger's intervention ensured the collaboration with Oscar, who anyway died in 1941, ceased.

In subsequent years MI5 regarded Deutsch as a priority and sought the help of liaison services, such as the FBI, to pursue leads and offer Deutsch's photograph, taken from his Home Office Aliens Registration record, to potential witnesses. Among those who were approached in the hope of corroborating Krivitsky's material were Leon Helfand, who defected in Paris in 1940; the celebrated NKVD defector Alexander Orlov, who said in 1955 he 'did not know this individual'; and the NKVD defectors Hede Massing and Elizabeth Poretsky.[4] However, some new information was elicited from Jacob Albam, a Soviet spy convicted in the United States in 1957. When interviewed in Lewisburg federal penitentiary in August 1957 he had much to say about Deutsch, whom he recognized as the NKVD officer who had recruited him in Paris in October 1937, where he had turned up bearing a letter from his brother Abram, then running his own import-export business in Vienna. In his distinctive handwriting Albam recommended that Jacob engage in 'anti-Hitler work'. Albam would later insist that he 'had no reason to believe that the work referred to by Abram was actually connected with Soviet intelligence activities'. His first task was to allow his address in the Square de Moulin to be used as a letter-drop, and he was instructed not to open any mail with envelopes marked 'AB' or 'SB'. Thereafter, once a week Deutsch would call or meet at a neighbourhood café to collect the mail.

Deutsch told Albam that he lived in a hotel and that receiving mail at the hotel was not convenient for him. Deutsch also told Albam that he was writing a book and spent a lot of time doing research work in the libraries.

After a month Deutsch introduced Albam to his replacement, a woman named Bella, who 'spoke only a little French and preferred to speak Russian'. When he was reunited with Deutsch and his wife in Moscow, he remembered that the couple had the unusual habit of tapping messages to each other on the table in Morse code. He also recalled that their daughter, known as Nina, had developed epilepsy, and Deutsch's main occupation was researching and writing a book on 'a history of the cinema relative to American and European movies in German', while ostensibly employed as a translator by the Academy of Agriculture and Research.

Additionally, the FBI commented:

> In connection with Albam's instructions to proceed to Moscow in 1938, his Soviet contact instructed him to proceed to Antwerp, Belgium, and take a Soviet freighter for Leningrad. He did so and found that among the passengers were Josefine Deutsch, wife of Arnold Deutsch, and her female child. Albam arrived in Leningrad and then travelled to Moscow by train. He was met in Moscow by Arnold Deutsch and thereafter placed in contact with a Soviet named George whose last name was not known to Albam.

When questioned further, Albam recalled that he had known Deutsch as 'Stefan Lang', whom he described as 'an Austrian who spoke French with a marked German accent'.

After Albam returned to Moscow in 1938 he saw Deutsch on a few occasions. On one occasion, Deutsch introduced him to a young man later identified as the brother of the wife of Vasili Zubilin.[5] Also at one of these meetings Deutsch showed Albam a passport with various markings which he indicated were in part forgeries. Deutsch stated that he was a handwriting expert and could copy any handwriting. Deutsch also told him that he had gone to school in England but had never been in the United States.

By February 1958 almost all trace of Arnold Deutsch had disappeared, but Nina was found by the CIA to be living in a Soviet housing block in Vienna's Obere Donaustrasse, where she was registered as a student, and was a member of the Free Austrian Youth movement. Although her father had been declared officially dead, the FBI suspected he might still be alive, living under the alias Stefan Lang, and perhaps active in the film industry.

The breakthrough for western intelligence agencies in relation to Deutsch came in January 1963 when, in acceptance of an offer of immunity from prosecution conveyed by his old friend and former colleague Nicholas Elliott, Kim Philby drafted what he claimed to be a comprehensive confession, which he prefaced with a beguiling but disingenuous caution:[6]

> This memorandum deals with events that occurred a very long time ago. It cannot, therefore, be taken as 100% accurate, especially with regard to dates. With that caveat it is to the best of my knowledge true in all particulars.

In his typed document, Philby insisted he had ceased working for the Soviets in 1946, and recalled his original approach to the CPGB's King Street headquarters as a membership candidate, and being frustrated at the lack of response.

> Before anything happened from that quarter, however, Lizzy came home that evening and told me that she had arranged for me to meet 'a man of decisive importance'. I questioned her about it but she would give me no details. The rendezvous took place in Regents Park. The man described himself as Otto. I discovered much later from a photograph in MI5 files that the name he went by was Arnold Deutsch. I think that he was of Czech origin; about 5ft 7in, stout, with blue eyes and light curly hair. Though a convinced Communist, he had a strong humanistic streak. He hated London, adored Paris, and spoke of it with deeply loving affection. He was a man of considerable cultural background.

Otto spoke at great length, arguing that a person of my family background and possibilities could do far more for Communism than the run-of-the-mill party member or sympathizer. In short, he proposed that I should work for an organization which I was able to identify later as the OGPU. (Krivitsky's statement was conclusive in that respect.) I explained my own position with great care, and he interrogated me at length. He maintained his offer and I accepted. His first instructions were that Lizzy and I should break off as quickly as possible all personal contact with Communist friends.

It may seem strange that, having rejected party discipline, I should have submitted willingly to the discipline of the OGPU, but the explanation is simple. None of the OGPU officials with whom I had dealings ever attempted to win my total acceptance of the party line. All they required was rigid adherence to instructions on the technical level. In short, I joined the OGPU as one joined the army. There must have been many British soldiers who obeyed orders at Passchendaele although convinced that they were wrongly conceived.

I then entered into regular contact with Otto. Our meetings always took place in outlying districts of London, such as Ealing, Acton, Park Royal, etc., and almost always in the open air. The regular drill consisted of synchronizing watches with a neighbouring clock, appearing at the rendezvous on the dot, taking at least three taxis to and from the rendezvous to ensure that nobody followed. At each meeting a time and a place was fixed for the next one.

My first job was with the *Review of Reviews* (I abandoned all thought of the civil service as a result of Professor Robertson's letter about which you know). For the first year or so I contributed very little and Otto devoted most of his time to lessons in tradecraft, emphasizing security above all things. He was always setting little traps for me in order to determine whether I had really broken off all connection with Communist friends, was following the taxi drill, etc.

One of my earliest tasks was to give him details of all my Communist friends at Cambridge. This I did. The list included Donald Maclean, Guy Burgess, Stott, Stevens, David Haden-Guest, Tom Pateman, and others I have now forgotten.[7] A few weeks after I presented the list, Otto turned up at a rendezvous with a senior official, whom he introduced as Big Bill. I later identified him fairly certainly as Krivitsky's Orloff. He was a bull of a man and struck me as being quite ruthless, an impression that Krivitsky confirms. But he had a good sense of humour and was always pleasant with me.[8]

Big Bill went over my list with me, concentrating finally on Donald and Guy. We had several meetings to discuss their potentialities. I was in favour of recruiting Donald, but entered strong reservations with regard to Guy, on the grounds of his unreliability and indiscretion. Finally, Bill instructed me to approach Donald, which I did. He accepted in the course of one meeting (I am not sure whether this was just before or just after his entry into the Foreign Office). I gave him instructions how to keep a rendezvous with Big Bill, and from that moment, except for one occasion which I shall come to later, he passed out of my life.

As soon as Donald had been recruited, Big Bill returned to the charge about Guy. I maintained my opinion, but was overruled finally. Guy made no more difficulty than Donald had done, and I duly arranged for him to meet either Otto or Big Bill – I am not sure which it was.

Although the OGPU officers constantly asked me to keep an eye open for potential recruits, Guy and Donald were the only two I actually recruited. I think that this was deliberate policy on their part as they did not want to put too many eggs into my basket. In any case my instructions were to have no contact with Communists, so that my access to likely material was strictly limited – in fact virtually non-existent.

The demonstrably tendentious statement created short-term and long-term problems. Firstly, Philby was contradicting Alexander Orlov, who in 1963 was living quietly under FBI protection in Ann Arbor, Michigan. According to Philby, he had met Orlov in London with Deutsch, probably in 1935, yet Orlov had already denied ever having met Deutsch. Why had Orlov lied? Evidently he had been in a position to compromise Philby, and maybe many others, yet he had never mentioned to his interlocutors that he had ever been to England, let alone knew the identities of important Soviet spies there. Years later, it would emerge that Orlov had replaced Reif as the illegal *rezident* in 1934, and had been succeeded in the post by Deutsch.

The second issue was Philby's talent for abbreviation. He had described his introduction to Deutsch by his wife Lizzy, omitting to mention the role of intermediary played by her Viennese friend Edith Suschitsky.

Clearly Philby had no intention of incriminating the mentally fragile Suschitsky, who was then living in Brighton where she managed an antiques shop. Similarly, Philby had admitted having recruited Burgess and Maclean, but both men were then safely in the Soviet Union. What about Anthony Blunt, the academic who had been involved in the 1951 defections? As regards Deutsch, Philby described a close relationship, illustrated by an episode that took place the last time he ever saw him:

> One evening our telephone rang, and Otto asked if we were alone at home. I replied that we were, and he told me that he would be round in half-an-hour. I was much astonished by this, since it was completely at variance with his normal security-mindedness. He arrived in a state of great agitation with a suitcase. He used my telephone to book an air passage to Paris and left the following morning. I never saw him again. I cannot put a date to this event, but I subsequently connected it in my mind with some major development in the Glading case. From then on, Theo took over direct contact with me.

This version of Deutsch's emergency departure did not stand up to much scrutiny because MI5 already knew from Deutsch's Home Office file that he had left the country by rail in November 1937, and not by air the following year. Percy Glading had been arrested in January 1938. Whether deliberately or accidentally, Philby's story was demonstrably untrue. However, his assertion about being run thereafter by 'Theo', thought to be Theodore Mally, the NKVD officer now known to have replaced Deutsch as the illegal *resident* in London, probably was accurate, although he was known (under the alias Paul Hardt) to have left the country suddenly in June 1937, while Glading was under investigation. When Philby mentioned 'Theo', he knew that he too was a worthless lead, as he had been liquidated in Moscow during the purge.[9]

MI5's Evelyn McBarnet, who investigated Deutsch for years, assessed that Philby's story of Deutsch's unexpected arrival was probably true, and was a consequence of an incident in which Edith Suschitsky reported that she had mislaid her diary in a taxi, and that the content was highly incriminating. This episode had caused considerable panic, and had prompted Moscow to recall Deutsch to Paris temporarily. In the event, the overreaction proved unnecessary as the diary had slipped into a sofa in Suschitsky's home and was recovered.

An assiduous researcher, McBarnet linked Deutsch to a mysterious figure who had briefly impinged on MI5's surveillance of Percy Glading.

Back in April 1937 MI5's mole inside the CPGB, Olga Gray, designated M/12 by her handler Max Knight, had reported at the time that Glading had attended a meeting with this individual, whom he had confided to her that he disliked, but had felt obliged to cooperate with him out of professionalism. In retrospect, it was realized that this unidentified figure had been Deutsch.

MI5 was also puzzled by the people Philby sought to implicate, such as the *Daily Worker* journalist Fred Pateman, David Haden-Guest, who was killed while fighting in the Spanish Civil War in July 1938, and the distinguished psychologist Denis H. Stott. Was this nothing more than a cynical ploy to waste MI5's resources on pointless investigations?

Countless molehunts followed and, apart from the Cambridge Five, several others were known to have been in contact with Deutsch, among them Alister Watson, Michael Straight, Arthur Wynn, Bernard Floud, Jenifer Hart and James Klugmann. An inspirational talent-spotter, Deutsch concentrated on finding leftist students at Oxford and Cambridge and persuading them to devote themselves to the Communist International.

Deutsch's full story would remain shrouded in mystery until 1988, when the Soviet authorities declassified his NKVD personnel file, which contained his own account of his life, dated 1935 and completed while he was on leave in Moscow.[10] He gave his date of his birth as 21 August 1904, his nationality as Austrian Jew, and his citizenship as Austrian. His education had been five years of primary school, eight in a gymnasium, followed by five in Vienna University's chemistry faculty. Party membership dated back to 1931, and membership of the Austrian Communist Youth Organization since 1922, and the Austrian Communist Party since 1924. He had been employed by the Comintern in Vienna from December 1928 to December 1931, and as an NKVD officer since August 1932 had been posted to Paris, Vienna and London. Under the heading 'knowledge of foreign languages', Deutsch had written 'German, French and English fluently, can read and write Italian and Spanish'. Between 1928 and 1932 he operated for the Comintern in Greece, Romania, Palestine, Syria, Germany and Czechoslovakia. His 28-year-old wife, Fini Pavlovna, worked from 1931 to 1935 as 'Liza Kramer' on special assignment in the Department for International Relations. She was a candidate member of the Communist Party, a member of the Austrian Communist Party, and was by profession a teacher. While in the Department for International

Relations in Moscow, she attended the Communist University for Western Youth.

Deutsch's file also contained a second document that described his operational experience, dated 15 December 1938:

I was born in Vienna (Austria) in 1904. My mother and father are Jewish and of Slovakian origin. My father was a country school teacher. After they moved to Vienna, he worked for a merchant. He was called to the colours in 1916 and served in the Austrian Army as an ordinary soldier till 1919. From 1919–20 he was a rag-and-bone man and later sold ready-made clothes and underwear from a stall as he did not have his own shop. In 1927 he hired a bookkeeper. After Hitler incorporated Austria and already under Schuschnigg, as a Jew he had to give up his business and live on the income from his house, which he had bought in 1931–32. On what means he lives at the moment, I cannot say as I have not heard from him for several months. Since about 1910 right up to its prohibition in 1934 he was a member of the Austrian Social-Democratic Party.

About my relations with my parents. My mother is the daughter of a courier. I have always had good relations with her. My father was a religious Jew and he tried to force me in every way, including beatings, to become one too. The final conflict with my father arose because of my political activities, which called forth all his wrath and hatred. My mother, on the other hand, defended me and helped me in this regard. At the beginning of 1929 I left my parents and from that time on I have maintained relations with my family only for my mother's sake. He persecuted my two younger brothers even more than me because they were materially dependent on him. He forced them to have nothing to do with the communist movement. They also hated him.

From 1910–15 I attended the primary school and from 1915 on the gymnasium in Vienna. During the first years, in as much as my father was serving in the army, I received a scholarship. Later, I did not have to pay any school fees at all because of my high marks. From 1923–28 I studied physics, chemistry and philosophy at Vienna University and got a degree of Doctor of Philosophy. In 1920 I became a member of the Free Union of Socialist Students, an organization of Communist and socialist students. In 1922 I joined the Austrian Communist Youth Organization, where I worked permanently as a leader of a propaganda group, partly in the district, partly in the Central Propaganda Department. In 1924 I became a member of the Austrian Communist Party. I did propaganda work in the district. Later I worked also in the MOPR (International Workers Relief Organization) and was a member of the Central Committee of the Austrian MOPR. Several comrades know me from the time I worked in the Austrian Communist Youth Organization and the Communist Party: Koplenig, General Secretary of the Austrian Communist Party; Fuernberg, representative of the Austrian Communist Party with the IKKI (Executive Committee of Comintern); Heksman, member of the Central Committee of the Austrian Communist Party, and his wife. All three are at present living in Moscow in the Hotel Luxe.

After my studies at the University in 1928, I was sent by the ACP to Moscow as a member of the Austrian workers' delegation to the Spartakiade. After my return to Vienna, I worked for about three months as a chemical engineer in a textile factory. In December 1928 comrades Koplenig and KONRAD, at that time Secretary of the Austrian Communist Youth Organization, recommended me for work in the underground organization of the Department for International Relations of the Comintern in Vienna. This was underground liaison and courier work. In October 1931, because of the bad work of some of the members of our apparatus, we were discovered.

In January 1932 I was summoned to Moscow. Up to May I remained without work. Then I was sent on a temporary assignment to Greece, Palestine and Syria. In August of that year I returned to Moscow and I was told that I had been sacked and would work in a factory.

The Head of the Department for International Relations was Abramov. Something about my attitude to Abramov, who later turned out to be an enemy of the people. I once said something to a colleague which implied criticism of Abramov's work. This colleague told Abramov about this and the latter forced me to write a statement to the effect that I would never again criticize his organization. Abramov sent one of his creatures, a certain 'Willy' to Vienna, with whom I and certain other members of the Department did not get on because he tried to introduce an anti-party, bureaucratic spirit into our organization. When 'Willy' later returned to Moscow, he encouraged, as far as I can judge, Abramov in his dislike of me. I heard recently that 'Willy' was arrested a year ago by our security people.

50

When comrade Georg Mueller heard that I had been sacked from the Department of International Relations, he offered me work in our department. Mueller was at that time already working in the department and I knew him from the time of his work in the Vienna organization. I was also recommended by comrade Urdan, who at present is Head of Department in the People's Commissariat for Heavy Industry.

In January 1933 (up to October 1932 I had been ill with typhoid fever in Moscow), I was sent by our department to Paris to work for Karin. I carried out technical tasks for him, photography, etc., and set up crossing points across the French frontier to Belgium, Holland and Germany. Apart from this, I tried to establish contact with fishermen in France, Holland and Belgium in order to use fishing boats to install radio equipment, in case of war. I invited comrade Luksy, the adopted daughter of the Hungarian revolutionary writer A. Gabor, and the daughter of the literary translator Olga Galperina to join in our work. Both are now in Moscow.

In October 1933 I was told that I would be sent to Britain on operational work. I then went to Vienna and recruited STRELA (GERTA) and JOHN in our organization. In February 1934 I went to London alone where I recruited EDITH, whom I already knew in Vienna.

In London I worked with Reif from April till June 1934 and from June till July 1935 with SCHWED (Alexander Orlov). In August 1935 I went to Moscow on leave where I remained till November 1935. After that I returned to London and worked there from November 1935 till April 1936 by myself, from April 1936 till the end of August 1936 with MANN [Theodore Mally], then up to January 1937 again by myself and till June 1937 again with MANN, and later, till November 1937, again by myself.

During my work in London I personally recruited a number of people. As a cover I studied psychology at London University. I completed these studies with the exception of the last examination. In London I found one of my relatives, a cousin, whom I had not met until then and who is the owner of a large British film company. I started working for him as a cover in the capacity of head of the psychological and advertising department. I worked for ten months for him and the monthly salary of twenty pounds sterling I gave to our organization. He agreed to obtain a work permit for me, necessary for foreigners, but as I had come to Britain on a student visa, the British police refused to issue me with a work permit and I was obliged to leave England in September 1937, together with my family. In November 1937 I returned for ten days to London in order to conserve our network there. On 23 November 1937 I returned to Moscow.

In 1932 I was transferred by a commission of the Central Committee of the All-Union Communist Party from the Austrian Communist Party to the ACP (b) and at the end of March of this year (1938) I passed the renewal of party cards successfully. In the beginning of 1938 I received Soviet citizenship.

About my wife Fini or Sylvia, born 1907. I have known her since 1922. We married in 1924. In the same year she joined the Austrian Communist Youth Organization. She worked at the time as a teacher in a children's home. In 1927 she became a member of the Austrian Communist Party. In 1931 she was sent to Moscow to attend the radio school of the Comintern and she remained there till 1932. Up to 1934 she worked as a radio operator at one of the Comintern stations. From 1934 till the beginning of 1936 she studied at the KUNMZ. In February 1936, i.e. only after Abramov's removal, who up to then because of his dislike for me had resisted this in every way, she joined me in London where she gave birth to a child. After my return to Moscow my wife and child, on the instructions of the leadership, remained abroad for another nine months. My wife arrived in Moscow on 1 September 1938.

I have two brothers. One is 27 years of age and the other 26. The elder was a tailor and was for some time a member of the Austrian Communist Youth Organization, but later left because of my father's opposition. Later he became a member of the Schutzbund and took part in the February revolt in 1934. My younger brother worked as an engraver but continued his studies at night. He passed the entrance examination to the University and studied at the medical faculty. He only had to pass a few more examinations when Austria was incorporated and he was obliged to abandon his studies. He was also a member of the Schutzbund and took part in the February revolt. During the administration of Dollfuss and Schuschnigg he worked in the underground organization of the MOPR. In August 1938 my brothers succeeded in obtaining visas for Argentina and leaving

Austria. Both are now living in Buenos Aires. One works as a tailor and the doctor became an errand boy.

I know English and German fluently, speak French fairly well and can read and understand Italian and Dutch.[11]

Deutsch also described how in 1920 he had become a member of the revolutionary group of the intelligentsia *Clarte*, founded by the French novelist Henri Barbusse, but in 1927 he had been rusticated from the university for six months because of his Communist Party activities. When Deutsch became active for the Comintern's international bureau in Vienna in 1931, he had to go into hiding for two months, after which he was summoned to Moscow. There, in the autumn of 1932, he was invited to join the NKVD to work in the Foreign Department, where he encountered Edith Suschitsky, a member of the Austrian Communist Party's Central Committee, employed by the TASS news agency as a photographer. Later Suschitsky would be implicated in espionage when photographic equipment, including a Leica camera, used by Percy Glading to copy classified documents was traced back to her through receipts dated January 1937. Additionally, Suschitsky was a close friend of Glading's Austrian (second) wife, Rosa Scharr. Suschitsky's flatmate in Brixton was another of her recruits, Margaret (Peggy) Moxon, who would in 1938 marry Arthur Wynn.

During this period Deutsch developed a talent for forgery and created a few recipes for invisible ink and obtained passports for the Vienna *rezidentura*. He was also talent-spotted by Alexander Orlov, who submitted a report to Moscow about him on 8 September 1935, while Deutsch was there on leave:

I am very pleased that he was of use to you and that you were attentive to him and treated him as a comrade. STEPHAN is a very serious worker and a devoted compatriot [Communist]. Very valuable for our work. He has already accomplished much and if directed rightly he can be of great use. He deserves that our organization showed appreciation of his work in such a way that it would increase his zeal tenfold and, most importantly, that he should know that for the Centre he is not some unknown technical assistant. I am therefore of the opinion that if our department awarded him a diploma, a revolver, a watch or something like that, that would be only just and very useful for our work. STEPHAN never lets one down and the trust put in him is fully justified.

This praise was followed a month later by a recommendation from Alexander Slavatinsky in Moscow who accepted Orlov's suggestion and approved the reward.

> Arnold Deutsch, an assistant of SCHWED [Alexander Orlov], is an Austrian citizen, a member of the Austrian Communist Party since 1924, a member of the All-Union Communist Party (B) since December 1931 under the name Stephan Lang, born in Vienna, 21 May 1904. In view of the fact that comrade Deutsch, due to the conditions of underground work, is not a Soviet citizen, he is not on the permanent staff of the Department and is listed as a secret employee. Comrade Deutsch has worked illegally abroad for the Foreign Department since 1932. During his work in group 'G' comrade Deutsch proved himself in various aspects of underground work as an extremely combative and loyal operator. Comrades SCHWED and MARR, who work with him, note his exceptionally meritorious work for the group such as, for instance, his recruitment of SOEHNCHEN [Kim Philby], his smooth contacts with ATILLA and HEIR, his great initiative in organizing the technical work of the group (photography, safekeeping of material, etc.). In view of the above, request that comrade Deutsch be awarded a revolver.

When Deutsch left London for the last time in September 1937, his first assignment in Paris was to put the NKVD *rezident* in Spain, Alexander Orlov, in touch with Kim Philby, who had travelled as a freelance war correspondent to the Nationalist front where he filed stories for *The Times*. Deutsch also arranged for Orlov to meet Guy Burgess in Paris, where the latter was to act as an intermediary between them, communicating by exchanging postcards.

Apparently Deutsch always intended to return to London but the recent defections of Ignace Poretsky and Walter Krivitsky in the summer of 1937 made this impossible as he was known to Krivitsky, or so Deutsch reported to Moscow from Paris on 23 October 1937:

> Comrade DUCHE (Sergei Spiegelglas) told me that I should put on record all I know about GROLL [Walter Krivitsky]. GROLL met my wife before I myself met him. He knew the name of my wife's mother from the Vienna days. When in June 1936 I was in Paris, MANN [Theodore Mally] first introduced me to him. He asked me for a cover address in Paris and also to find an Austrian communist

girl who could help him in his work. I introduced him to Luksy and her husband. When I lost contact with him, he rang me up in my hotel, having presumably got my address from MANN. GROLL was a little aware of the nature of our work in London: he knew that we worked with young people and he knew about the man in the F.O.

According to his Moscow file, Deutsch returned once more, very briefly, to London to put his agent network on ice, and later he reported to Spiegelglas on what had happened in February 1938:

When in the beginning of November I went to London, I received instructions from you to put all our people on ice for a period of three months. I paid them all their salary up to 1 February and arranged with them that by that time somebody would get in touch with them. It is now already the end of February and as far as I know only PFEIL and JOHN have been contacted. For various reasons I consider it of great importance to renew contact with our comrades, if not personally then at least by letter. All our people are young and do not have much experience in our work. For them a promise by us can be relied upon as something absolutely certain. Many of them count on our money, as they depend on it for their livelihood. In the interest of our further work, I told them that I was going to Spain, which to us is a more important battlefield than Britain. If they do not hear from us they are bound to be disappointed. They are all working for us out of conviction and with enthusiasm and they may start thinking that they have been turned down. I don't want to be alarmist but in the interest of our further work we should avoid anything that could cause them to become disappointed, that could shake their faith in our reliability and punctuality. Particularly in view of the recent events (GOT) [Percy Glading] it is essential to show them a) that this has nothing whatsoever to do with us and b) that we are in place and continuing the work which for all of them has become their life's mission.

I should like to point once more to the special composition of our group. They all believe in us. They are convinced that we are always in place, always everywhere, that we fear nothing, never leave anybody to their fate, that we are first and foremost accurate, exact, reliable. The success of our work has been based on the fact that we have so far never disappointed them. It is just now very important from a psychological point of view that they hear from us even if we do not start working with them at once.

Deutsch remained temporarily inactive although there were repeated attempts to send him abroad on a mission, the first being in December 1937, almost as soon as he had arrived in Moscow, when Abram Slutsky suggested to Nikolai Ezhov that he should be posted to the United States as illegal *rezident*. A second, similar proposal was made on 15 March 1938 by Spiegelglas to Mikhail Frinovsky. No action was taken, but on 11 October 1938 the new Head of Intelligence, Zelman Passov, sent a minute to his chief, Lavrenti Beria:

> At the end of 1937, the eminent recruiter of the illegal apparatus, the temporary employee, Comrade Lang, Stephan Georgievich, was summoned back to the Soviet Union. His recall was connected with the treachery of RAYMOND, who knew where he worked. For eleven months he has been without work being maintained at our expense. Bearing in mind that the question of his work abroad cannot be decided now, I request your agreement to finding work for comrade Lang outside our organization.

Two days later Beria confirmed his approval, and Deutsch slipped into obscurity at a time when the NKVD was to be paralysed by purges, arrests and liquidations. Somehow Deutsch escaped attention, and it was not until March 1939 that the NKVD invited him to write a series of essays on Britain, beginning with one on the country's political structure, and an account of the former illegal *rezidentura* in London. This was an opportunity for Deutsch to demonstrate his skills as a psychologist and he assembled insightful profiles of Philby, Maclean, Burgess and their co-conspirators. Upon completion of this task, Deutsch approached Pavel Fitin, the new Head of Intelligence, reminding him that he had been inactive for twenty-one months. Suitably prompted by this, Fitin wrote to Beria on 31 December 1940 recommending that Deutsch be sent to the United States as illegal *rezident*, with Boris Krotenschild acting as his assistant, on a mission to re-establish contact with three specific sources codenamed '19th' (Laurence Duggan), NIGEL (Michael Straight) and MORRIS (Abraham Glasser), and to recruit new agents, perhaps in the government or defence industries.

The network in America to be managed by Deutsch and Krotenschild included Straight, who had been recruited while a prewar undergraduate at Cambridge by Anthony Blunt, then working in the US State Department; Abraham Glasser, who was fired from the US Department of Justice in 1941 on suspicion of espionage; and Laurence Duggan, a senior

Department of State official in charge of the Latin America Division, who committed suicide in 1948 after having been compromised by VENONA traffic, in which he featured with the codenames SHERWOOD and PRINCE.

Deutsch's rehabilitation occurred soon after Anthony Blunt, by then ensconced in MI5's B Division as assistant to the director, Guy Liddell, had removed Deutsch's dossier from the registry and passed a copy to his handler, Anatoli Gorsky, for onward transmission to Moscow. This slim volume accurately reflected MI5's relative ignorance of the master-spy and failure to identify any of his contacts. Astonishingly, there was no indication that MI5 had even bothered to investigate Oscar Deutsch. Satisfied that OTTO had escaped relatively unscathed from his role in London, he was cleared for a further mission to the United States.

The plan called for the pair to travel to America posing as Jewish refugees from the Baltic. According to his NKVD file, in 1941 Deutsch embarked on SS *Kayak*, but only reached Bombay and when war broke out in the Far East he was stuck in India. He was obliged to return to Moscow via Teheran, arriving on 1 April 1942, and a second attempt to reach the United States by sea ended tragically on 7 November 1942 when SS *Donbass* was sunk by a U-boat in the Atlantic. However, this version is contradicted by naval records which show that the tanker *Donbass* was sunk by a German destroyer, *Z-27*, en route from Archangel to Reykjavik.

Chapter 5

Renato Levi

... a natural liar, capable of inventing any story on the
spur of the moment to get himself out of a fix.

[Evan Simpson, September 1942[1]]

The longest-serving British agent of the Second World War was an
Italian playboy from Rapallo, who came from a privileged background.
Born in Split in Croatia, he was brought up partly in Bombay, where his
family owned a very successful boat-building business, was educated in
Zug, Switzerland, with his brothers Mario and Paulo, and spent fourteen
years before the war in Australia. Truly cosmopolitan, he possessed a
British passport and a beautiful Italian mistress, and worked for the
French, German and Italian intelligence agencies, as well as SIS.[2]

Levi's extraordinary wartime success in Cairo, achieved in partnership
with his British case officer, the peacetime theatrical impresario Evan
Simpson, created the modern concept of strategic deception. Although
tactical, short-term deception, to exploit the element of surprise, is as old
as warfare itself, the idea of integrating numerous channels of information
to convey an entirely bogus, long-term scenario was both sophisticated and
novel, embracing camouflage, emulated wireless traffic, disguised vehicles
and coordinated diversionary feints. To pull off such a ruse required the
careful management of false broadcasts, the construction of fake installations for the benefit of the enemy's aerial reconnaissance and, perhaps
most dangerous of all, the manipulation of controlled enemy agents.

Hitherto, no security or intelligence apparatus had ever enjoyed the
means, let alone the ambition, to perpetrate a fraud on a massive scale,
involving imaginary military units and fabricated intelligence for the purpose of diverting an adversary from one's true intentions and objectives.
Such Machiavellian schemes required top-level authority and great imagination, rare qualities indeed, especially within the military establishment.

Initially codenamed LAMBERT and then CHEESE, Levi's information helped lift the siege of Malta, misled Erwin Rommel's Afrika Korps at

El Alamein and persuaded the Axis during the battle for Normandy to divert precious reinforcements to Greece. The campaign, supervised by Dudley Clarke, was so successful at duping the enemy, which grossly over-estimated Allied strengths in the Mediterranean and Middle East, that a similar strategy was adopted to convince German military analysts that the long-expected D-Day landings would take place in the Pas-de-Calais. Using the same techniques pioneered by CHEESE in Cairo, Hitler's High Command became convinced that the initial invasion, on 6 June 1944, was merely a diversionary feint.[3]

Two sequential files in MI5's wartime Middle East records provide a contemporaneous outline of how the case developed:

INTRODUCTORY

The so-called CHEESE (or LAMBERT) case may be said to have begun with a letter from the War Office (PF.4-5241 of 3 June 1940) informing Cairo that a certain Renato Levi, described as a British subject whom the French had used as a 'double-cross agent', was on his way to Egypt. It was suggested that he would need help, but must be carefully watched, as his loyalty to the Allied cause was not above suspicion.

On 12 September 1940 and again on 15 October 1940 CHEESE visited the British Embassy, Belgrade, which reported that he was about to make his way to Egypt via Istanbul. He returned to Italy before doing so, and did not reach Turkey until 26 December 1940. He reported to our Embassy there, but his journey was delayed by the fact that the Turks arrested him on a charge of belonging to a gang engaged in passport and currency frauds. His release was secured and his journey to Egypt facilitated. Meanwhile the account he gave of himself and his mission (set out in the next section of this report) had been communicated ahead of him to Cairo.

II. PREVIOUS HISTORY OF CHEESE

Though classed as a British national by the War Office, CHEESE might be better described as an international adventurer. Born in Italy in 1902 of Italian-Jewish parents, he had spent his life in India (1903–13), Switzerland (1913–18), Italy (1916–26) and Australia (1920–37). In 1937 he returned to Italy. In November 1939 he was living at Genoa (where his mother owned a hotel) when he was approached by Dr Hans Travaglio, a leading member of the German Secret Service in Italy, who asked him to go to France as a spy. He claims that he immediately informed the British Consul at Genoa (who encouraged him to accept the German offer), and he certainly reported later to British authorities in Paris. He worked for the Germans in France, 'double-crossing' them by contact with the French authorities. The French are said to have mishandled his case, but detailed information is lacking. After the collapse of France he returned to Genoa. Here Travaglio approached him again, introducing him to his colleagues Major Helfferich and a certain Rossetti, whose Christian name he gave as Clemans. He was instructed to go to Egypt, taking with him a W/T set, and an operator to work it, and to set up an organisation for collecting military intelligence and transmitting it back to Italy. Messages were to be written in French, and enciphered. The plan was approved by Count Sirombo, head of the Italian Intelligence Service in Italy. A visit was paid to Bari where it was arranged CHEESE's W/T signals were to be received and answered. The Italians made one change in the plans: CHEESE was not to take a W/T set with him; one was to be sent to him, perhaps by diplomatic bag (?Hungarian). He was given two questionnaires, one Italian, one German, and Sirombo provided him with the names and addresses of those to whom he could apply for assistance at Budapest, Belgrade and Sofia (a certain [Otto] Eisentrager). He was told that in any neutral country except Turkey, he could get help from the German consul by enquiring for 'Abwehr Abteilung' and saying that he came on behalf of 'Emile of Genoa'. He was warned to avoid the German consulate in Turkey for fear of drawing on himself the suspicions of the Turks or the British. Arrived in Cairo, he was to expect a message at the Carlton Hotel, enabling him to get possession of the promised W/T set. He was also to make contact with two former acquaintances of Sirombo – George Khouri and Madame Lina Vigoretti-Antoniada. Acting on Sirombo's instructions, CHEESE travelled to Istanbul on a German passport, made out in the name of Renato Ludovici. At Sofia he interviewed Eisentrager. At Istanbul he visited the British Embassy and volunteered all the information about himself and his mission given in this section. He was accompanied by a wireless operator of the name of Fulvio Melcher. This man shared CHEESE's ill-luck in being arrested by the Turkish Police. He spent three weeks in gaol and, losing heart, returned to Italy as soon as he was released. CHEESE himself, provided with a British passport, finally proceeded to Haifa by sea. He was taken to Jerusalem and there interrogated by a representative of SIME, but no fresh information of any importance was obtained. He was then flown by RAF plane to Cairo, where he arrived on 19 February 1941.

III. CHEESE in Egypt

On arrival CHEESE was placed in a hotel, not under surveillance, but in daily contact with an officer of SIME to whom he made his reports. He had brought with him £500, in Sterling notes of £100. The promised note from the enemy was not awaiting him and there was no sign of the W/T set. He was instructed to approach the two people in Cairo whose names had been given him. He did so unaccompanied. He reported that Madame Vigoretti-Antoniada was of no consequence. She was unintelligent and quite unresponsive to his hints and suggestions. (She has been kept under observation since, but without result.) He represented George Khouri as more promising. This man is a Syrian-born moneylender, who was already known to us, having assisted to organise anti-British activities in connection with the pre-war troubles in Palestine. He introduced CHEESE to a well-known Egyptian journalist, Habib Jamati, from whom CHEESE obtained a little information about Egyptian politics, which he passed on to SIME. CHEESE stated that he asked for further assistance from Khouri and even paid him money in return for a promise to collect information for transmission to the enemy.

NOTE. The officer who handled CHEESE at the time was very uncertain how much of CHEESE's accounts of his conversations with Khouri could be believed. Khouri, when arrested in 1941, denied ever having met CHEESE. While this is undoubtedly a lie, it is considered possible that CHEESE met Khouri on one or perhaps two occasions, that Khouri refused to have anything to do with him, and that the accounts CHEESE has given of subsequent conversations with Khouri were sheer invention on CHEESE's part. Before leaving Cairo CHEESE told SIME that he had informed Khouri of the setting up of W/T communication, arranged for him to supply the operator with reports for transmission by means of a postbox, and promised to send him more money. In actual fact, no information was ever supplied through this postbox.

With or without Khouri's co-operation, communication with the enemy had to be set up. The promised W/T set from Italy had never turned up, but an amateur-built one was found, the work of an NCO at GHQ signals. The book-cypher code suggested to CHEESE by the Italians proved clumsy and unsuitable: a SIME officer devised a new substitution cypher. It was arranged that SIME should act as an imaginary spy-ring in Egypt, transmitting false information to Italy, while CHEESE returned to take charge of the reception at Bari. He was to stop en route at Istanbul and visit the German Embassy; he was provided with some misleading information on general matters, and a story was concocted about his own mission for the benefit of the enemy. This was, briefly, as follows,

(i) that after great difficulty he had found an amateur W/T set which an Italian had been hiding in his house, and had bought it for £200;
(ii) that he had set it up in a flat in Heliopolis, that he had secured the services of a certain (imaginary) Paul Nicossof as Morse (key) operator. This man was left rather vague; he subsequently told the Germans 'I believe he is a Syrian, but he told me he was born in Egypt;'
(iii) that transmissions should begin on 25 May 1941 and continue twice weekly;
(iv) that CHEESE had given to Nicossof and his accomplices the balance of his £500 – after deducting expenses, the £200 for the W/T set, the money given to Khouri, and many incidental items. This balance was reported as no more than £150. It is to be noted that, if the enemy takes the trouble to look back at their records of the case (supposing they have any proper records), he will conclude that he has a spy-ring working for over a year, paying considerable sums to agents and contacts, with no financial resources beyond this original £150.

IV. Return of CHEESE to Italy

CHEESE's passport was 'cooked' to show his entry and exit from Egypt. He was flown back to Palestine, and sailed from Haifa to Turkey on 19 April 1941. As arranged, he visited the German Embassy at Istanbul; it proved necessary to pay a number of visits. CHEESE took with him written statements of his activities since leaving Italy, embodying the concocted story given at the end of Section III, These were given to [Kurt] Zahringer at the Embassy, but copies were left with our authorities, to whom CHEESE also gave written reports of his interviews with Zahringer.

CHEESE reported that Zahringer seemed very pleased with the work done in Egypt, and wanted to send him back there immediately, in spite of his own insistence that he must return to Italy for private reasons; but that finally Zahringer received instructions from Berlin to facilitate CHEESE's return to Italy.

CHEESE left Istanbul for Rome at the end of May 1941. With the doubtful exception of one telegram (see section V) no further communication has ever been established with him. What hand he has had in the W/T messages from Bari, and what his other activities have been, are matters of guesswork only.

NOTES ON CHEESE

The following comments made by the officer who handled CHEESE during the two months he was in Egypt, and who was in daily contact with him, may be of interest:

(i) CHEESE"s motives in working for us are difficult to fathom. He is, of course, a Jew, and says he wants to do something to help the Allied cause because it is fighting on behalf of the Jews. In addition, he obviously has considerable love of adventure and enjoys the work for its own sake. He is very fond of women, and the work gives him opportunities of travel, and of handling large sums of money, which he would not otherwise get. He showed no particular dislike for the Germans or the Italians; in fact he often described the good times the Germans had given him, and how friendly he was with Travaglio.

(ii) As a result of his successful activities in France, Italy, Turkey and then in Egypt , he had acquired an amazing self-confidence and complete belief in his own ability to travel anywhere and deceive anybody.

(iii) He is a natural liar, capable of inventing any story on the spur of the moment to get himself out of a fix. He has very considerable intelligence and an inventive mind. For example, he invented cyphers of his own, but immediately grasped the advantages of one which was nut up to him and mastered it in a very short time.

(iv) I think there is little doubt that if he turns up after the war, he will ask as a reward for his services, to be given British citizenship and allowed to go to Australia, As far as we can say at the moment (1942) he has done us well and deserves consideration.

V. Establishment of W/T Communication

The initial attempts at transmission beginning, as arranged, on 23 May, proved unsuccessful: no reply or acknowledgement was received. After a technical examination, the conclusion was reached that the frequencies agreed upon were unsuitable and would need altering.

Arrangements had been made, in case of W/T difficulties, for telegrams to be sent to CHEESE in Rome, via Istanbul, in a simple code, suggesting commercial dealings. By this means, the new frequencies were communicated. Further attempts at transmission were then made, and successful contact was at last established on the 14th, 17th and 21st of July. Since that time, for a little over a year, messages have been sent and/or received on most Mondays and Thursdays. Occasionally, by special arrangements, messages have been exchanged on other days, and since early July 1942 there has been almost daily communication. The occasional lapses from the twice-weekly standard – particularly in the first three months of 1942 – may have been due to technical difficulties or to enemy slackness and loss of interest. But even in these months, our signals were acknowledged at least once a week. In the first three months (July–September 1941), the messages sent out were not of any great importance: the art of deception by W/T agents had not yet been fully developed. During this time the amateur set was found unsatisfactory and abandoned in favour of an ordinary Army set. The operator had also to be changed, at least twice, owing to illness. The enemy do not seem to have allowed these changes to arouse their suspicions. The organisation at Bari appeared to be very bad. The encoding was particularly careless (it has improved a little since, but has never attained a reasonably good standard), and there was much repetition of questions, etc. The slipshod methods suggested that CHEESE himself was handling the job at the other end.

In October–November 1941 the organisation of deception was rapidly developing. Advanced Headquarters, 'A' Force saw in CHEESE a possible opportunity for a decisive stroke. The information despatched was gradually put on a far higher level, and close liaison was maintained between 'A' Force, SIME and the operational authorities.

One device developed at this period is well worth a mention. As Heer's reports to Zahringer had been vague on the subject of the personnel of his spy-ring, it was difficult to be precise about the methods supposedly being used to collect information in Cairo without queering his pitch in Italy, where he might have been elaborating stories of which we had no knowledge. It was therefore suggested in our second message (21 July) that we had got into touch with a 'good South African contact' from whom information was forthcoming. He was later (29 September) replaced by a South African NCO, confidential secretary to a general, and in a position to acquire first-class information. Experience shows that the enemy is curiously unwary and eager to accept stories of the disloyalty of disgruntled Colonials, Irishmen, etc., and even of the supposed ex-members of the Fascist organisations in England. Our imaginary figure (nicknamed PIET) was, however, provided with subsidiary motives, and represented as in great difficulties over women and money. Owing to the extreme meagreness of the funds that CHEESE had left behind, PIET had to act his part on promises rather than cash. But he appears to have done so convincingly. As far as we can judge, the enemy swallowed PIET whole. He certainly proved a useful excuse for transmitting high-grade Intelligence which would have been quite beyond the reach of CHEESE's associates.

It is not possible to give details of this intelligence, nor of the actual deception practised in November 1941. It is best summed up in a telegram despatched much later (6 January 1942) to 'Snuffbox, Oxford' from which the following is an extract: 'Have been officially informed that LAMBERT was main source by which successful deception recently achieved, resulting in complete strategic surprise at outset of Western Desert campaign. Without LAMBERT, main theme of deception plan which was put over on 20 October and 27 October could not have reached enemy before 18 November. This very satisfactory and completely justifies care and trouble taken. LAMBERT still in touch but doubt further utility ...'

VI. CHEESE Discredited

It will be noted that the above-quoted telegram was not despatched till January 1942. During November–December 1941 there was no indication in the W/T traffic that the enemy realized how seriously he had been fooled. He still sent promises of money and demands for military information in much the same style as before, and on 1 January 1942 even sent good wishes for 'bonne collaboration dans la nouvelle année'.

Information reached us from other, most secret, sources that the enemy had lost confidence in ROBERTO: the details given, though not all applicable, enabled us to identify ROBERTO with CHEESE. From similar sources came the report that CHEESE himself was arrested (we subsequently heard that he was released after some 2–3 months), presumably on suspicion of having had a hand in the deception.

After the New Year message of good wishes, there was a marked change. The enemy frequently failed to reply to, or even acknowledge, our signals, and contact was seldom established more than once a week. His messages showed far less interest in military matters, and few questions were asked on military subjects. Traffic continued sporadically on the subject of the money which was said to be on its way, but enemy messages were such as to lead us to suspect that traps were being set. It was, for instance, proposed that the enemy should send the money to Istanbul, and that we should send someone to fetch it. This looked very like an attempt to kidnap a British agent on the Venlo pattern, or at least to learn more of our organization. We toyed with the suggestion over some messages, pleading lack of money for the journey and suggesting that we might find a 'neutral merchant' to act as intermediary. A scheme was tentatively laid on for action at Istanbul, but the enemy appeared to lose interest, and it was not thought wise to persevere.

In retrospect, it is perhaps not fanciful to describe the enemy's messages as those which might be expected from one who was trying to keep the source still open, for its own sake, with little or no assistance (e.g. questionnaires) from those who were interested in it as a reliable channel for military information. And in spite of occasional spurts of energy, the business was conducted in a somewhat half-hearted way. But the period January–June 1942 is more conveniently dealt with in the following section.

VI. Re-establishment of CHEESE

This section covers the period between January and July 1942 – between the time when we reported 'LAMBERT still in touch but doubt further utility', and the time when we began to receive reports, from most secret sources, that the enemy was regarding the source as 'credible' (4 July) and 'trustworthy' (12 July), and arranging for direct communication of our messages from Athens (which was presumably over-hearing the Cairo-Bari traffic) to the HQ of the Panzer Armee in Libya. These reports coincided with the messages we began to receive, indicating a renewed eagerness on the part of the enemy for military information and the unprecedented request (on 2 July 1942) for daily transmissions in place of the usual twice-weekly ones.

It is obviously impossible to be certain how this re-establishment was effected. The probable contributory factors, apart from the general unwariness and inefficiency of the enemy, were: the building-up of a new 'spy-story'; the handling of military information; W/T procedure. These are best discussed under separate headings:

(a) Unwariness of the Enemy. All outside evidence goes to show that since the Italian declaration of war and the prompt internment of Italians suspected of espionage, the enemy has been starved of reliable and up-to-date intelligence from Egypt. He is consequently doubly greedy for it, inclined to swallow bad (in the absence of good) information, and careless in his correlation and checking up.

Travaglio was concerned in the Venlo affair.

RDF researches in late July seemed to show that the acknowledgements and replies to our messages were still coming from Bari.

Though CHEESE was originally recruited by a predominantly German organisation, it seems that the arrangements for his journey, W/T set, etc., were in Italian hands, and he himself complained to Zahringer of the inefficiency of the arrangements. The handling of the CHEESE messages was done at Bari, and linguistic evidence (the very Italianate idioms embedded in the French of the messages) seemed to show that the translation, and possibly the writing, of the messages was in Italian hands. Perhaps the whole case was being handled by Italians, and handled with a laziness and carelessness that Germans would not have tolerated.

It has been plausibly suggested that sometime in the early summer of 1942 a new director of intelligence took over (perhaps in view of Rommel's offensive) and demanded more information from Egypt. Since this demand could not be satisfied from really reliable sources, CHEESE was quoted as at least a working proposition. His murky past may have been concealed or minimized, the deception of November 1941 explained away or ignored. It is possible that CHEESE, released from prison with a new stock of plausible ingenuities on his tongue, may have had a hand in re-establishing what he had originally foisted on his employers, and found them once more ready to be deceived. All this must naturally remain pure conjecture. If true, it leads to the pleasing conclusion that 'wishful thinking' is not a monopoly of the democratic peoples.

While on the subject of enemy methods, it may be remarked that had the enemy been handling genuine, loyal agents (instead of a pertinacious British organisation), he would also certainly have soured their loyalty and lost their co-operation at a much earlier stage. The constant carelessness in encodement, and (still more) in W/T procedure, endangered the whole communication, and strangely enough, it rose to a climax of inefficiency in early June, just when the directorate of enemy Intelligence seemed most eager for the information which was being transmitted. Meanwhile the failure to send money, the hollowness and monotony of the promises to do so, and the apparent indifference to the dangers which inefficiency would have brought on real spies concealed in Cairo, indicate a really lamentable lack of imagination and common sense.

(b) Building-up of a new 'Spy-Story'. As the events of November 1941 had presumably discredited CHEESE's imaginary spy-ring in enemy eyes, it was clearly wise to represent it as falling (and finally fallen) to pieces. The fact that no money had been received for a year made this story plausible – indeed somewhat overdue. The fact that the enemy had never enquired into the membership or circumstances of the ring made it easy to fabricate. Constant whines for money were sent. The enemy's suggestion that CHEESE himself might return with funds was warmly welcomed. When neither he nor the money appeared, the gang was represented as finally dissipated. The (true) fact of George Khouri's internment was reported, the other absconding members were left in their original anonymity. But the enemy was encouraged to conclude that the agents who had so sadly misled him in November would no longer be sending inaccurate or poisoned intelligence.

Attention was concentrated on the one name that CHEESE had left us – that of Paul Nicossof, the W/T operator. It was implied that he was ignorant of military matters and only able to answer such questions as were within the range of the ordinary man in the street. When more difficult matters were broached, he pleaded lack of funds to hire agents. He transmitted 'Suis seul' and 'Suis à bout'. He threatened to sell or pawn the W/T set to pay the debts which he implied he had accumulated. He grew sarcastic and even impudent about the never-ending stream of false promises to which the enemy treated him.

It is possible that (but for an unforeseen event) these efforts to keep him ' in-character' and make his story consistent might have landed him in an impasse. He could hardly carry on indefinitely without money. His patience (like Hitler's) would have had to be exhausted sooner or later. He would have had to close down. Such a closing down would not, at the time, have been regarded as a great loss. The value of the military information sent was negligible; the attempt to use his appeals for money in order to trap other enemy agents (or at least learn more of enemy organisation) seemed quite unsuccessful. The failure to obtain any money meant that Paul could not go on indefinitely, but it also seemed a sign that the enemy had lost interest, and that it was not worth our going on.

(It is possible that we underestimated the success of our own security measures in the Middle East, and consequently under-estimated the enemy's difficulties in getting, or even attempting to get, a large sum of money to a spy in Egypt.)

The unforeseen event occurred justifying our pertinacity. The Germans began to advance on the Libyan front. Their Intelligence service naturally became hungrier than ever for Egyptian information. At the same time, Paul was provided with a new and excellent motive for continuing, and feverishly multiplying his activities. He could now begin to picture himself as 'the man who brought Rommel into Egypt', dream of the entry of the Panzer Armee into Cairo and imagine high German officers hastening to his hotel to thank him, pay all his debts, and load him with money and medals.

While protesting violently against the inexplicable inefficiencies of Bari, and the danger into which they put him, Paul began to show a new energy and enterprise. Messages were even prepared to indicate that he was beginning to suffer from the monomania common among successful spies; it was not thought advisable to send these, and it was clearly becoming unnecessary to do so. CHEESE seemed to be com-pletely re-established, and on the most favourable lines. The enemy had been given every excuse for forgetting the past: new contacts, which Paul represented himself as making, could be continued or dropped at will; mistakes and deceptions could be explained away on the plea of lack of funds, or of Paul's unfamiliarity with the business of collecting military information. Prospects were good either for a renewed course of misleading and fogging enemy intelligence, or, with good luck, for a large and more decisive stroke. It still remains to be seen whether these hopes can he fulfilled. At the time of writing, CHEESE appears to be in a most healthy condition.

(c) Handling of Military Intelligence. As can be deduced from the foregoing section, the W/T messages between January and June 1942 contained the minimum of military information. Few questions and no formal questionnaires were received from the enemy. Doubt whether or no he was trusting us made it dangerous to answer what was sent, or to volunteer information. And the particular spy-story which was being 'put across' naturally confined military intelligence to the lowest grade and the meagrest proportions.

Between 1 January and 25 June 1942 only three items of military intelligence were sent:

(i) Planning of an American aircraft factory near Cairo. (Enemy enquiries about site, capacity, etc., were first evaded, then answered with the excuse that the agent who supplied the original information had disappeared.)

(ii) American officers and soldiers seen in streets. (Enemy enquiries for further details were met with a brief reply giving three shoulder-badges noticed.)

(iii) The address of GHQ in Cairo was correctly given. (This had been asked for, and correctly answered, nearly a year before. The address is such common knowledge throughout the Middle East that a trap was suspected. But it is possible that the enemy is even more ignorant of conditions in Egypt than we suspect. His second enquiry may imply that he had lost record of the first, or that he thought there had been a move.)

This was the sum total of military information transmitted. The enemy's questions on other points (location of 23rd Infantry Division, location of Polish, Free French and Colonial Units, and shipping intelligence from the Canal zone) were either ignored or answered with the plea 'No money: no agents to collect information'. It was not till the latter half of June that anything further was transmitted. Even then, the matter supplied was at first of low grade, though, in order to build up confidence, it had to contain a high proportion of truth. Advanced HQ, 'A' Force was fortunately able to supply the enemy with information that he already possessed, new items that were unlikely to be of use to him, or truths that would probably confuse him more than a deliberate lie.

(d). W/T Procedure. It had been arranged with CHEESE that, while the actual messages were to be put into the newly-devised cypher, discussion over the air of such things as frequencies, times of contact, requests for repetitions, etc., should be carried on in what is called the Amateur Code, an international convention established among W/T amateurs before the war. It is safe to say that, had this arrangement not been made, and had all traffic been restricted to cyphered messages, communication would have repeatedly broken down altogether.

It was discovered that this Amateur Code gives scope, not only for technicalities, but for a quite surprising range of familiarities – apologies, greetings, confidences, and even such messages as 'Hope to meet you after the war!' It was occasionally so used by the extremely intelligent Sergeant of Signals (an ex-amateur) who has represented Paul Nicossof in his capacity of W/T operator during the last nine months. Latterly, he was taken into confidence about the particular mood in which Paul would be transmitting. It is believed that much verisimilitude was added to the enciphered messages by timely suggestions of danger and urgency and, on other occasions, of ease and good-fellowship. It is certain that something was learnt of the enemy's W/T operators and of how best to deal with their vagaries.

This correspondence between the matter of the enciphered messages and the encoded comments on the manner of sending was most continuously maintained during the period of actual re-establishment. An officer familiar with the whole background of the case was present at each transmission, giving the sergeant a rough outline of what was required and dictating such things as promptness or delay in replying, courtesy, irritation or warnings.

It has been already stated that, as the enemy's requests for fuller and more frequent information increased, his mistakes in cyphering, failure to keep appointments and general inefficiency of W/T procedure increased to such an alarming extent that it was at one time feared we were going to lose contact altogether. The W/T experts called in to advise on this curious aberration came to the conclusion that the fault lay almost entirely with the enemy. This greatly strengthened the impression that there was extremely imperfect co-operation at Bari between the Directors of Intelligence, eager for information from Egypt, and the staff at their disposal, disinclined to take much trouble or ensure its proper reception. Paul was made to send protests and pathetic appeals, but it was thought inadvisable to make them too emphatic, in case the culprits should begin suppressing his messages to conceal their own inadequacies from their superiors. The trouble gradually cured itself, but there is little or no guarantee that it may not recur.

VII. Conclusion

This report can only give the more salient facts of an extremely complicated case, and nothing but guesswork about the reasons why an apparently discredited source has recently regained the confidence of the enemy. Even the facts are capable of other interpretations than those given, and there are some questions of detail that have never been satisfactorily explained. It is also too early to form any decisive judgement on the case. CHEESE is still in action, and it is hoped that he will long remain so, to the better confusion of His Majesty's enemies.

This rather bland account of CHEESE's origins lays bare three developments of historic proportions. Firstly, there was CHEESE's value as a counter-intelligence asset in his identification of several Axis intelligence officers, among them Count Carlo Sirombo, Clemens Rossetti, Kurt Zahringer, Hans Travaglio and Erich Helfferich. All would reappear in ISOS intercepts and play important roles in their respective intelligence agencies. Indeed, Travaglio was of considerable interest to SIS as he was known to have participated, under the alias of 'Major Johannes Solms' in the notorious Venlo incident in November 1939, when a pair of British officers were abducted at the Dutch frontier. A Luftwaffe officer attached to Ast Stuttgart, Travaglio was married to the celebrated Viennese opera singer Hildegard Ranscak. He had masqueraded as an anti-Nazi to lure Major Richard Stevens and Captain Sigismund Payne Best to a rendez-vous close to the German frontier.[4]

Similarly, Count Sirombo was not entirely unknown as the Venetian nobleman had been one of the SIM delegation that had travelled to Spain during the Civil War on SS *Leone Pancaldo* to offer *materiél* support to Franco's forces.

Secondly, CHEESE found a potential solution to the familiar problem of finding methods for the Germans to pay their agents. The challenge of creating a practical conduit through which to fund espionage had always presented a major obstacle and invariably threatened to undermine a promising double agent's credibility. CHEESE, however, encouraged the idea of employing an intermediary in neutral Istanbul, and explained away inaccurate information by pleading he was unable to pay for top quality material. Shifting responsibility for the collection of demonstrably false information from the spy-rings to their German paymasters was a shrewd ploy to persuade Berlin to justify an increase in its financial commitment to networks under Allied control.

In addition, CHEESE pioneered the concept of the notional sub-source, in the persons of his Greek girlfriend, his radio operator Paul Nicossof, and the South African source known as PIET. There were obvious risks in employing such tactics, as the enemy might seek independent verification of the individual's *bona-fides*, or take measures to authenticate their alleged status or access, but there was an equally great danger in a requirement to indoctrinate a nominee to act a particular role. Significantly, CHEESE was the first time any British organization had attempted such a large-scale hoax, and the evidence available on ISOS indicated that the fraud had been successful. It soon became evident that CHEESE's advantage was that the Axis simply did not have the ability to double-check on his activities. Isolated in Egypt, at the centre of a region of increasing strategic importance, CHEESE was exercising a virtual monopoly on intelligence collection, giving SIME the unprecedented advantage of ISOS to gauge Berlin's reactions. Theoretically at least, ISOS greatly reduced the danger of CHEESE imploding, thereby compromising the entire deception campaign.

A second SIME report, covering CHEESE's activities between August 1942 and February 1943, continued the narrative from the British perspective:

CHEESE SUMMARY

The following report summarizes CHEESE's activities for the period 1 August 1942 to 16 February 1943 under the following headings:

(1) Notional background
(2) Operational
(3) Money
(4) W/T transmissions
(5) Code

1. NOTIONAL BACKGROUND

The previous report presents no clear background of CHEESE. This vagueness is deliberate, for we had no knowledge of what was said about Paul Nicossof when he returned to Turkey.

The successive 'money plans' showed the necessity of a clearly etched 'notional' background for CHEESE: how he lived – where he lived – the circles wherein he moved and gathered his information and so forth.

His 'crise de nerfs' in mid-July 1942 indicated that his mode of living wasn't normal. A man of mixed Caucasian and Syrian parentage – temperamental – shrewd – not without considerable courage – a skilled W/T operator and mechanic – living in hourly danger of detection and death yet proud of his ability to elude the attention of the British Intelligence Service – he lived on his wits – awaiting the reward for his services to the Axis.

In July he found an 'amie' – a Greek girl animated by hatred of the British – well-educated, intelligent, witty and courageous, sustaining him when discouraged or disgruntled – she aided and abetted him by forming a series of friendships – and possibly 'alliances' – with British and American officers – military and Air Force.

From these she extracted information of varying degrees of reliability and importance. This enabled CHEESE to supplement information gleaned from Greek military friends and other acquaintances.

Without funds – he could no longer employ reliable agents. All information – whether high level or low – true or false – he passed on to his Axis friends – leaving them to sift the chaff from the wheat. Those sources that misinformed him he discarded, and thus always had the requisite retort if and when accused of passing on false information.

For instance – on 7 August 1942 he said that he was sorry giving false information but without money he had to collect such information as his friends told him and report what he saw himself.

He chose a flat in Heliopolis from which to work, because its proximity to military W/T installations guaranteed his transmitting set from detection.

He was suspicious of his neighbours and said so on 23 September 1942. On several occasions he has declined to transmit over extended periods because of the danger in which his prolonged use of direct current from 'mains' might involve him.

Uncertainty of livelihood – curtailment of his Black Bourse [Black market] activities and the non-arrival of funds from his Axis partners finally forced him to find regular employment.

After trying from 7 December 1942 until 25 December he secured a post as an interpreter in the OETA, commencing his duties on 1 January 1943.

His amie continues to collaborate. He mentioned her first to the Germans on 24 July and on 27 July he said that she could decode already and was learning to transmit.

At the moment she is the active intermediary for collecting the money due to him – and both are anxiously awaiting its arrival.

2. OPERATIONAL

'A' Force Advance HQ provides purely military information (this includes Naval and Air Force items and movements of highly important individuals).

Special Section, SIME, provides domestic items, 'build-up' of sources and deals with W/T problems.

During the period under review (1 August 1942 to 16 February 1943) the informal committee – which (under the direction of the Commander, Advance HQ 'A' Force) really constitutes CHEESE – has built up, and passed over successfully, no less than six major items. These, we believe, engendered six serious headaches!

Despite these items, most secret sources inform us that CHEESE is still quoted as 'reliable' and 'authentic'. In addition CHEESE maintains a steady stream of low-level information, of which a high proportion is true.

The following analysis shows the volume of W/T traffic that the a/m has involved.

Month	Messages Sent	Messages Received	Nights 'On the Air'
August 1942	21	6	21
September	15	7	21
October	20	10	25
November	13	17	28
December	13	6	27
January 1943	8	7	28
February	3	2	13
(to date)	92	15	26

3. MONEY

The table of messages below gives CHEESE's complaints about money, and some embodied details of plans to get money to him.

Month	From CHEESE	From Enemy
August 1942	6	3
September	6	5
October	6	2
November	6	3
December	6	5
January 1943	5	3
February	3	2

These messages give a good picture of CHEESE's temperament. They run the gamut of his emotions; rising from pathetic whines to a crescendo of angry – not to say violent – accusations of hypocrisy and deliberate deceit; then dying down to a disgruntled 'no money – no information'.

In response to the enemy's provocative replies to his complaints in August 1942 he had evolved and the enemy had accepted a plan by mid September, whereby a Greek merchant friend went (27 September) to Aleppo to collect CHEESE's money.

The friend, scared by the execution of five Axis spies at Aleppo a few days previously – returned 4 October and CHEESE abandoned this plan. He was very discouraged.

During October a plan complete in detail to dates, times, place, recognition and passwords – was evolved. The money was to be expected between 10–15 November. This plan fell through also (possibly because of the 8th Army's activities).

On 21 November CHEESE 'blows up' and as a result receives on 7 December the news 'that the money is already in his town'. This electrifies CHEESE. He finds a friend's flat ('amie' having given up hers through lack of funds) whereat 'amie' can receive the money. This is to be delivered by a 'hamel' (porter or native labourer) in either a 'bottle of milk' or in 'a packet'.

The flat is (factually) raided by the Egyptian police. This gives CHEESE a severe attack of the 'jitters'. He passes on this news 17 December, and says his 'amie' is looking for another and safer place. On 20 December he tells the enemy that the police raid was a domestic affair; but he is badly frightened.

However, he borrows the money for and finds another (quite safe) flat – installing 'amie' by 15 January 1943. He asks the enemy to divert the courier to the new address. They reply that they will try their best, but doubt whether it will be possible to do so.

On 6 February the enemy confirms that it is impossible to effect the desired change, and, filled with an increasing anxiety, CHEESE now awaits the courier's arrival at the former address.

4. W/T TRANSMISSIONS

During the period under review, CHEESE – in the person of Sergeant Shears, RCS – has faced and overcome numerous technical difficulties. Of the 163 occasions when he was 'on the air' as many as 24 transmissions were unsuccessful due to four causes,

(1) Bad atmospheric conditions (particularly October–November);
(2) Heavy interference;
(3) Incompetence or laziness of enemy operator;
(4) Enemy 'not on the air'.

The third cause became so bad that on 21 October he registered a complaint in no mean terms. This had the effect of bringing new operators into action.

The enemy are now using 6 operators whom we call:-

The 'original', for whom CHEESE has a high regard;
The 'goon' – a dull-witted and lazy operator;
'Curt' – so called from his style;
'Good' – an expert 'Ham' operator;
'New Good' – first appeared late in December 1942;
'Square Morse' – a good operator who sends in continental style.

Wave lengths have been changed three times. We can now work two alternative frequencies. Call signs have been changed five times and hours of transmission three times.

5. CODE

The code is somewhat cumbersome, and is based upon the 'Playfair' system. An explanation of this code is attached.

We have evolved a style – over a period of several months – that is distinctive, and which can be picked up in a day by a new cipher officer – if need be. This style uses the 16 variants for each letter – before any one is repeated.

We believe that to break down this code – so used – would entail very considerable trouble over a prolonged period.

The shortest message sent contains 15 groups and the longest 270.

The enemy uses two encoders – one of whom is lazy and careless – sometimes shockingly so. He causes endless trouble when we have to decode his 'messages'. Neither displays any desire to use more than a minimum of variants for any given letter, and from a Security 'intercept' point of view – both are criminally careless.

EXPLANATION OF CYPHER DEVISED FOR CHEESE

The cypher may best be described as an extension of the familiar Playfair system.

The keyword is written down (omitting any repeated letters) as the beginning of a square of 5 letters by 5. This square is then filled by writing down the rest of the alphabet omitting all letters already used. In order to reduce the alphabet from 26 letters to 25, it is also necessary to omit 'K'. Thus, if the keyword is ELEMENTS the square will be:

```
E  L  M  N  T
S  A  B  C  D
F  G  H  I  J
O  P  Q  R  U
V  W  X  Y  Z
```

Each letter of the 'clear' is represented by a pair of cypher letters. The first letter of the pair may be *any* letter in the same vertical line as the letter to be enciphered; the second is any letter in the same horizontal line. Thus LD represents A, UM represents T, etc.

It will be noted that the cypher differs from (and has one great advantage over) Playfair, in that there are 16 alternative ways of enciphering any given letter: B can be enciphered as SL, SM, SN, ST, FL, FM, FN, FT, OL, OM, ON, OT, VL, VM, VN or VT.

'K' being omitted from the square is the signal for numerals. The first two lines of the square following 'K' become the figures 1 (E), 2 (L) etc., up to 0 (D). The signal for ''numbers off' is the letter G encoded,. i.e. AH, WJ or the equivalent. The letters standing for numerals must also be encoded. 1 is not represented by B but by SL, OT or its equivalent.

It was arranged that the third word of each message should be the keyword for the next. Thus if a message (say on Monday) began with the words 'Argent pas encore rive ...' the square for Thursday's message would be as follows:

E N C O R
A B C F G
H I J L M
P Q S T U
V W X Y Z

In case of emergency or doubt, a standard keyword was arranged. If it was not known whether the other side had or had not received the last message, or was likely to make any mistake about it, the square was to be constructed on the keyword EQUINOX. To indicate that this was being done, the first group of the message was to be SCOOI. This precaution proved a wise one. Owing partly to the incompetence of the enemy, partly to technical troubles, the emergency codeword has had to be used over and over again.

It will be clear to the expert that, in spite of the alternatives, the cypher does not present any very grave difficulties to the 'cracker'. This did not matter, so far as we were concerned, though it should have caused the enemy some anxiety, had he been alive to our W/T security precautions. Meanwhile it was easy and quick to work, and (with a little care) free from possible ambiguities.

Special Section, ŞIME

After his astonishingly brave decision to return to Italy in April 1941, Levi's SIME handler, Evan Simpson, could only catch glimpses in ISOS of his experiences as he travelled from Istanbul to Rome, only to be arrested, convicted of black-marketeering, and imprisoned on the island of Tremiti, where he was incarcerated in November 1941. Thus ended the first part of CHEESE's remarkable odyssey. Over the following two years, categorized as a political prisoner, he endured terrible privations that broke his health. What baffled the distant observers in Cairo was the nature of the charges against Levi. Why had not the Abwehr intervened with their Italian colleagues to help him? Was he suspected of greater crimes? Bizarrely, the German attitude towards Nicossof appeared to be unaffected.

When the Allies eventually arrived in San Severo, on the mainland, in October 1943 CHEESE was in the town gaol, having been transferred from the local hospital. Although he made many attempts to re-establish contact with his British handlers, the chaotic conditions then prevailing prevented his messages from reaching SIME until February 1944, when steps were taken to bring him to Cairo under the alias 'Mr Rose'.

Following a period of recovery in Egypt, SIME decided that CHEESE's clandestine career was far from over and once again he was put to work in the Allied cause, this time in Greece, in a scheme code-named JACOBITE. According to the proposal made by Nicossof in September, CHEESE would travel to Athens to create a stay-behind network to report on Allied activities across the Balkans. The Germans welcomed the idea and promised to bury a quantity of gold, together with a transmitter, in a cache secreted in Chillabdariou Street in the suburb of Physhiko. However, when a team of SIS officers visited the site, described in minute detail by the Abwehr, neither money nor radio could be found, so it was decided, finally, to terminate CHEESE once and for all. Even though the Germans continued to transmit to CHEESE during March 1945, the call-signs went unanswered, and thus the case was, as the intelligence professionals termed it, 'liquidated', despite protests from MI5 in London which recommended that a further attempt should be made to revive CHEESE.

Levi returned to Italy to be reunited with his wife, Michaela Villa, and their son Luciano, and with his mistress Lia Socci, a dancer from Livorno, by whom he had a son, Roberto. Levi would eventually divorce Michaela, and rarely spoke of his wartime activities. His health had been broken during his imprisonment on Tremiti. Levi died in St Pancras Hospital, London, of a cerebral haemorrhage on 6 September 1955, at the age of 52, and his death certificate gave his occupation as hotelier, and his address as 3 Richmond Buildings, Dean Street, a block of flats in the centre of Soho. The informant was his son Luciano. Levi is buried at Kensal Green Cemetery, his role as one of the century's greatest spies to remain under wraps for another sixty years.

Chapter 6

Richard Wurmann

U.35 does not feel that Major Wurmann is the type of
person he ever wants to see again once the orange has
been squeezed dry

[Klop Ustinov, April 1943[1]]

Prior to the Allied invasion of North Africa in November 1942 very little
was known about the enemy's intelligence apparatus, apart from some
pre-war manifestations, and the interrogation of low-level spies captured
during the 'invasion summer' of 1940. It was understood, mainly through
reports from German-occupied territory, that the Germans appeared to
run several different, fragmented intelligence and security agencies,
among them the Abwehr, the Sicherheitsdienst and the Gestapo, which
were largely uncoordinated and often appeared to be in competition with
one another. The development of the cryptographic source ISOS by the
Radio Security Service seemed only to muddy an already confusing
picture. This situation would change dramatically when, on 8 November
1942, a senior Abwehr officer was captured by British troops near the
Tunisian border and indicated his willingness to cooperate with his
interrogators.

Major Richard Ernst Heinrich Wurmann, married but in the process of obtaining a legal separation from his wife, told his captors that
he hoped for an opportunity to negotiate peace by contacting his former
chief, Admiral Wilhelm Canaris. Although the Allies had heard of this
mysterious figure, not much was known about him, nor even the structure
of his organization, but this lack of detailed information was about to
change, thanks to the source whose true identity would be concealed under
the codename HARLEQUIN for decades after the end of the war.
Wurmann's background was carefully documented during a series of interviews conducted throughout December by the Prisoner of War Interrogation Service (MI-19) at the mansion in Kensington Palace Gardens

known as the London Cage. The result was a lengthy report which was circulated on 5 January 1943:

A Chartered Accountant by profession, and his identity under the name of Wurmann has been checked in a 1939 edition of the Cologne telephone directory.

An ex-officer of the last war, when he was badly wounded twice, he holds the Hohenzollern EKI, and the Hohenzollern Yerlienstkreuz for bravery in the field. At the conclusion of the last war, he joined one of the freikorps, and took part in the civil war against the revolutionaries in Germany in 1919 and 1920.

In 1920 he joined the Stahlheim, of which he was an active member until he went to Chile in 1929. He had in the meantime qualified as a chartered accountant, and in 1920/21 was recalled to the Colours for a period as German Liaison Officer to the British Armistice Commission in Berlin.

He was subsequently employed in Valparaiso and various other South American towns, partly by Mannesmann AG and partly by Siemen-Schuckert. He denies any political activities during his stay in South America, which ended in 1933. On his return to Germany, he found that the Stahlheim had been incorporated in the Party, and he thus became a Party member.

In 1937 he was recalled to the reserve, and took part in the manoeuvres of that year as Company Commander in a machine-gun battalion.

In 1938 he was transferred to the Abwehr and participated in the 1938/1939 manoeuvres as an officer of the services at Ast Wehrkreis Munster. At the outbreak of war he was mobilized, and served in the Abwehrstelle Koln until May 1940, when he was lent to the Headquarters of the Army Group Von Kleist for the interrogation of British prisoners. He served in that capacity until Dunkirk, and after the Franco-German Armistice was first sent for three weeks to Paris, then to Biarritz to organize an Abwehrstelle, where he was stationed until November 1941. Details of Biarritz re given above. From December 1941 until March 1942 he worked in Berlin. Before being transferred to Algiers he was sent to Paris, where he was employed until the end of May 1942. Politically, he represents in its entirety the view of the German General Staff, i.e. that while they are grateful to the Party for having rebuilt the German armed forces, they dislike the excesses committed by the Party. If they could find a strong enough man amongst the General Staff, they would speedily eject Hitler and his satellites. The man chosen for this part was Brauschitsch, but since his disgrace there is no other strong enough.

It is of interest to note that many of the intimate and highly secret details in this report concerning the Abwehr had been furnished by Wurmann despite the fact that he is a major in the German SIS and an officer of many years' standing.[2]

Having established Wurmann's credentials, and learned from SIS's Section V that he had appeared in fifteen ISOS intercepts and that his Abwehr codename was BLANCO, the MI-19 interrogators proceeded to describe, for the very first time, the Abwehr:

ABWEHRDIENST

1. General. The German SIS or Abwehrdienst has no executive power. It is divided up into:

Gruppe I   Espionage
Gruppe II   Sabotage
Gruppe III   Counter-espionage

In peacetime Gruppe II is practically non-existent. Gruppe l is largely a skeleton service which is only expanded to its full strength during manoeuvres or periods of general mobilization and the greatest numerical strength lies in Gruppe III. Gruppe III carries out very extensive counter-espionage measures, both in the armed forces and in industry, but relies on the Gestapo for its executive powers at home. The Gestapo also carries out extensive counter-espionage work, even though its main and ostensible interest is political, and not military or economic. There is a considerable clash between the two branches as to the limits of their prerogatives.

It would appear that in practice the boundaries of their respective spheres have never been defined. In war time, counter-espionage activities of the Gestapo both in Germany and in occupied countries were intended to be confined to political matters; in practice the Gestapo has become the executive arm of Gruppe III.

There is now, however, a movement to transfer Gruppe II and Gruppe III of the Abwehrdienst to the Sicherheitsdienst. The Sicherheitsdienst is Gestapo Abteilung Ausland and, on paper at least, is concerned exclusively with political as opposed to military activities.

It has sections in the same towns as the Abwehrdienst, unknown to and uncoordinated with the Abwehrdienst. It is a fact that in Paris Gruppe III has already been transferred to the Sicherheitsdienst, whose Chief is Himmler. Canaris, the head of the Abwehrdienst, does not combat this tendency as he is principally interested in Gruppe I.

2. Germany.
The Abwehramt is a portion of the Oberkommando der Wehrmacht and is divided into three main groups, I, II and III. Each group is headed by a Leiter (indicated by 'L'); each group is divided into three main sub-sections: 'h' = Heer, 'm' = Marine, and Luft (Air). Gruppe I and Gruppe III have, in addition, numerous ancillary sub-sections, such as Wi = Wirstchaft, 'p' = Presse, 'f' = Funk, etc.

The Abwehramt in turn has under it a considerable number of Abwehrstelie which control Nebenstellen and Meldektipfe. All information, irrespective of origin, is passed by the Abwehrstelle concerned to the Abwehramt, where it is collated and passed to the appropriate department of the Army, Navy or Air Force, and not to the OKW. For instance, information procured by Gruppe I h is passed to the OKH, Abt, 1, Fremde Heere. The whole is commanded by Admiral Canaris, whose second-in-command is Oberst von Piekenbrock. Von Piekenbrock is also head of Gruppe I and a most intimate friend of Canaris.

Canaris takes no interest at all in administrative matters, nor in Gruppen II and III. His major interest is in Gruppe I, and in the many highly placed agents he has in various countries. He visits these latter regularly in person, and is usually accompanied by von Piekenbrock.

Canaris is described as a friendly individual, with an ice-cold brain, who knows every single subordinate of importance personally and fairly intimately. These, he always addresses as 'Du'. In private life he is a domesticated man, not given to intrigues, either private or political. He entertains a lot in his Berlin flat, but Party officials are never seen there. His intimates are believed to be Von Keitel, von Brauschitsch and particularly von List. He is on bad terms with Himmler and Ribbentrop, on no terms at all with Goering, and his attitude towards Hitler is described as 'diplomatic'. Hitler entrusts him with diplomatic missions of major importance, particularly in Spain, where his connections are first class.

He has no known vices, and is thought to be at heart a despiser of the Party. He shows no preference to naval officers in the matter of promotion.

The functions and status of an Abwehrstelle in Peace.

NOTE: Although for the sake of clarity the word 'Abwehrstelle' is used throughout this report, all such Stellen outside Germany are called 'KO' = 'Kriegsorganization'

It appears that in peace time the Abwehrstelle is either part of, or identical with, Section l(c) of the Wehrkreiskommando. It is not entirely clear whether the officers of Gruppe I h of the Abwehrstelle are identical with the officers of Section l(c) of the Wehrkreiskommando, but this certainly is the case with the smaller sections such as Wi, i, p, etc. Each Abwehrstelle works independently of any other Abwehrstelle, and while it may have a particular country or countries allotted to it, this does not prevent the Abwehrstelle from sending agents to any other country, except to those countries in which a properly organized Abwehrstelle exists.

The functions and status of an Abwehrstelle in War.

At the outbreak of war each Abwehrstelle takes in the numerous reserve officers who were attached to it during manoeuvres, and forms a number of Nebenstellen and Meldekopfe. It is usual for a Nebenstelle to have a Gruppe I and Gruppe III, but no Gruppe II officer. A Meldekopf usually consists of one officer only, who is placed near a frontier for the purpose of collecting messages brought across that frontier by agents. A Meldekopf does not appoint agents, but, as the name indicates, simply collects messages.

It is the Abwehrstelle which recruits agents, trains them and sends them to the particular country for which they are best suited. This is done without reference to anyone unless the country in question already possesses an Abwehrstelle. In this case, the Abwehrstelle of the country concerned must be consulted. Thus, the Abwehrstelle Cologne can send agents to the United Kingdom on its own initiative, but before sending an agent to Spain, it would have to consult the Abwehrstelle Madrid. No confirmation can be found of the theory that each Abwehrstelle specializes in one particular subject. Wurmann thinks that this impression may have arisen from cases where a specialist, sitting in one or other of the Stellen, has betrayed abnormal interest in some particular subject. The large number of officials at any one Abwehrstelle is accounted for by the extreme importance attached to Gruppe III.

Abwehrstelle WIESBADEN. This is located at the Hotel Vier Jahreszeiten, where one of the senior officers was a Major Hebelein. It occupied quarters in the same hotels as the Armistice Commission, and its W/T officer in 1941 was Leutnant Blim, who certainly did the W/T work both for the Armistice Commission and for the Abwehr.

It controls the Abwehr in North Africa, via Casablanca, but does not appear to have any direct connection with, or control over, the Abwehrstelle Paris.

Its cover address is 1a, Afrika, Waffenstillsstandskommission. It has a close liaison with Stuttgart, but which of the two holds precedence could not be ascertained.

Abwehrstelle STUTTGART. The Abwehrstelle at Stuttgart is on the second floor of Olgastrasse 13, which is opposite Post Office No. 9.

The Gestapo office is in the Watsenhaus in Charlottenplatz (now called Danziger Freiheit).

The Stuttgarter Rundfunk is in the same building, the whole of which is guarded by an SS Wache, whose Haupttruppe is also quartered there.

A detailed sketch of the layout of the buildings is attached.

Tuition in W/T is carried out at the former Schurgeschaft Heere in the Friederichstrasse, near the Post Office, where Morse is taught in the Kunstgewerebe Schole, at the Waldenhof where technical theory is taught, and at a place in the Necharstrasse, almost opposite the State Theatre, coming from Charlottenplatz. The name on the door is 'Georgi', who is a hauptmann in the German Army. The instructors wear mufti, but they are all thought to be army NCOs.

Abwehrstelle Munster. The Abwehrstelle in Munster is definitely the same department as the Ic of the Wehrkreiskommando VI. The total strength in peace-time is 10/15 officers. Nothing is known of the allegation that Munster specifically directs operations against the United Kingdom and the USA, nor is this thought very likely.

Nebenstelle Cologne. The Nebenstelle Cologne comes under Munster; it is located in the Reiterstrasse close to the Oberlandeagericht and not the Stollwekhaus. The front door bears the cover name of 'Institut fur Wirtschaftsforshung'. It is commanded by

Dr Falkner (probably with the rank of Oberstleutnant) whose real name is Focke.

This man is an ex-officer from the last war and is director of a machine tool factory. Gruppe Wi is Haupt Dr Ernst Dornheim, a well known Cologne solicitor and the brother of a chartered accountant in Cologne. Borheim is his real name. The head of Gruppe II is thought to be Dr Becker.

From 3 September 1939 to 13 May 1940 Wurmann was in charge of a Meldekopf at Hellenthal which came under Cologne, and which was concerned with collecting information from Belgian agents.

France (Biarritz). Wurmann ran the Nebenstelle at Biarritz from August 1940 until November 1941. Biarritz controls the area Bayonne, St Jean de Luz and Hendaye. It is in turn responsible to the Abwehrstelle Bordeaux.

Its main function is the supervision of frontier traffic, the collection of information from Spaniards who had facilities for travelling to Madrid or England, and the protection of German Abwehr officers who crossed the frontier to and from Spain. Wurmann originally ran both Gruppe I and III under cover of 'Liaison Officer to Spain', from his villa Alma Nova, Rue Falaise, Biarritz, but subsequently Gruppe III was taken away from him and the whole Stelle under the charge of the officer i/c this Gruppe. These were in turn Major Heckel until March 1941, Fregattenkapitan Stobbe until May 1941. This officer is now at the Abwehrstelle at Royan, and was succeeded at Biarritz by Major Heidschuk, now in charge of Gruppe III at Naples, with the rank of Oberstleutnant. He was there until December 1941.

The main office of the Abwehr then moved to the Carlton Hotel.

Spain

The Abwehrstelle in Madrid is located in the German Embassy in Madrid, and maintains communications with Berlin, Tangier, and various Spanish Nebenstellen by means of powerful W/T transmitters also located at the German Embassy. The Leiter is Kov. Hap. Lenz (cover name SUMMER). Gruppe I is handled by von Kuhlenthal, said to be the son of a former German military attaché in Paris. There is no Gruppe II and Gruppe III used to be directed by Major Heim but the name of the latter's successor could not be ascertained. For a long time past Gruppe III has suspected von Kuhlenthal, who is reputed to be a relation of Canaris, of being in the pay of the British

SIS. Quite recently Major Heim, then head of Gruppe III, addressed a confidential report to Canaris setting out his suspicions and the reasons for them. Canaris refused to take the report seriously, and Heim was subsequently transferred.

Other officers employed by Gruppe I are Korv. Kpt. Gardemann (cover name GUDE) and Lang. Dily. Working hours at the KO Madrid are 9–1pm and 4–8.00pm. The principal figure is von Kuhlenthal who is described by Wurmann as 'Madchen fur Allies'. One of his chief assistants is Joaquin Canaris who is a nephew or stepson of the Admiral. Von Kuhlenthal only interests himself in the Spanish Nebelstellen, but is also active in providing agents for the United Kingdom, USA and North Africa. He is said to have had some considerable successes, particularly in the USA.

The German Abwehr officers frequent the bar of the Palace hotel in Madrid and invariably wear plain clothes. They are often in the company of Oberstleutnant Wilhelmie, the German assistant military attaché in Madrid but it is not known how far the latter is concerned with Abwehr duties. The Ambassador himself takes a keen interest in the work and once visited Wurmann's Abwehrstelle in Biarritz. From his conversation it was obvious that he was completely *au fait* with local Abwehr matters.

A lot of information is obtained by the German SIS from the Spaniard upper classes who frequent the Ritz bar in Madrid. Some of these are reported to move in circles close to the British Embassy. Among those mentioned as close to the British Embassy are:

Martinez de Kamposie (of Spanish SIS)
Conde Charas (ex-diplomat)
Tony Clavico
Marchese Orrizaga
Contessa Ileves
Serge Dinim
Conde Simera
Vejarrovo (a Falangist, and active in procuring the return of objets d'art)
Trias (brother-in-law of the above)

Bilbao

One of the Nebenstellen controlled from Madrid is that of Bilbao. Gruppe I is run by the honorary German consul, named Otto

Mesner, and Gruppe III is run by Otto Henrichren. It is alleged that Mesner is also the representative of the Gestapo in Bilbao. The work is carried out from the private addresses of these two people. But the addresses could not be ascertained. Erhardt & Co., local suppliers and exporters, are the local suppliers of Thyssen of Phoenix. Erhardt is a great friend of Mesner, and is reputed to be also known to Furch.

San Sebastian

This Nebenstelle comes [under] Bordeaux. For some reason this Nebenstelle is frequently visited by senior members of the Abwehramt, Berlin. It is very possible that these visits are connected with the dispatch of agents from Spain to England and other countries. Head of Gruppe III is Alfred Cencerowski, who used to work at the German Consulate in San Sebastian, but who may now have moved. He conducts an import and export business as cover for his Abwehr work. Head of Gruppe I is Fritz Furch, not Furche, as given in GLIST.[3]

Almost immediately, Wurmann demonstrated the depth of his knowledge, and his willingness to answer detailed questions. On 21 January 1943 Guy Liddell minuted the acceptance of Wurmann's offer to help the Allies in return for permission to remain in England after the war:

Reference the document at 9A in which Wurmann offers his services to the democratic powers in a capacity except that of a fighting soldier, consideration was given at the Joint meeting between SIS and the Security Service on 20 January 1943 to the possibility of making use of Wurmann as a reference library in all matters affecting the Abwehr. For these services it was agreed that he would have to be granted a certain measure of liberty and that possibly some provision would have to be made for looking after him after the war. It was felt, however, that no definite offer should be made to him until we had had an opportunity to assess his character and extract from him all the information that he is bound to possess.

It was agreed that the Security Service should undertake this work and explore, through Major Scotland, the possibility of getting Wurmann handed over by the American authorities, whose prisoner he is. We would also arrange for him to be housed and interviewed by someone suitable for the purpose.

The present position is that we should get him transferred from the hotel near Oxford where he is resident with an officer from MI-19, to the house of U.35, who strikes me as being in every way suitable to conduct the preliminary enquiries.[4]

Acceptance by MI5 and SIS of Wurmann's terms, which included an annual salary of £300 and the occupation of a rent-free flat, began a relationship that, in the end, only lasted some five months, but was to be of immense value to both intelligence agencies. Wurmann's experience dated back to before the war, and his postings to Berlin, Paris, Italy and Athens gave MI-19 a hitherto unprecedented glimpse into the Abwehr's innermost secrets. Of particular interest to his interrogators was the period he spent on the Spanish border supervising the transit of agents destined for England, and his recollection of KO Madrid personalities had the potential of triggering local counter-intelligence operations. Furthermore, Wurmann remained willing to act as a human encyclopedia, disclosing details of the Abwehr's relationship with the Spanish personalities. However, in April 1943 MI5's Herbert Hart and Dick White took Wurmann out to dinner in London and observed that

> HARLEQUIN has an extremely bad conscience. Much of his mental energy appears to be absorbed in persuading himself that he is only acting in the highest interest of the German people by collaborating with us. He is obsessed with the idea of a compromise peace. He appears to suppose that this can be brought about by means of negotiation with Admiral Canaris with himself and possibly Prince Hohenlohe acting as intermediaries.
>
> In view of the uncompromising terms in which HARLEQUIN recognizes the necessity of the overthrow of the National Socialist Party as a precondition of peace, this Hessian line was felt to be decidedly out of place.

Wurmann's conscience would eventually get the better of him, but while he was still in a cooperative mood he provided the key to Allied counter-intelligence success. He was able to identify individual officers from (heavily disguised) ISOS reporting, and provide reassurance about Abwehr concerns regarding hostile penetration by double agents, and the lack of assets already in England. When eventually other Abwehr sources became available, such as Erich Vermehren in January 1944, Wurmann adopted the role, although he was unaware of it, of a method of verification. In March 1943 MI5's Helenus Milmo referred to the 'copious intelligence which HARLEQUIN has supplied me to date' and commented to

Charles Stuart, his Section V counterpart in SIS, 'his general description of the leading personalities of the Abwehr is so clearly correct that I do not really think it stands in need of amplification'. As a peacetime barrister with the reputation of being MI5's toughest interrogator, Milmo added 'I have not the slightest doubt that he is being entirely frank.'[5] As for his motivation, it was noted that Wurmann recalled having attended a conference held at the Hotel des Ambassadeurs in Paris in May 1942 attended by all the Abwehr officers in France where the audience listened to a very candid assessment of the military situation delivered by the Chief of Abteilung Fremde Heer. 'HARLEQUIN states that, as a result of this lecture, all Abwehr officers realized after the German offensive in the summer of last year had failed, that the war was lost.'[6]

For ten days following his release from MI-19's custody, Wurmann was questioned gently by Klop Ustinov, known to MI5 as U.35, at his country home in Gloucestershire. Ustinov, who asserted that 'Wurmann is overcome occasionally by feelings of being a traitor', found his task disagreeable, but nevertheless completed a comprehensive report, lavishly illustrated with organizational charts, the contents page of which shows its breadth:

> Abwehr Terminology; Organization and personnel of Amt Ausland/ Abwehr, Berlin; Organization and personnel of 'Asts', 'Nests' and 'Meldekopfe'; Abwehr organization, France (occupied territory); Asts Brussels, Athens; KOs Spain, Portugal, Switzerland, Turkey; Organization of staffs of Divisions, Army Corps, Army; Women (secretaries, shorthand typists) employed by Abwehr; Agents employed and Agents mentioned by Wurmann (excluding the Algiers net exhaustively covered by another section of the War Office); Recruitment and running of Agents; General Intelligence; Prewar Abwehr vis-à-vis England; Function of Abwehr offizier at Army Headquarters on front; Relations of Abwehr – Gestapo – Sicherheitsdienst; Professions favoured by Abwehr for 'V' work; Particulars of all persons of interest known to Wurmann (in alphabetical order); Curriculum vitae of Major Wurmann; General Conclusions re (a) the Abwehr (b) Major Wurmann personally.

Among the topics covered by HARLEQUIN, quite apart from the numerous questionnaires submitted by other branches of British Intelligence, were such issues as British wireless agents in France run as double agents; leakages of information from indiscreet members of the British

Embassy staff in Madrid; Canaris's trusted 'gentlemen agents', such as Prince Max Hohenlohe and the controversial French businessman Charles Bedaux, and the Portuguese spy Rogeiro de Menezes. He was also invited to complete personality profiles on his colleagues, friends and agents, and offer opinions on a myriad of other subjects. The result was, for the first time, that the many branches of British Intelligence began to develop a sense of quiet confidence that they might have the measure of their opponents. In particular, Wurmann made comments relevant to the double agent cases of WATCHDOG[7] (then in Canada), DRAGONFLY[8] and FATHER[9], without giving the slightest hint that they had been compromised. Additionally, he made some shocking disclosures, describing the Abwehr's reliance on signals intelligence to identify the Allied order-of-battle, remarking on the very poor security exercised by wireless operators, and explaining how the Abwehr routinely recruited Jewish refugees as agents. As Herbert Hart reported, after an interview conducted in February 1943:

> According to Wurmann, England is badly covered by the Abwehr. The best information comes from the Funk Uberwaching. Wurmann has seen the periodical results of this W/T traffic and says he was terribly upset when he realized how useless the pure Abwehr work was compared to the splendid W/T interception service. He says that by means of this service everything is known to the Germans about the distribution of the different divisions in England, their numbers, etc. He saw similar results in Athens from the W/T interception service in Egypt. This information came from Rommel who also sent it to Berlin.

HARLEQUIN's comments about lax signals security, and the Abwehr's reliance on interception, evidently touched a raw nerve in London where MI5's Guy Liddell reacted by reporting the matter to his minister, Duff Cooper. This was followed in April 1943 with a special report prepared for the Prime Minister, one of only two such documents specifically for his eyes only, without a copy being retained by the Cabinet Office.

By May 1943 Wurmann had developed a severe case of cold feet, as was described by Helenus Milmo, who took him out to dinner. Clearly he had been greatly affected by the widely publicized dismissal of Admiral Canaris, and he had come to suspect that MI5 had only promised him British citizenship as an inducement. Meanwhile, the British had concluded that they had extracted just about everything of value, and readily agreed to his request to be returned to the general PoW population, which meant a transfer from his flat in Chelsea to a prison camp in the United States, and a welcome release from a potentially lengthy and unrewarding commitment to the man now living at liberty as 'Heinrich Steinbock'.

I took HARLEQUIN for dinner tonight. My purpose was to bring it home to him that his transfer to a prison camp, which I had fore-shadowed in my last meeting with him, was rapidly approaching. HARLEQUIN's reaction tonight was characterized by the same sense of inevitability and the same satisfaction at having regained his conscience, which he had displayed the other day. His only hope was that the transfer should not take place before Friday. As the reason for this wish was, however, nothing more than the arrival of the laundryman, I could reassure him about the fate of his laundry by pointing out to him that it could always reach him in hospital, where he would have to pay a flying visit in order to be examined for the complaint which will provide the excuse and cover for his prolonged separation from his playmates. To this too HARLEQUIN readily agreed and even provided a genuine affliction in the shape of appen-dicitis, which had caused him pains and trouble in recent weeks. HARLEQUIN wishes it to be known, however, that the hospital doctor should not be given a free hand to follow his vocation in the normal way and to appropriate his appendix. HARLEQUIN wishes to keep his appendicitis. HARLEQUIN also wishes to remain the owner of the money which he seems to have at his bank and hopes that Major Caroe, whose absenteeism of late he has not failed to notice, will visit him, if possible today, in order to discuss with him the fate of his personal belongings such as clothes, which he cannot take with him into full captivity. The prospect of migration to the USA does not seem to astonish or worry HARLEQUIN. He shows, however, some predilection for not being in the same camp as the men with whom he came over. HARLEQUIN would also be grateful for some hint to the Americans that he is 'a good boy', without the slightest suggestion regarding the extent to which he was helpful. I made it perfectly clear to HARLEQUIN that not a word about the questions that were discussed with the British or the persons with whom these questions were discussed must come from his mouth and this he promised me solemnly, adding that if anyone had an interest to remain silent about the 'intermezzo' it was he himself. I repeated to HARLEQUIN Major Caroe's remark that one does not want to 'play the dirty' on him but expects too that he will play fair with us. To this HARLEQUIN agreed from all his heart, not quite seeing at the same time how he can do anything else. As HARLEQUIN's mind is, at the present moment, and possibly under the impression of the crushing events in Tunisia, travelling far ahead, he expressed the hope that, when general repatriation starts for prisoners of war, he may be allowed to return home via the UK in order to fetch his civilian clothes, (which he hopes Major Caroe will store for him in the meantime) and to take counsel with his British friends re the part which he might play in an occupied Germany. I told HARLEQUIN that he must consider this problem a 'cura posterior', but assured him at the same time that the services he had rendered would be remembered for all future eventualities. Everything is therefore set for HARLEQUIN's change of status.

In retrospect, Wurmann's contribution to the Allied cause was immense, although he probably never understood his true impact. In May 1945 Milmo explained the background to the case to the FBI, which had belatedly taken an interest in him:

> It is unnecessary to go into the details of the events leading up to this climax and it will suffice to say that HARLEQUIN became increasingly conscious on the one hand that our only interest in him was what we could get out of him and, on the other, that public opinion in this country is such that Germany will be completely crushed following upon the inevitable Allied victory. In consequence he commenced to experience difficulties with his conscience and asked to be relieved of his obligations under the bargain which was struck with him.
>
> On our part, we felt that there is little, if anything further, to be extracted from this particular source whereas our commitments, if the arrangements were to continue, remained very substantial. It was clearly entirely to our advantage to call the whole thing off at this stage and so we are putting no obstacles in HARLEQUIN's way and are parting with him on good terms.
>
> We have, however, taken the precaution to warn that we expect him to play fair with us as we intend to play with him. He fully realizes the weakness of his own position and that he has infinitely

more to lose than we have by any leakage with regard to what has taken place. We have fitted HARLEQUIN up with a cover story to account for his disappearance from the [PoW] camp for the past three or four months. Notionally he will have been transferred to an ordinary civilian hospital for treatment in connection with abdominal complaints.

In order that HARLEQUIN may never have any cause to complain that we have let him down, we would be very grateful if you could notify your Bureau of the position so that when HARLEQUIN reaches the States, as he no doubt will do in due course, no one will do anything which will 'blow' the period of his collaboration over here. I may say that we regard him as squeezed practically dry of any useful information which he possesses and in any event you may take it that he is now a 'reformed' character and is no longer prepared to talk freely if at all.[10]

This effectively ended HARLEQUIN's short-lived career as a defector, although in December 1943 the German government approached the Canadians, in the belief that Wurmann was in that country, seeking his release as part of a prisoner exchange, on the grounds that he had been a member of the Armistice Commission. When consulted, MI5 recommended against allowing Wurmann to be sent back to Germany, arguing that his Armistice Commission role was merely an Abwehr cover. Wurmann's MI5 file indicates that at the end of May 1945 he wrote to his initial MI5 case officer, Waldemar Caroe, to let him know that he anticipated his imminent release from his PoW camp at Ruston, Louisiana, and would be in touch again when he reached Cologne. There is no indication in the file that he ever did either.

INFANTRY UNIT

Officers   Soldiers   Horses   Carts

ARTILLERY UNIT

Officers   Soldiers   Horses   Guns   Ammunition Wagons

CAVALRY UNIT

Officers   Soldiers   Horses   Carts

BRIDGE TRAIN

Officers   Soldiers   Horses   Pontoons and Carts

Silhouettes showing composition of trains conveying constituted units.
Multiply all wagons and flat trucks by three to get requisite numbers
Retain one officer coach per train

A train-watching guide as issued by the British SIS to the WHITE LADY network in enemy-occupied France and Belgium during the First World War. The organization collected accurate intelligence about German troop movements and conveyed the information to GHQ over a chain of couriers.

Olga Gray, the MI5 agent designated M/12, who penetrated the Communist Party of Great Britain to expose a spy-ring and compromise the codebook used to encrypt messages transmitted on a clandestine radio channel to Moscow.

Westminster Bridge in September 1931 as Christopher Draper flies underneath the centre arch at low tide to draw attention to the plight of army veterans.

Christopher Draper's 1962 memoir *The Mad Major*, in which he described his role as an MI5 double agent engaged in a scheme to pass false information to the Abwehr.
The operation lapsed because of a reluctance to compromise classified information.

THE MAD MAJOR

THE AUTOBIOGRAPHY OF
Major Christopher Draper D.S.C.

Arnold Deutsch, the NVD illegal *rezident* in pre-war London, who was responsible for the recruitment of the Cambridge Ring-of-Five and a dozen other crypto-Communists.

Thedoore Maly, the NKVD's inspirational illegal *rezident* in London, who took over after Deutsch failed to renew his visa.

Josefine Deutsch acted as her husband's secretary and radio operator while he was the NKVD's illegal *rezident* in London. Their daughter Nina was born during their posting in London.

Edith Suschitsky, the veteran Comintern agent who arranged the introduction of her friend's husband Kim Philby to Arnold Deutsch in Regent's Park.

Renato Levi, the double agent codenamed CHEESE, whose network based in Cairo created the concept of strategic deception by inflating Allied strength across the Middle East.

Klop Ustinov, the MI5 agent designated U.35, who interrogated Erich Wurmann at his Gloucestershire cottage for ten days to obtain the Allies' first inside account of the Abwehr. Here he is pictured with his wife, the celebrated artist Nadia Benoist.

Al Sarant, a key figure in the Rosenberg spy-ring in New York, betrayed the secrets of airborne radar to the Soviets and managed a covert photographic studio to copy documents for the Rosenbergs. When they were arrested he had been interviewed by the FBI, so he fled to the Soviet Union where he would develop a micro-electronics industry.

Pavel Fitin, the NKVD Chief of Foreign Intelligence, masterminded Soviet espionage throughout the Second World War.

Engelbert Broda, the Austrian physicist and NKVD spy codenamed ERIC, who was Lizzy Philby's lover, recruited Alan Nunn May and influenced Klaus Fuchs.

Clyde Conrad faces conviction in a Federal German court for his involvement in a Hungarian network that stole NATO's defence plans for Europe.

Ex-Army Officer

PENTAGON SPY ARREST

THE WEATHER
Bay Area: Fair, except for morning cloudiness and drizzle near the ocean. High Wednesday, 60 to 70; low, 52 to 57. Westerly wind to 20 m.p.h. in the afternoon. See Page 40.

San Francisco Chronicle
THE VOICE OF THE WEST

★★★★
FINAL

102nd Year No. 194   CCCCAAA   WEDNESDAY, JULY 13, 1966   10 CENTS   GArfield 1-1111

In Broad Daylight

Jon Cresslia and Linda McKinnie staged a very realistic robbery

A Bad Place To Be a Victim

By Maitland Zane

A make-believe crime was staged at Powell and Sutter streets yesterday—and it showed what a cinch it is to get away with strongarm robbery in broad daylight.

Designed to alert the public to the dangerously high rate of crime in San Francisco's streets, the stunt was conducted by the Optimists Club.

The results were, however, depressingly negative.

The experiment showed that:

• Most people just stand and gawk when a woman is robbed and the thief runs off down the street.

• Most people pay no attention whatever to the victim's screams, or her cries of "Stop, thief!" They just walk on by.

• Those men who do come to the victim's aid are more or less ineffectual about it, and don't follow through by notifying police.

The pretty, gutsy gal for yesterday's robbery staged across the street from the St Francis Drake, was Linda McKinnie, 20, a bill, pretty secretary.

HOPE

The "crook" was Joe Cresslia, a muscular, well-spoken Post street jeweler who says that "our program is directed at apathy and non-involvement — law enforcement should be everybody's job, not just the cops' job.

"We are hoping that people will realize they ought to wake up and not be so selfish."

New Dispute Spikes Hopes In Air Talks

Times-Post Service

Washington

A dispute in Tokyo involving eight to ten men led to the collapse of negotiations to end the five-day-old airlines strike yesterday.

Negotiators for the International Association of Machinists abruptly walked out of a Federal mediation session when a charge that Northwest Airlines, one of the five struck carriers, had violated an agreement protecting the handful of union members working in Japan.

Assistant Labor Secretary James J. Reynolds was trying to resolve the matter and again to hopes that mediation could be resumed at 10 a.m. today. Even if what he

See Page 8, Col. 4

A Deadly Heat Wave Sizzles Over Midwest

Associated Press

St. Louis

A searing heat wave took a heavy toll of lives, trip-

To Ireland— By 12-Foot Sailboat

United Press

Ferrit, Ireland

A lone American sailor brought his homemade 12-foot sailboat into this small port on Ireland's west coast yesterday after a 65-day crossing of the Atlantic from Florida.

William Verity, 40, of Fort Lauderdale, Fla., made the voyage in his tiny sloop "Nonoalca" to fulfill his goal of crossing the Atlantic in the smallest boat on record.

Robert Manry, a Cleveland, Ohio, newsman crossed the Atlantic last year in a tiny boat without the Tinkerbelle.

IRISH

Verity said he also wanted to show it was possible that

nearly 11 inches of rain.

Unseasonably hot, sticky weather made life miserable

'Drowned' Lawyer's Return

By George Draper

A wealthy Maine lawyer, whose life was insured for $500,000 and who disappeared last April, turned up yesterday in San Mateo.

He is Philip S. Bird, 26, of Waterville, Maine, who presumably drowned while testing an outboard motor boat on the Kennebec river on April 4.

The boat was found washed up on the river bank but there was no sign of Bird, who is married and the father of three children.

NOTES

The attorney, who once ran unsuccessfully for mayor of Waterville, left no notes, apparently did not communicate with his family, and did not draw on his bank accounts.

Although the insurance companies did not pay off on his $500,000 policies pending further investigation, Bird's will was admitted to probate. In so doing last week, Kennebec County Probate Court Judge Lewis L. Naiman declared:

"A reasonable inference of death arises from his disappearance under such circumstances as would warrant the presumption that he died at the time of his disappearance."

FACTS

"Death is established by the showing of facts inconsistent with the continuance of life and such as would leave no conclusion that death had taken place."

Yesterday, however, Bird entered the San Mateo County General hospital and was placed under observation. A hospital spokesman said a formal psychiatric hearing

See Page 18, Col. 1

Police Kill 5 At India Protest

Lucknow, India

Police opened fire yesterday on a crowd of demonstrators protesting rising prices, killing five and injuring 60.

The demonstration in Banda, 120 miles south of here, was mounted by helping parties as part of a 24-hour general strike in Uttar Pradesh state. India's most populous.

Reuters

Strategic Secrets Sold To the Soviets, FBI Says

Ex-Aide to Joint Chiefs Indicted

New York Times

Washington

A retired Army lieutenant colonel was arrested yesterday for conspiring to spy for the Soviet Union while he served in a highly sensitive position with the Joint Chiefs of Staff.

William Henry Whalen, 51, was arrested by FBI agents on an indictment that accused him of conspiring with two Soviet Embassy employees to pass high-level defense information to the Soviet government.

The maximum penalty is death.

CONSPIRATORS

The Russians, identified in the indictment as Colonel Sergei Edemski and Mikhail A. Shumaev, were named as co-conspirators but not defendants since both have left the country.

According to the indictment, Whalen, who was decorated several times during his Army career, was paid $5000 in five instalments of $1000 and one payment of $500 between December, 1959, and March, 1961.

Whalen was said to have conspired to supply the Russians data on a wide range of sensitive subjects. It listed the following:

"Information pertaining to atomic weaponry, missiles, military plans for the defense of Europe, estimates of comparative military capabilities, military intelligence reports and analyses, information concerning the retal-

See Page 18, Col. 5

WILLIAM HENRY WHALEN, FREE ON BOND, REJOINED HIS WIFE
'I don't believe it,' she said. 'I don't believe it, I'll never believe it'

Johnson Opens Door to China

New York Times

Washington

President Johnson last night held out to Communist China the prospect of eventual reconciliation but emphasized that the war in Vietnam may last a long time.

White House officials characterized the President's speech as his first major statement on Communist China.

In it, they said, the President sought to look beyond the immediate conflict in Vietnam to the situation that could emerge in Asia after the war ends.

The President's statement on the long-range attitude of the United States toward Communist China was essentially a reiteration of what other Administration officials, such as Secretary of State Dean Rusk and Vice President Hubert H. Humphrey, have been saying recently.

REPORTS

And both the President in his speech and Rusk at a news conference earlier in the day, sought to counteract what the Administration regards as excessively optimistic interpretations in the

'A Lucrative Day' for U.S. War Planes

Associated Press

Saigon

The Communists launched nine missiles and two MIG-21 fighters Monday in an effort to curb intensified United States air attacks on North Vietnam, but a spokesman announced yesterday that Air Force pilots outmaneuvered all of them to press raids on missile, radar and fuel sites and other targets.

Navy fliers were officially credited with a "lucrative day."

They wrote off 99 barges and cargo junks as destroyed or damaged. One missile site was reported destroyed but the results of fuel site strikes was not given.

In all the Americans flew 101 missions, only a dozen short of the record 113 last Wednesday.

The U.S. Command announced the destruction of

The Poles Won't Run Either

Another track meet has become a casualty of the Vietnam war.

The Polish Sports Ministry said that Poland's track and field team, as a protest to U.S. policy in Vietnam, has adopted a "unanimous resolution" to withdraw from a meet against an American team that had been scheduled for this weekend in Berkeley.

For details, see the Sporting Green.

And in Moscow, the U.S. ambassador protested against a similar cancellation by the Russians of a

The Index

Arrested in July 1966, Lieutenant Colonel William Whalen was betrayed by Dmitri Polyakov and confessed to having sold classified information on five occasions between December 1959 and March 1961.

John Walker's spy-ring effectively neutralized the US Navy's submarine-launched nuclear deterrent and gave Moscow a 'first-strike' capability. His espionage lasted from 1967, when he approached the KGB in the Washington DC *rezidentura,* to his arrest in May 1985.

John Scarlett, the SIS officer who met Vladimir Kuzichkin on the Turkish side of the Iranian frontier and drove him to Ankara in June 1982 as part of the KGB officer's exfiltration plan.

John Walker, before his arrest, wearing his toupee.

Ayatollah Khomeini was alerted to the KGB plan for a Tudeh Party coup after Vladimir Kuzichkin defected and betrayed the Soviet plot to seize the country in 1982. Consequently the mullahs rounded up the membership and executed thousands of opponents of the regime.

A Soviet-built Scud missile. Two were fired at Israeli positions in the Sinai on the last day of the Yom Kippur War. CIA analysts feared nuclear warheads had been delivered to the Egyptian army on the SS *Mozhduechenck*.

Three weeks after Marwan's role as a Mossad spy was exposed he was killed in June 2007 by two Libyan visitors at his London flat. His lifeless body was found beneath his sixth floor balcony in Carlton House Terrace, and his killers escaped to Tripoli.

Ashraf Marwan with his wife Mona and his father-in-law President Nasser at their wedding in July 1966. Six years later he made three attempts to contact Mossad to warn of Anwar Sadat's plans to launch a surprise attack on Israel in 1973.

Gennadi Vasilenko (left), codenamed MONOLIGHT by the CIA, was freed from a Russian prison in 2010 as part of an elaborate exchange for a group of illegals arrested in the United States by the FBI. To achieve his release the FBI and CIA concealed his past role as a mole recruited in 1979 by Jack Platt (right).

Chapter 7

Al Sarant

We decided that the best way to convince Sarant was to use a simple idea, that the Soviet people were giving their blood in the struggle against fascism for the common good of all humanity.

[Aleksandr Feklisov, *The Man Behind the Rosenbergs*[1]]

Born in New York in September 1918 of Greek parentage, Sarant studied physics at Cornell University and was employed during the war by the US Army Signal Corps on highly secret radar research at Fort Monmouth in New Jersey until September 1942, when he was 'dismissed with prejudice'. He was also an important member of the NKVD spy-ring headed by Julius Rosenberg, although relatively little has been written about him because he never faced criminal charges and, until his death from a heart attack while on a visit to Moscow in March 1979, the FBI hoped to arrest him if he ventured out of the safety of the Soviet Union. His wife Louise Ross, whom he married in July 1945, also shared his political views, and was in 1934 an employee of the Soviet Purchasing Commission in New York.[2]

Much of what is known about Sarant's espionage was revealed to American investigators through analysis of the VENONA traffic in which he appeared under the codenames AL and HUGHES. He had studied electrical engineering at Columbia University between October 1942 and September 1946, and at the time of the VENONA intercepts, was a radar expert working for Bell Telephone Laboratories in New York on highly classified computer systems for the B-29 bomber. That some of this data, relating to the AN/APQ-7 high resolution airborne radar developed by the Massachusetts Institute of Technology, was compromised by a spy codenamed HUGHES emerged unmistakably in part two of a long text dated 13 December 1944 from New York which also referred to

99

LIBERAL (Julius Rosenberg), WASP (Ruth Greenglass), CALIBRE (David Greenglass), YOUNG (Theodore Hall), ARNO (Harry Gold) and METER (Joel Barr). Clearly the burden of running these agents was becoming too much for one man, and on 5 December 1944 his NKVD handler, Stepan Apresyan, warned Moscow about overworking Rosenberg:

> Expedite consent to the joint filming of their materials by both METER [Joel Barr] and HUGHES [Al Sarant] (see our letter no. 8). LIBERAL [Julius Rosenberg] has on hand eight people plus the filming of materials. The state of LIBERAL's health is nothing splendid. We are afraid of putting LIBERAL out of action with overwork.

Accordingly, the NKVD's New York *rezidentura* sought to introduce two additional handlers, Aleksandr Raev and Aleksandr Feklisov:

> Further [14 groups unrecovered] Both are COMPATRIOTS [Communists]. Both are helping us and both meet LIBERAL [Julius Rosenberg] and ARNO [Harry Gold] [3 groups unrecovered] HUGHES handed over 17 authentic drawings related to the APQ-7 (postal despatch No. 9). He can be trusted. The transfer of HUGHES to LIGHT [Aleksandr Raev] is no way out of the situation. It will be necessary to put LIGHT in touch with CALISTRATUS [Aleksandr Feklisov] in order to bring material for photography into the PLANT [Soviet Consulate]. I cannot carry material in and out of the PLANT late in the evening. I insist on bringing HUGHES [Al Sarant] and METER [Joel Barr] together, putting the latter in touch with CALISTRATUS or LIGHT and separating both from LIBERAL.
> In TYRE [New York] [16 groups unrecoverable] round the clock. There are no major contradictions between letters 5 and 7 about LIBERAL. They complement each other. LIBERAL's shortcomings do not mean that he will be completely useless for photography. He is gradually getting used to photography.

Unfortunately for historians trying to piece together the exact sequence of events, to establish who knew precisely what, and when they learned it, the VENONA traffic remains tantalizingly elusive because the modern custodian of the traffic, the US National Security Agency, has only released the final version of each text, making it impossible to understand the genesis of its development or, more relevantly, exactly what information was available to investigators pursuing particular leads. The date stamp on the final intercept might be 1957 but some of the content may have been issued a decade earlier. The secrecy surrounding the investigation process was thought at the time to be essential so as not to alert the adversary to the source, and thereby terminate it as a source of demonstrably reliable intelligence. Naturally, the FBI came to rely on VENONA, although only two counter-intelligence officers were fully indoctrinated into the cryptographic nature of the material.

As the VENONA project expanded postwar, and more of the traffic was 'broken out', additional leads were made available to the Special Agents conducting the field enquiries who pieced together the tangled links between the various strands of the Rosenberg network, which had certain common components. Many of the participants were members of the CPUSA, or had been members of the Young Communist League, or their front organizations. Many of the suspects knew each other, socialized together or were related. Many were Jewish, and came from impoverished, immigrant families.

Two additional, unexpected sources have emerged in recent years to assist in the analysis of the VENONA intercepts. The first, in 2001, was the publication of Aleksandr Feklisov's memoirs, *The Man Behind the Rosenbergs*.[3] Feklisov worked in both the London and New York *rezidenturas*. He never met Sarant, but handled him through his friend Joel Barr, and stated that 'between 1943 and 1945, Barr and Sarant gave us 9,165 pages of secret documents relating to more than one hundred programs in the planning stages'. One such item was the SCR-584 anti-aircraft microwave radar designed to detect and destroy German V-2 ballistic missiles in flight.

> I was meeting with Barr every two weeks on average. Once a month, early in the morning, he would slip me a roll of about twenty films representing about 400–500 pages of documents.

The second unexpected counter-intelligence windfall was the removal by a KGB officer, Alexander Vassiliev, of a large quantity of notes he had taken in the KGB archive while working on the history project that had produced *The Haunted Wood*, his collaboration with two American historians, Harvey Klehr and John Earl Haynes.[4] Vassiliev's material, which complemented the VENONA collection, was published in 2009 as *Spies: The Rise and Fall of the KGB in America*, and revealed the true identities of NIL (Nathan Sussman); PERS (Russell McNutt); and the brothers Oscar

(GODSEND) and Stuart Seborer (GODFATHER) who had fled to Israel, and then Moscow, in February 1951.[5]

The VENONA texts were hugely incriminating, as was demonstrated by a message from Apresyan dated 26 July 1944 which identified Max Elitcher as a vital member of Rosenberg's network:

> In July ANTENNA was sent by the firm for ten days to work in CARTHAGE [Washington DC]. There he visited his school friend Max ELITCHER, who works in the Bureau of Standards as head of the fire control section for warships (which mount guns) of over five-inch calibre. He has access to extremely valuable materials on guns.
>
> Five years ago Max ELITCHER graduated from the Electro-Technical Department of the City College of NEW YORK. He has a Master of Science degree. Since finishing college he has been working at the Bureau of Standards. He is a COMPATRIOT [Communist]. He entered the COMPATRIOT's organization [Party] after finishing his studies.
>
> By ANTENNA he is characterized as a loyal, reliable, level-headed and able man. Married, his wife is a COMPATRIOT. She is a psychiatrist by profession, she works at the War Department.
>
> Max ELITCHER is an excellent amateur photographer and has all the necessary equipment for taking photographs.
>
> Please check ELITCHER and communicate your consent to his clearance.

A childhood friend of Morton Sobell, Elitcher had graduated as an electrical engineer from the City College of New York in 1938, where he had studied alongside Julius Rosenberg and Morton Sobell, and had joined the US Navy. In 1948 the Office of Naval Intelligence had investigated Elitcher as a possible Communist, prompting him to buy a house next to Sobell in Queens, New York, and join his friend at the Reeves Instrument Company. When the FBI interviewed him in July 1950 he admitted having been approached by both Sobell and the Rosenbergs, but denied having passed any classified document to either. Instead he agreed to give evidence against them, and appeared as a prosecution witness at their trial in March 1951. Although the FBI had some doubts about the extent to which Elitcher had refused to help Morton and Julius, there was no further VENONA material to incriminate him, and the single text in which he was mentioned by Apresyan gave no indication that he had subsequently become an active member of the network.

Initially codenamed ANTENNA, Rosenberg and his wife Ethel were at
the heart of a massive spy-ring, and the FBI would conclude that he had
been a spy since his discharge from the Army Signal Corps in March 1945.
His organization is best known, of course, for its theft of the Manhattan
Project's atomic secrets, accomplished through Ethel's brother David
Greenglass, employed as a machinist at Los Alamos, and his wife Ruth.
Greenglass would be compromised by his 'cut-out' Harry Gold, having
been identified by Klaus Fuchs from FBI surveillance photos. Others
involved in the network, such as Morton Sobell, did not have access to
atomic information and limited their espionage to whatever classified
material they could steal, in his case advanced radar designs. Similarly,
Joel Barr was an electrical engineer (codenamed METER in the
VENONA intercepts) employed by Western Electric at Bayonne, New
Jersey, on the design and development of a Sperry Gyroscope bombsight.
His friend and fellow CPUSA member William Perl (who appeared in
fourteen VENONA texts as GNOME and then YACOV) was an expert
on jet propulsion and worked for Westinghouse.

Based on recently declassified documents, it appears that at least three
of the *apparat*'s spies escaped relatively unscathed. Nathan Sussman (codenamed NIL) was a CPUSA member employed as an engineer at Westinghouse. Russell McNutt (codenamed VOGEL and PERS) was a contractor
for the Kellex Corporation which built the Manhattan Project's gaseous
diffusion separation plant at Oak Ridge, Tennessee. In addition, there was
a construction engineer, Harry Steingart, who acquired a thin FBI file and
was only suspected of having engaged in espionage.[6]

Sobell would be arrested in Mexico in August 1950 and returned to the
United States, where he was convicted of espionage and sentenced to
thirty years' imprisonment. Perl was convicted in May 1935 of perjury,
having lied to a Grand Jury about his association with Sobell and Rosenberg, and sentenced to three years' imprisonment.

Two other members of the spy-ring, Lona Cohen (codenamed
LESLEY) and her husband Morris (codenamed LUIS and VOLUN-
TEER), disappeared overnight in June 1950 and fled to Mexico before
being exfiltrated to Moscow. Their removal beyond the FBI's reach meant
severing contact temporarily with several sources, among them Dr Theo-
dore Hall, the youngest physicist on the staff at Los Alamos. By the time
Hall (codenamed YOUNG) and his friend and former room-mate Saville
Sax (codenamed OLD) came under suspicion, the FBI had completely lost

the Cohens, who would not reappear until January 1961 when they were arrested in London.[7]

At the end of the war Saville Sax returned to Harvard, and was replaced as Hall's courier by Lona Cohen, who maintained irregular contact with him until 16 March 1951, when Hall was visited at the Institute for Radiobiology and Biophysics at Chicago University by two FBI special agents. During a three hour interview Hall denied any involvement with espionage, but refused the FBI permission to search his home. At a second interview, two days later, Hall declined to answer any further questions, and soon afterwards he took up a research post at Memorial Sloan-Kettering in New York. Sax, who had given up running a copy shop and was then driving a taxi in Chicago, was also interviewed by the FBI on 16 March, but denied espionage, claiming that his occasional visits to the Soviet Consulate in New York had been in connection with relatives still living in the Soviet Union, and his single trip to New Mexico had been taken after he had dropped out of Harvard, to consult his trusted friend Ted Hall about another university course. Sax denied ever having received a list of atomic scientists from Hall, and consented to a search of his home, which revealed nothing incriminating.

In 1953 Hall broke off all contact with the Soviets and eleven years later he was offered a twelve-month contract at the Cavendish Laboratory at Cambridge University. At the end of the year, instead of returning to the United States where his friend Sax had died, Hall remained at the university, and he stayed in the town with his wife Joan and their daughter until his death in 1999. Taken together, the VENONA texts amount to as comprehensive an indictment of Hall's espionage as could be asked for, but the necessity to protect the source's integrity meant that Hall was allowed his liberty. All he was prepared to say before his death was that 'in 1944 I was nineteen years old – immature, inexperienced and not too sure of myself'.

> I recognize that I could easily have been wrong in my judgement of what was necessary, and that I was indeed mistaken about some things, in particular my view of the nature of the Soviet state. The world has moved on since then, and certainly so have I.

After his death in November 1999 in Cambridge, his wife confirmed that Hall had indeed spied for the Soviets, and expressed her support for him.

In retrospect, the NKVD's failure to compartmentalize the Rosenberg network looks catastrophic, especially considering that the Cohens were given the responsibility of acting as intermediaries for a sonar engineer, Joseph Chinilevsky (codenamed SERB and RELAY), who had lost a leg while fighting with the Republicans in the Spanish Civil War. Of Ukrainian and Polish parentage, Chinilevsky was a 26-year-old CPUSA member, recruited by Morris Cohen in August 1942, and later handled by Semyon Semyonov (TWAIN) and then Aleksandr Feklisov (CALISTRA-TUS), both working under consular cover in New York.

SERB/RELAY appeared in four VENONA texts and on 11 July 1944 a message indicated that he did not live in New York, and could only remove documents from his workplace temporarily:

> With a view to reducing the time required for the receipt and handing back of RELAY's [Joseph Chinilevsky] materials we consider it would be a good thing to make it his job to photograph his own materials and bring to TYRE [New York] only undeveloped films.

In a text dated 4 July 1944 Stepan Apresyan (MAY) in New York evidently tried to appoint RELAY as 'group leader' for Enos R. Wicher (codenamed KEEN), a scientist then working in the Wave Propagation Group at Columbia University's Division of War Research, and an as yet unidentified spy, FISHERMAN.[8]

A Russian immigrant by background, Wicher had been a CPUSA organizer under the alias 'Bill Rain' in Wisconsin, and both his wife Maria Wicher (codenamed DAShA) and his stepdaughter Flora Wovschin (codenamed ZORA) were Soviet spies. Although VENONA shed no light on the information this family trio was supplying, Wovschin worked in the US State Department where she was instrumental in recruiting her colleagues Judith Coplon (codenamed SIMA) and Marion Davis (codenamed LOU). While these spies may have worked in isolation from the Rosenbergs, it is clear that their network was far more extensive than even the FBI suspected at the time.

While Julius Rosenberg was incarcerated at the detention facility on West Street in New York awaiting trial, the FBI placed a microphone in his cell to monitor his conversations with a 'jailhouse snitch', Eugene Tartakow, a CPUSA member and convicted car thief and armed robber, who was befriended in prison by Rosenberg to act as a discreet conduit to Eugene Dennis, the CPUSA General-Secretary who was serving a prison sentence for contempt of Congress. When the spy had started confiding in Tartakow in December 1950, the petty criminal had approached the FBI, offering to become an informant. His subsequent reports over the first half of 1951 showed that Rosenberg apparently had no hesitation in sharing the most compromising information with the younger man, referring indirectly to Joel Barr as being safely in Europe, having headed one of his networks, and mentioning that Al Sarant and William Perl also had been members of his organization.

Sarant had been interviewed in July 1950, when he had acknowledged his friendship with the Rosenbergs and had named Joel Barr as having introduced them. During the course of the interrogation, Sarant named Hans Bethe as the person who had sponsored his entry into Cornell in September 1946, having been introduced to the professor by his father-in-law, Victor Ross. Sarant had married his step-daughter Louise earlier in the year, and clearly Ross had attempted to help Sarant leave his job at Bell in New York and move upstate to Ithaca.

Both Sarant and Barr had fled the country, but Tartakow had revealed a link between Sarant and Bethe. Allegedly, Rosenberg had mentioned Sarant's wealthy father, and had claimed that Sarant knew both Bethe and Morrison well at Cornell University. This coincided with a statement made in prison by David Greenglass in July 1951, to Special Agent John Harrington, about a meeting he had held with Harry Gold on 4 June 1944. According to Greenglass, he had recommended Bethe as a candidate for recruitment because William Spindel, a colleague in the US Army's Special Engineering Detachment (one of the Manhattan Project's military covers), had identified Bethe as a Communist. Supposedly Bethe's name had been passed on a list of recommended prospects to Gold, then Rosenberg and finally to Anatoli Yatskov, but there was no direct evidence that the Soviets had acted on the tip.

While Sarant claimed to have met Bethe in July 1946, the FBI traced a draft board letter, dated a month earlier, in which Sarant had disclosed to his board that he was to take up a research fellowship with Bethe at Cornell later the same year. With Sarant's consent, the FBI had searched his home and come up with a couple of items that appeared to contradict his version of his ostensibly casual relationship with Bethe, who was his next-door neighbour, and to link him to Morrison and William Perl. One document was a receipt for an airline ticket in Morrison's name, which Sarant was unable to explain was doing in his possession. Another was a baby book registering a gift from Hans and Rose Bethe upon the birth of their child. There was also a personal letter from Perl.

Hans Bethe was interviewed by Special Agent William Tower in Seattle in July 1950 and acknowledged his friendship with Victor Ross, a lawyer who had done some work for him unpaid, whom he described as holding views 'very close to the Communist Party line'. He also recalled a meeting with Ross and Al Sarant in his office in May 1946 (whereas Sarant had remembered it occurring two months later) but claimed that he had not sponsored Sarant for a post at Cornell, and in fact had told him he was not sufficiently qualified for postgraduate work in the Physics Department, acknowledging it to be 'strange' that despite being rebuffed, Sarant nevertheless had moved up to Ithaca. 'Bethe denies close relationship with Sarant, stating has not talked to Sarant for even one hour during entire time he has known him' reported the FBI agent. He expressed surprise that Sarant had subsequently applied for, and obtained, a job as an electrical engineer at the Cornell Physics Laboratory in November 1946, but denied that he would have had any access to classified information. During Tower's interview with Bethe he asked whether the physicist had been in contact with an impressive list of Soviet spies, and seemed to obtain an acknowledgment that he may have been a target of Soviet espionage:

> BETHE denies ever knowing or contacting JULIUS ROSEN-BERG, WILLIAM PERL, JOEL BARR, MAX ELITCHER, MORTON SOBELL or HARRY GOLD. Denies that any approach in any manner ever made to him or any person to furnish information to an apparent espionage agent. Possibility that BETHE may have been target of Russian espionage and given to SARANT as an assignment in espionage ring presented to BETHE, and he stated that SARANT did not pursue the development of his friendship and BETHE never got the impression that SARANT wanted technical data nor did SARANT ask for such. BETHE states his impression of SARANT is that SARANT is 'leftist in his ideology'.[9]

The FBI was suspicious of Bethe and found it hard to accept that the physicist had engaged in violent political disagreements with his friend Victor Ross, and was able to characterize Al Sarant as a left-winger if he had only spoken to him briefly. As for Morrison, it was equally odd that Tartakow should have offered his name, along with Bethe's, in connection with Perl and Sarant, as members of Rosenberg's organization. The FBI investigated the possibility that Sarant had some covert relationship with Bethe and Morrison, and in July 1950 undertook a handwriting analysis of Bethe and Morrison to see if they had been responsible for some cryptic postcards found at Sarant's home in New York.

107

Philip Morrison remained the subject of FBI interest for many years, and as late as July 1954 an informant in Tampa, who before the war had been a member of the CPUSA branch in Alameda County, California, identified the scientist as a probable Communist. Morrison was also reported by an FBI confidential informant run by Special Agent Randall McGough to be a Communist. When confronted by the Senate Internal Security subcommittee in May 1953, Morrison conceded that he had been a CPUSA member in 1942, at the time Professor Eugene Wigner had invited him to join the Manhattan Project, but insisted that 'atomic security officers and his superiors had known of his Communist background'.

One of the VENONA messages that incriminated Sarant was dated 5 May 1944, in which his NKVD handler, Stepan Apresyan, requested Moscow:

> Please carry out a check and sanction the recruitment of Alfred SARANT, a lead of ANTENNA [Julius Rosenberg]. He is 25 years old, a Greek, an American citizen and lives in TYRE [New York City]. He completed the engineering course at Cooper Union in 1940. He worked for two years in the Signal Corps laboratory at Fort MONMOUTH. He was discharged for past union activity. He has been working for two years at Western Electric [45 groups unrecoverable] entry into the COMPATRIOT [Communist Party]. SARANT lives apart from his family. Answer without delay.

As well as drawing in members of his family, his neighbours and many of his oldest friends, Rosenberg was revealed to be his network's key figure, even to the point of handling his sub-agents' data himself, as was disclosed in a telegram to Moscow dated 22 May 1944, which showed that his productivity had increased during the year, and also established a direct link with Anatoli Yakovlev at the Soviet Consulate:

> Study of the work of the KhU [Economic Directorate] connected with the receipt of bulky materials is attended by great risk particularly the secret materials which were coming in during 1943 and are coming in now. The danger has increased because of the periodic surveillance of the cadre workers and the increasing surveillance of the PLANT [Soviet Consulate] to which the materials are being brought for filming. It has become impossible to bring [18 groups unrecoverable] to film at ALEKSEI's [Anatoli Yakovlev] apartment

108

to which a portable camera had been brought earlier. It is intended in the future to practise such filming only now and then. What is your opinion? We consider it necessary to organize the filming of ANTENNA's [Julius Rosenberg] PROBATIONER's [agents] materials by ANTENNA himself. Again the question of a camera for ALEKSEI has been raised. Exceptionally secret materials are conveyed in the original or in manuscript which is more dangerous than the presence of a camera at ALEKSEI's. It is incomprehensible why one cannot do this in the course of the next half year (your No. 2031). We assume that it is connected with conservation and not the danger of ALEKSEI's disclosure [34 groups unrecoverable].

On 2 September 1944 Moscow changed many of the cryptonyms assigned to the New York *rezidentura* as a security precaution and listed a total of twenty-two in a VENONA text. Among them was ANTENNA, who became LIBERAL. Another was William Perl, codenamed GNOME, a member of Rosenberg's ring who was transformed into YAKOV, but on 14 September Apresyan was still referring to him as GNOME:

Until recently GNOME was paid only the expenses connected with his coming to TYRE [New York]. Judging by an appraisal of the material received and the last [1 group garbled] sent to us GNOME deserves remuneration for material no less valuable than that given by the rest of the members of the LIBERAL group who were given a bonus by you. Please agree to paying him 500 dollars.

On 20 September Moscow gave Apresyan permission to pay Perl, still referring to him as GNOME:

Your No. 736. We agree to paying GNOME 500 dollars [12 groups unrecovered] September on trips to TYRE [New York] [2 groups unrecovered], and [211 groups unrecoverable]

Perl had shared a room at Colombia University with Al Sarant, and had studied with Elitcher, Barr, Sobell and Julius Rosenberg at the City College of New York. An expert on supersonic flight and jet propulsion, he was supervising a team of fifteen scientists working on a research project at the National Advisory Committee on Aeronautics, at Cleveland, Ohio, when he was interviewed by the FBI in July 1950. Perl denied knowing Sobell and Rosenberg, and it was for this lie that he was sentenced to five years' imprisonment on a perjury charge in 1950, but the

FBI remained convinced that he had been responsible for the leakage of several classified files on the subject of advanced jet propulsion that David Greenglass mentioned as having reached Julius Rosenberg, and that he was a key figure in his spy-ring. While at Columbia University in 1946 and 1947, Perl had occupied an apartment at 65 Morton Street, Greenwich Village, which had been rented in Al Sarant's name, had been occupied by Joel Barr's former girlfriend Vivian Glassman, and had been used as a photographic studio by Rosenberg. On 23 July 1950 she had visited Perl and while sitting on a couch had written him a series of notes, so as to avoid being overheard. In them she identified herself as a friend of Julius Rosenberg and offered him money, asking him to flee to Mexico. Perl had dated Vivian's sister Eleanor, so he knew who she was, and clearly was connected to the Sidorovichs, with whom he was seen in Cleveland negotiating the purchase of a car. Anxious about what he suspected was heavy FBI surveillance and maybe an attempt to entrap him, Perl rejected Vivian's proposal and told his lawyer to inform Special Agents John A. Harrington and John B. O'Donoghue about the incident. In the absence of any other evidence, or the damning request for payment to GNOME in September 1944, Perl was convicted of perjury in May 1953 and sentenced to five years' imprisonment for having lied about not knowing Rosenberg and Sobell.

The FBI's investigation of Vivian Glassman revealed that she too had been an important spy, and had been classmates at CCNY with Sobell, Perl, Elitcher, Barr, Rosenberg and Sidorovich. A mathematician by training, she had been employed by the US Army Signal Corps from May 1942, and had worked on sensitive projects at the General Development Laboratory at Long Branch with her sister Eleanor, and at Fort Monmouth in New Jersey where she 'had access to material of a secret and confidential nature'.

On 14 November 1944 a VENONA message from Leonid Kvasnikov introduced yet another member of the Rosenberg ring, Joel Barr, code-named METER:

LIBERAL has safely carried through the contracting of HUGHES [Al Sarant]. HUGHES is a good friend of METER [Joel Barr]. We propose to pair them off and get them to photograph their own materials having given a camera for this purpose. HUGHES is a good photographer, has a large darkroom and all the equipment but he does not have a Leica. LIBERAL will receive the films from

110

METER for passing on. Direction of the PROBATIONERS [agents] will be continued through LIBERAL, this will ease the load on him. Details about the contracting are in letter No. 8.

Barr had much in common with others in Rosenberg's network. He had studied electrical engineering with Sobell and Elitcher, graduating in 1938. He had worked alongside Al Sarant in the Army Signal Corps laboratory at Fort Monmouth until his discharge in 1942 because of his political activities on behalf of the Communist Party, and then had found a job as a radar specialist with Western Electric, designing systems for the B-29 bomber. In 1946 he had switched to Sperry Gyroscope, with a reference signed by Al Sarant, but had left a year later when his security clearance was declined. By the time the FBI linked him to the source codenamed METER, Barr had been living in Paris since January 1948, but he promptly disappeared and moved to Finland, well beyond its reach. Obviously the NKVD had cultivated Barr as a spy in November 1944, but there was no further VENONA evidence apart from a single reference in the text dated 5 December 1944 which certainly implies that Barr and Sarant (METER and HUGHES) were highly productive.

There can be no doubt of either Rosenberg's industry, for he was managing two apartments in Manhattan, at 65 Morton Street and at 131 East 7th Street, as photographic studios, nor of his ideological commitment, but Moscow was always keen to reward effort, and a telegram on 6 March 1945 refers to a financial inducement, and mentioned another source, codenamed NIL, now identified as Nathan Sussman.

> [66 groups unrecovered] decision was made about awarding the sources as a bonus the following sums: to LIBERAL 1,000 dollars, NIL [Nathan Sussman] [58 groups unrecoverable] either the purchase of valuable gifts for the PROBATIONERS [agents] or payment to them of money on the basis of well thought out cover stories. [28 groups unrecovered].

As the FBI researched the links between LIBERAL's organization, and started building the legal case against the Rosenbergs, doubt was expressed about the wisdom of charging Ethel, for the proof against her, apart from testimony from Ruth Greenglass, was contained in a VENONA text dated 27 November 1944 from Kvasnikov:

> Your 5356. Information on LIBERAL's wife. Surname that of her husband, first name ETHEL, 29 years old. Married five years.

111

Finished secondary school. A COMPATRIOT [Communist] since 1938. Sufficiently well developed politically. Knows about her husband's work and the role of METER [Joel Barr] and NIL [Nathan Sussman]. In view of delicate health does not work. Is characterized positively and as a devoted person.

In 1948 Sarant had taken a post at the Cornell nuclear physics laboratory, and when interviewed by the FBI's Peter Moxson at his home in Ithaca, New York, in 1950 he acknowledged having been a Communist and having known Julius through their union, the Federation of Architects, Engineers, Chemists and Technicians. Sarant denied any involvement in espionage and claimed not to have seen the Rosenbergs since 1946. Moxson's investigation of Sarant led to the discovery of his CPUSA 'Party name' Raymond Cooper, and the belief that he had habitually adopted the alias 'Walton'. Moxson reported:

Subject resides with wife, LOUISE, and infant sons at RD1, Cayuga Heights Road, Ithaca, NY, and is self-employed as painting contractor. He was interviewed during the period from 19 July 1950 to 25 July 1950 in connection with JULIUS ROSENBERG espionage network. Denied ever engaging in espionage for the Russian government or working as an agent for JULIUS ROSENBERG. Admits acquaintanceship with ROSENBERG while he (SARANT) was resident of New York City from 1942 to 1946. States ROSENBERG 'propositioned' him, adding 'I did not bite'. Denies he can recall any further details of this meeting and believes ROSENBERG was sounding him out politically. Denies any contact with ROSENBERG since moving to Ithaca in September 1946. Address of JULIUS and ETHEL ROSENBERG, 10 Monroe Street, NYC, found in address book in search of Subject's residence. Admits close friendship with JOEL BARR from 1941 to 1946, believing he met ROSENBERG through BARR. Denies knowing BARR was Russian espionage agent and denies doing any photographic work with BARR for the Russian government. Claims he met WILLIAM PERL through JOEL BARR. SARANT resided in Apartment 61, 65 Morton Street, NYC, from 1 October 1943 to 1 September 1945. States he lived alone at this address until marriage of 6 July 1945. Claims this apartment held in his name from September 1946 to January 1950 while he resided in Ithaca, that he received rent payments from BARR, PERL and VIVIAN GLASSMAN, and that he made payments to 65 Morton Street Realty Corporation by check from Ithaca. States this arrangement made by BARR with understanding that PERL or BARR would use apartment, since apartments scarce at time Subject moved to Ithaca. Denies returning to apartment since 1946 and denies any knowledge of the use to which apartment was put during period from 1946 to 1950. Check of postal money orders, Ithaca, N, reflects payments in amount of $45.50 (rental figure) received by SARANT from PERL, GLASSMAN and HENRI-ETTA SAVIDGE. Subject denies close association with SAVIDGE and claims he met her on only one occasion. Admits being associated with BARR in hobby shop known as SARANT LABORATORIES, 227 East 11th Street, NYC, for at least 5 months in 1946 prior to leaving New York. Denies use of this shop for any purpose other than pursuit of joint hobbies. Denies ever residing at or knowledge of apartment at 112 East 7th Street, NYC. Denies knowing MORTON or HELEN SOBELL, MAX or HELENE ELITCHER, MIKE or ANNE SIDOROVICH, HARRY GOLD or RUTH or DAVID GREENGLASS.

Sarant's FBI file had at its heart the incriminating search and interviews conducted in Ithaca from 19 July 1950, two days after the arrest of Julius Rosenberg:

At Ithaca, New York:
ALFRED SARANT, RD1 Cayuga Heights Road, was interviewed in connection with the investigation of the JULIUS R0SEBERG espionage network.

He was first interviewed on July 19, 1950, by SA's JOHN D. MAHONEY and PETER F. MAXSON. Subsequent interviews were conducted on July 20, 21, 22, 24 and 25 1950; between SARANT and Agents MAHONEY and MAXSON. Early in the course of the first interview, SARANT was asked for permission to search his residence. He consented to this and executed a written permission dated July 19 1950 authorizing Special Agents MAHONEY and MAXSON to perform such search. This search was conducted during the night of July 19 and the early morning of July 20 1950. During the course of the search, when it was found that it was going to take considerable tine, SARANT executed a second consent to search directed to SAs NICHOLAS L. DUNBAR and PAUL R. BIBLER. These Agents then assisted in the search. On July 21 1950 SARANT, by written consent, further authorized Agents MAHONEY and MAXSON to conduct an additional search of his premises on the same date. Various material was obtained during both searches, and appropriate receipts dated July 20 and July 21 respectively, were furnished Subject.

Information received during the course of these interviews and searches will be hereinafter set forth under various captions as the material; applies to points of pertinency relative to the JULIUS ROSENBERG network.

SARANT was willing to furnish background information concerning himself, such information being set forth later in this report. He, however, though expressing a desire to cooperate, was vague and furnished contradictory information in many of his answers to questions put to him. He at all times positively denied performing espionage on behalf of the Russian government, or permitting espionage in his apartment at 65 Merton Street, New York City. He further denied any knowledge of this apartment being used for espionage from 1946 to 1950, after he had left the apartment but while it was still rented in his name. This information will be set forth later in detail.

SARANT, when questioned concerning his membership in the Communist Party, stated emphatically that he is not now a member of this Party. He did state that he was a member of the Communist Political Association for approximately 18 months sometime between 1943 and 1945, that he was a member of a club in Greenwich Village. He stated that he did not recall how he happened to join or any of the circumstances connected with his joining.

He recalled that he was a member of the American Student Union while at Cooper Union Institute of Technology and was a delegate from Cooper Union to a national convention held in Washington DC in 1941. He advised that starting with his college days he considered himself a 'liberal and a progressive'; and that many of the ideas of the Communists seemed to him to be right at the time. When he moved to New York City he just happened to join the Communist Political Association. He did not recall where he attended meetings, who got him to join the Party, or the names of any other members of the club or branch to which he belonged. He stated that JOEL BARR and JULIUS ROSENBERG were not members of this branch. He stated that he never was a member of any other branch. According to

114

SARANT, when he found that the meetings consisted chiefly in arguments and lengthy discussions, he just stopped going. He denied being a Party member or going to any Party meetings since that date. He denied ever knowing his wife was a member of the Communist Party.

Subject was questioned concerning any trips made by him to New York City since moving to Ithaca in September 1946. He stated that he could not recall with any degree of clarity the dates or nature of any such trips made by him, with the exception of perhaps one, but that he thought he may possibly have made in the neighbourhood of six to seven trips.

Sarant was caught in numerous lies, not the least of which was his denial of having met Julius Rosenberg at an address on East 7th Street. The search of his home revealed a classified manual entitled *Microwave Transmission Design Data* which he had evidently removed from the Sperry Gyroscope Company.

Clearly unnerved by the FBI's interest in his contacts with the Rosenbergs, and his friendship with Joel Barr (who had moved to Czechoslovakia in 1948), Sarant denied any knowledge of his apartment at 65 Morton Street in Manhattan, which he had transformed into a photographic studio.

When Sarant realized he was under intensive FBI surveillance, he fled to Mexico, where he made contact with the NKVD through the Polish embassy. Acting on instructions, he waited in Mexico City for six months while passports were forged, and then he slipped over the porous Guatemalan border to join a ship destined for Casablanca, and travelled by air from Spain to Prague. Accompanying him on this remarkable journey was not his wife Louise, the mother of his two children, but his next-door neighbour Carol Dayton. Then married with two children to a physicist, Bruce Dayton, her participation in Sarant's last-moment panicked escape had been completely spontaneous, although they had been conducting an illicit affair for some months.

Once in the Soviet Union Sarant resumed his exploitation of classified information by disclosing details of his past work for the US government and under his new identity of 'Phillip G. Saros' became a senior research scientist, helping in 1955 to found the Zelenograd micro-electronics centre in Leningrad to develop computer systems for Soviet submarines and anti-aircraft systems at their LKB laboratory, which would employ

2,000 staff. Sarant's role as a pioneer of the modern Soviet integrated circuit and semiconductor industry is well documented, and his defection would have a lasting impact. In particular, he was credited with the design of the UM-1, the first Soviet-designed digital computer, and the *Uzel*, a device for calculating torpedo launch solutions on Red Banner Fleet submarines.

Whereas Sarant's espionage in the United States effectively ended when he lost access to classified information, it seems he took on the role of photocopier for other members of the Rosenberg ring and his value to the Soviets remained very high until his death at the age of 61.

Chapter 8

Engelbert Broda

During the period of his co-operation with us he supplied
an enormous quantity of most valuable, genuine
documents in the form of official American and British
reports on the work on ENORMOZ and, in particular,
on the construction of uranium piles.

[NKVD assessment of ERIC, August 1945.[1]]

The combined NKVD and GRU effort to penetrate the Allied atomic
weapons research programme, known in England under the cover name
Tube Alloys and from 1942 in the United States as the Manhattan Project,
was directed by Lavrenti Beria, who initiated Operation ENORMOZ
and established a new intelligence discipline designated 'XY' to collect
and collate the technical information through both, hitherto separate,
organizations.

In New York the XY line was headed by Leonid Kvasnikov, who was
posted to Amtorg from March 1943 to October 1945. His position in
Moscow was taken by Lev Vasilevsky and the scheme was supervised by
the Head of the 3rd Department of the NKVD's First Directorate, and
later by the Deputy Head of Intelligence, Gaik Ovakimyan, while a staff
intelligence officer, Major Yelena M. Potapova, was given responsibility
for processing and translating the agent material. At certain stages she was
assisted by André Graur, a 3rd Department officer who had been implicated in an espionage case in Sweden before the war, and had fled London
in June 1943 following the arrest of Douglas Springhall, a CPGB activist
and one of his key sources in London. According to the NKVD archives,
Yelena Modrzhinskaya, Dmitri F. Ustinov and an aide named Cohen were
initiated into certain purely operational aspects of the case, and Ovakimyan reported directly to the Head of the First Directorate, Pavel Fitin,
on all operational questions and intelligence material received. Either

through Fitin or through the Head of the NKVD, Vsevolod N. Merkulov, all the material reached Beria, who coordinated the entire operation.

In 1943, as part of his XY assignment, Vladimir Barkovsky, an NKVD officer who had trained as a locksmith, established contact with a valuable source, codenamed ERIC, of information on atomic research in Britain. ERIC had been discovered in December 1942 when the *rezidentura* had reported that a Communist sympathizer had passed on a detailed report on atomic research in Britain and America. The source was an Austrian physicist, Engelbert Broda, who declared to his lover his intention to send the material to the CPGB, but she had promptly delivered the material directly to the NKVD.[2] With ENORMOZ in mind, the *rezident* Anatoli Gorsky had sought Moscow's permission to establish direct contact with this scientist and, when approval had been given, Gorsky asked his contact to meet the scientist again and have him agree to a meeting with a Soviet intelligence officer. In a letter to the Centre dated 10 March 1943 the *rezidentura* reported on the meeting with ERIC, recalling that,

> At first he hesitated, saying that he would have to think it over and that he saw no need for meeting anybody since he had already written all he knew about the atomic problem. Later in the conversation his attitude changed and he said that he hoped it would not be an Englishman since his English comrades were very careless. Finally, after assurances that everything would be properly organized, he said that he would be glad to meet our comrade.

The meeting took place in January 1943 at a London tube station, and after the usual signs and passwords had been exchanged, the scientist was judged to be straightforward and friendly, although obviously nervous. He verified all the arrangements for the meeting and it lasted more than an hour and a half, during which nothing was called directly by its name, but 'ERIC knew with whom he had agreed to cooperate', concluded the *rezidentura*. Barkovsky, codenamed GLAN, later recalled that when he met his new source for the first time he had been asked whether he understood nuclear physics and, upon receiving an unsatisfactory reply, the scientist said that he wanted his contact not to be just a transmitting channel, but to understand what it was all about. He urged him to study *Applied Nuclear Physics* by Ernest Pollard and William Davidson, and Barkovsky took his advice, and was grateful to ERIC for insisting on this as the American textbook turned out to be a great help to him in running his source. 'He told me, "We'll go through the book together, and then it will be considerably easier for you to deal with me".' I also did not see any other way out. I was completely swamped with work, but I started poring over the textbooks. Thanks to ERIC, Barkovsky became the key figure in the London *rezidentura*, where he served from 1940 to 1946. He would subsequently be posted in 1956 to Washington DC for seven years.

The document received by Barkovsky was a report relevant to the British War Cabinet's recent decision to develop an atomic weapon. News of this momentous commitment had been disclosed to the NKVD by John Cairncross, then working in the Cabinet Office, who had obtained a copy of the MAUD Report and given it to his contact.

> EDITH sent us a detailed report through MARY on the results and status of work on ENORMOZ, both in England and in the USA. ERIC had given her this report on his own initiative to pass to the FRATERNAL [CPGB]. The materials will be sent out in the near future. According to additional information that has been gathered ERIC, who since January 1942 has been Professor Halban's assistant in a special division (devoted to ENORMOZ) of the central laboratory on explosives in Cambridge – is completely informed about all the work being done on ENORMOZ both in England and in the USA. He has access to American materials on ENORMOZ that the English had received as part of an information exchange ... ERIC is a long-time COMPATRIOT [Communist] who understands the need for such work.

Suitably impressed by the material supplied by Gorsky, Moscow authorized him to maintain contact with his new source: 'We instructed EDITH to conduct a preliminary conversation with him and get him to agree to meet our comrade.'

When the meeting had taken place successfully, the *rezidentura* sent Moscow a detailed report of Barkovsky's first encounter with Broda:

> ERIC met GLAN cordially and carried himself with great ease and friendliness, although it was obvious that he was nervous. He carefully verified all of the rendezvous terms. At the outset of the meeting, ERIC said that he had only been notified of the meeting the day before and therefore was unprepared for a serious discussion about ENORMOZ. Because GLAN's primary objective was to strengthen ties with ERIC, obtain his direct consent to work with us, and determine the course of this work, GLAN did not press him for

information right away and instead set about achieving the afore-
mentioned objectives. The first conversation with ERIC lasted over
an hour and a half. As a result of the conversation ERIC gave his full
consent to work with us. During the conversation, nothing was called
by its proper name but ERIC knows who it is he agreed to work for.
ERIC reports that in their field of work the Americans were
significantly ahead. As part of a technical information exchange, their
laboratory received bulletins from the Americans on the progress of
work on ENORMOZ in America. Owing to the nature of his work,
ERIC has access to these bulletins, and the information he gives us
reflects American achievements in this field as well as English ones.

ERIC passed on the secret material to which he had direct access and,
being something of an adventurer, he took what was kept in the safes of his
colleagues. Barkovsky recalls how, when the scientist told him about this
opportunity, and brought him the impression of a doorkey, a duplicate
was required. It was too dangerous to have this work done in a local shop,
and it would take too long to send the impression to Moscow, as the
wartime diplomatic bag had to be sent via the United States and the Far
East and took months to reach Moscow. However, as a young man
Barkovsky had been a sixth-grade fitter, and he did the job himself and
made a duplicate that fitted perfectly:

> As a result of the decision taken by us we manufactured a copy of
> the key for ERIC and worked out arrangements for meetings so
> that we can contact him three times a week in London without prior
> notification. As a result we managed to remove from ERIC all the
> available American materials and other interesting materials on
> ENORMOZ.[3]

Describing ERIC's relationship with the NKVD, Barkovsky noted in a
letter to Moscow that he had been motivated by ideology, and was
scrupulous when it came to money:

> ERIC as before works for us with enthusiasm, but still turns down the
> slightest hint of financial reward. Once we gave him more to cover his
> expenses than he had asked for. He showed his displeasure and stated
> that he was suspicious of our desire to give him financial help. He
> asked us to stop once and for all our attempts to do so. In view of this
> we fear that any gift to him as a sign of gratitude for his work would

have a negative effect. ERIC is completely unselfish and extremely scrupulous in regard to anything that might appear as 'payment' for his work.

Barkovsky recalled that ERIC had claimed in 1943 that 'the Americans are far ahead' in the field of atomic research, and declared that he was 'a person who had come to us by himself, without any recruitment. He wanted to help and correct the injustice.'

> In his opinion, justice lay in preventing Russia's allies from knowing very important work of a defence nature. At our first meeting he began explaining something to me with much enthusiasm, but I had only the slightest idea about the structure of the nucleus. . . . He not only gave me technical data, but explained the sense of it, so that I could comprehend what we were discussing. I prepared my own glossary that proved to be extremely useful. All the terms were new ones that no one had ever heard of before. And these people did not cost the treasury one pound. They were our kind of people, brave people with initiative who considered that giving aid to the Soviets was a moral and political duty. Understandably this pertains, I hope, not only to atomic scientists.

Barkovsky described ERIC as 'extremely well-informed about the most diverse aspects of the work that was being done by the English in that area. He is the person with whom I worked. He was an excellent person and it was very pleasant to work with him. I remember him with gratitude. He was two years older than me.'

However, while Barkovsky was praising ERIC's dedication and motivation, MI5's Roger Hollis recorded his concerns about Broda, and in May 1943 complained that it was difficult to offer an assessment of his reliability unless investigators were told about the relative sensitivity of his research:

> As we cannot be told the nature of the work for which Broda is required we can only state that we know of Broda's connection with the Communists, and mention the definite risk that any information which he gets will be given to the Communists.

A note in Broda's MI5 personal file, added in July, stated that 'He now knows a considerable amount of the more secret aspect of work. DSIR is anxious about Broda' and several days later stated that it was 'agreed that

121

we should keep a careful watch for any references to Broda's work during our investigations upon the Communist Party's espionage activities'.[4]

MI5 kept tabs on Broda through a source recruited inside the Austrian Centre, codenamed KASPAR. He was a Jewish Austrian writer, Josef Lemmel, who had arrived in London from Vienna aged 59, and was recruited by B5(b)'s Claud Sykes, formerly an academic, German translator and author.

Although not a Communist, Lemmel was an ardent anti-Nazi and, while acting as the Centre's librarian, with his wife Renate, became close to Edith Suschitsky, providing first-hand, eyewitness accounts of his contact with her, and in November 1945 generated this report to MI5's F Division:

On 3rd November a Conference of Scientists for the promotion of Austrian Science took place at Burlington House under the auspices of the Association of Austrian Engineers, Chemists and Scientific Workers. The whole conference was stage-managed by Dr E. Broda, and it is said in Austrian Communist circles that the object of this meeting was to establish contact with scientists engaged on atomic energy research. Although I have no definite proof, I have always suspected Broda of being engaged in scientific espionage, and according to Edith Tudor Hart [Suschitsky] he has for some time occupied himself with secret scientific research at Cambridge connected with atomic energy. She stressed Broda's importance to the party in view of his qualifications and connections. In view of the intimate relations existing between Edith Tudor Hart and Broda, it must be presumed that she is well-informed of her lover's activities. As Chairman of the Association of Austrian Engineers, Dr Broda maintains close contacts with Austrian and foreign engineers and scientists and with Austrian students in the provinces, through whom he links up with British Communist student circles. Although outwardly the above conference appeared above board and non-political, I learned that secret meetings took place afterwards at which Dr Broda presided. At the official Conference Professor (Sir D'Arcy) Thompson took the chair, and speeches were made by Professors Blackett, Donnan, Hogben and Karl Przibram.[5]

During this period, when Broda had split from his wife but used the excuse of visiting his son in London to meet his Soviet contact every two or three weeks, he drew further attention to himself, unintentionally, when he wrote to his protégé Alan Nunn May upon his return from the United

States in September 1945. Unaware that May's mail was being intercepted, he wrote:

> Dear May, I am glad to hear you are back safely. Will you come to Cambridge some day or may I look you up in London? I shall love to see you. Yours, E. Broda.

Ostensibly, this request was innocent enough, but MI5 was very conscious that the Soviets were likely to warn May that he had been compromised by the defection the previous September of Igor Gouzenko and this connection was considered highly suspicious. Indeed, this intercept was regarded as so significant that it was shown by John Marriott to the recently appointed Deputy Director-General Guy Liddell on 2 October:

> John Marriott showed me an intercept saying that Engelbert Broda, an atomic physicist in Cambridge who is known to be a Party member, is in touch with Nunn May whom he is anxious to see.

At this point MI5 was quite convinced that Broda had engaged in espionage, even if there was no direct evidence, and certainly none on which to justify an arrest or prosecution.

When it became obvious that May had been tipped off to Gouzenko's defection, as evidenced by his failure to attend a pre-agreed rendezvous in London, MI5's Len Burt finally interviewed him on 15 February 1946. He confessed during a second interview five days later. Apparently May preferred to risk a short prison sentence in England than face a trial in Canada, or even a death sentence in the United States. The news of his arrest would be the subject of a report from Lemmel, codenamed KASPAR:

> On 8th, at about 7 p.m., in the presence of [XXXXXXX] Edith Tudor Hart answered the door bell, and had a conversation with the caller which lasted for about ten minutes. She then returned rather irritated and [XXXX] that a man had just called, introducing himself as Mr Francis, and enquired about Alexander Tudor Hart, who he thought was living at her place. When she told him that Tudor Hart was not staying with her, and that she [did not] know his whereabouts either, as it was none of her business, the man pretended to be surprised, and tried in a very clumsy way to start a conversation with her, asking her if she was Alexander's sister. She stopped him by saying that she was not his sister, but his ex-wife, as she had realized that the caller was nothing more than a snooper, not an ordinary one, but a

special one, judging by his Oxford accent. Edith seemed rather worried, and [thought that the] incident must be in some way connected with Broda, or with one of his friends who might have got into trouble with the police. She then wondered whether she would be forced to give evidence against Broda, and accused of being too careless. 'When a man is involved in such a business as he is,' she added, 'he ought to be careful and not endanger his friends by writing to or visiting them.' The following Wednesday, the 13th, early in the morning, Broda came up from Cambridge by the first train, and told her that a man had been caught by his landlord in the act of trying to get into his room. Broda suggested that this might have been a general check-up [and] added: 'All of our people are all right, don't get alarmed, don't write and don't phone.' A note was added: 'Any discussion about intelligence work or even the mention of anything of the sort is now strictly prohibited.'

Lemmel may have been encouraged to concentrate on Broda and Edith Suschitsky (Tudor Hart), because on 10 April he submitted another report:

Broda is still very careful, refrains from meeting people and using the telephone. He is in contact with Ilona Suschitzky, wife of Wolfgang Suschitzky, Edith's brother, whom he knows from Moscow. She is active at the Austrian Centre.

The precise role played by Ilona Suschitsky (née Donat), who was of Hungarian birth, is uncertain, but she lived in Moscow between 1931 and 1936 where she had taught in a school and stayed at the Hotel Lux with her lover, Hans Goldschmudt. In September 1946 KASPAR[6] was still enjoying access to Edith and Broda:

According to Broda, the Russians have already solved the problem or are near a solution. Broda states that, contrary to the Anglo/American method, the Russian scientists have found a way of releasing atomic energy through the combination of [XXXXXXX] four hydrogen atoms to helium which proves to be much cheaper and more efficient.

Lemmel would remain in England, running a travel agency, until 1962, when he returned to Vienna, where he published an 'autobiographic novel', *The Indestructible*[7], in 1981. He died in July 1980, his role as KASPAR unknown to anyone outside MI5. His book drew on many of his own experiences, such as his temporary internment at Mooragh on the Isle of Man, and his constant but unsuccessful political struggle, as a Christian social democrat, against the Communists.

Broda had arrived in England as a refugee in April 1938 and was employed at the Cavendish Laboratory in Cambridge, where he recruited a young colleague and fellow CPGB member, Alan Nunn May, but when May was posted to Canada as part of the Manhattan Project, he was handled in Ottawa by the GRU *rezidentura* headed by Nikolai Zabotin. Dr May, codenamed ALEK, would be betrayed in September 1945 by Zabotin's cipher clerk, Igor Gouzenko, whose defection led to May's arrest in London in March 1946. Under interrogation, May declined to identify his recruiter, thus allowing Broda's espionage to continue uninterrupted, if not undetected, for MI5 had harboured deep suspicions about Broda for years, not least because of his lengthy love affair with Edith Suschitsky. Indeed, Broda had also played a role in the NKVD's handling of another spy, Klaus Fuchs, who ultimately would be identified in 1949 by analysis of several incriminating VENONA texts.[8]

Born in 1910 in southern Austria to a family with Jewish antecedents, Broda was educated in Berlin where he joined the Kommunische Partei Deutschland (KPD) as a student, and was arrested at a Communist demonstration in Vienna in June 1931. In September 1935 he married another Communist, Hildegarde Gerwing, from a Jewish family in Aachen, and together they travelled widely, including to the Soviet Union, where he stayed for about nine months between 1935 and 1936. Finally, they moved as refugees to London in March 1938 and lived in a flat in Highgate Road. Broda would become active in the Austrian émigré community and, as a fervent undisguised Marxist active at the Austrian Centre at 126 Westbourne Terrace, he came under MI5's scrutiny. In July 1938 a Special Branch report noted:

> A group of the Austrian Communist Party composed principally of refugees who have come to England has been functioning in London for several months and meeting at regular intervals. Mrs Edith Tudor Hart [Suschitsky] has now been delegated by the Central Committee of the Communist Party of Great Britain to act as a liaison between the Central Committee and this group and to assist in its control. The leader of the group is Engelbert Broda, an Austrian whose address is kept secret from all, even Mrs Tudor Hart, who only knows his telephone number and communicates with him by that medium.

Until last week this was Primrose 3456; since then it has been Paddington 5443.[9]

At that stage MI5 was unaware that Edith Tudor Hart, née Suschitsky, was an experienced Comintern agent whose best friend, also from Vienna, was Lizzie Friedmann, married since 1934 to an impecunious freelance journalist, Kim Philby.

Broda was interned as an enemy alien in October 1939 but was released in December after just ten weeks. He was then detained again in July 1940 and sent to a camp at Huyton, but was freed after thirteen weeks. In December 1941, when MI5 received a request from the Directorate of Scientific and Industrial Research (DSIR) for a permit to employ Broda, it was explained that Broda was 'an active member of the Central Committee of the Austrian Communist Party of which party he was Cell Leader in Vienna', but DSIR's director, Sir Edward Appleton, decreed that 'the exigencies of this Department do override objections on security grounds to Mr Broda's employment on the work for which his services are desired'.

In these circumstances, days before Christmas 1941 Broda reported at the Cavendish Laboratory in Cambridge to work for another Austrian Jew, Hans von Halban, and a French scientist of Russian origin, Lev Kowarski, and was indoctrinated into the Tube Alloys project at a crucial moment, just a fortnight after the Americans had embarked on what would become the Manhattan Project. In moving to Cambridge, leaving his wife to work as a nurse at Stoke Mandeville Hospital in Buckinghamshire, Broda largely removed himself from MI5's immediate purview but MI5's Regional Security Liaison Officer, Major Dixon, was alerted by Millicent Bagot to what she described as a delicate case:

> In view of the nature of his work I am anxious that Broda should not be aware that he is the subject of suspicion, but if you should obtain any information to show that he is taking part in any political activities I should be grateful if you could let me know immediately.

Thus Broda was fully involved in the development of a British nuclear weapon when Alan Nunn May became a member of the team in early 1942 from the physics department at Bristol University. May had joined the CPGB in London in 1936, having graduated from Cambridge, where he had been a contemporary and friend of Donald Maclean, and had visited the Soviet Union in the same year, so was easily persuaded to begin attending the weekly meetings of a local cell of Communist scientists. He and Broda thus became colleagues and would work together until May was posted to Montreal in January 1943, making the transatlantic voyage on SS *Bayano*, and it was during this period that both men became spies and May began an affair with Broda's wife Hilde.

Born in Vienna in 1908 to William Suschitzky, a radical socialist who advocated birth control and sex education and owned a bookshop in the working-class district of Petzvalgasse, Edith had trained as a Montessori kindergarten teacher and in 1925 had travelled to England to work in a junior school.[10] Two years later she was back in Vienna, and studied photography under Walter Peterhans at the Bauhaus in Dessau. In 1931 she had been deported from London after she had been spotted at a CPGB rally.

In 1933, at the height of the political repression, she married Dr Alex Tudor Hart, a left-wing Cambridge-educated medical practitioner, at the British consulate, and moved first to Brixton in south London and then to the Rhondda Valley.[11] As well as being an active member of the banned Austrian Communist Party, she was also undertaking missions for the NKVD and in 1929 had completed two, to Paris and London.

Upon their return from South Wales, Alex Tudor Hart joined the Republican forces in Spain as a surgeon, while his wife opened a photographic studio in Acre Lane in Brixton and began to specialize, after the birth of her son Tommy in 1936, in child portraits. It was during this period, while active in the Workers Camera Club, contributing to *Picture Post* and organizing the Artists against Fascism and War exhibition, that she maintained contact with her friend from Vienna, Lizzie Friedmann, who was by then separated from Kim Philby, and liaised closely with Bob Stewart of the CPGB, who was himself acting as a clandestine link between the CPGB headquarters and the Soviet embassy. In March 1938 a Leica camera originally purchased by her was discovered in a police search of the home of Percy Glading, who was subsequently convicted of organizing the Woolwich Arsenal spy-ring, but when questioned by Special Branch detectives she simply denied any involvement. In 1940 she was divorced from Alex, and had acquired a substantial MI5 file which listed her aliases as Betty Gray and Edith White.

After the war Edith worked as a commercial photographer and briefly for the Ministry of Education, but her mental condition deteriorated and she suffered a breakdown, her son Tommy already having been institutionalized with schizophrenia, an illness he was thought to have developed during the London Blitz. She also had an affair with his psychoanalyst, Donald Winnicott of the Tavistock Institute, who would go on to treat her for a psychiatric illness involving persecution mania. According to the family, Edith was escorted to the hospital by her sister-in-law, Ilona, on the instructions of her Soviet handler; Ilona would not be forgiven for the act. Later Edith opened a small antiques shop in Bond Street, Brighton, where she was traced by MI5 following Anthony Blunt's confession in April 1964, but was deemed not to be a threat. She died of liver cancer in May 1973 aged 64, her remarkable espionage role largely undiscovered, despite an interview with MI5 conducted in February 1947 in which she reportedly acknowledged having been in contact with the Soviets in Austria and Italy back in 1932 and 1933, but made no incriminating admissions, and apparently maintained silence about Lizzie and Lizzie's (by then) ex-husband. She was also unhelpful in December 1951 when she was interviewed again at her ground floor flat in Abbey Road by Skardon, on the pretext of a background check on Lizzie Friedmann's new partner, the German journalist and editor of the *Berliner Zeitung* Georg Honigmann.[12] Originally from Frankfurt, Honigmann had been the Berlin correspondent for *Voss* until 1933 when he had come to London, later to be appointed head of Reuter's European service.

During a lengthy period of surveillance on Edith the MI5 watchers never spotted any incriminating activity, apart from fare-dodging on the bus to Golders Green. After her encounter with MI5's genial interrogator Jim Skardon he reported that 'This woman prevaricated from one end of the interview to the other.' She admitted having known Friedmann but insisted that she had long resigned from the Communist Party. MI5 had hoped that she might be panicked by the interview, in which she claimed not to recognize Philby's photo, into contacting him, but she did not rise to the bait.

As a celebrated photographer, Edith enjoyed a wide range of contacts within British society, and her expertise as a recruiter is confirmed in a letter dated 8 October 1936 from the London illegal *rezidentura* to Moscow Centre noting a recent significant success:

EDITH. Through EDITH we obtained SOHNCHEN [Kim Philby]. In the attached report you will find details of a second SOHNCHEN who, in all probability, offers even greater possibilities than the first. Edith is of the opinion that [name deleted] is more promising than SOHNCHEN. From the report you will see that he has very definite possibilities. We must make haste with these people before they start being active in university life.[13]

Three months after his confession in April 1964, Anthony Blunt was asked about Suschitsky and he told his MI5 interrogator, Peter Wright, that

> Edith Tudor Hart was a close friend of Lizzy Philby and he had always believed that it was Tudor Hart who first recruited Kim Philby. He thought Philby's recruitment preceded that of Burgess. Certainly Tudor Hart was involved in the whole affair and, as one source put it, was probably 'the grandmother of us all'. He thought Tudor Hart would know of his involvement although he had never met her.[14]

Alan May, having entered a guilty plea, was sentenced to ten years' imprisonment, some of which was spent at Camp Hill, the prison on the Isle of Wight which, coincidentally, also accommodated Douglas Springhall. In August 1953, following his early release from Wakefield prison in December 1952, benefiting from the statutory one-third remission for good behaviour, he married Hildegarde Broda, her husband Engelbert having moved to Vienna in April 1947. The circumstances of Broda's departure were duly reported by Lemmel:

> According to Mrs Tudor Hart, Broda has just returned from a visit to Rome. He flew to Rome about three weeks ago where he contacted a certain woman called Ada Drakovitch, Jugoslav, employed by UNRRA [the United Nations Relief and Rehabilitation Agency]. Broda was in touch with this woman about ten years ago in Belgrade when he visited Jugoslavia on orders from the Party. From what Tudor Hart said it would seem that Ada Drakovitch is employed by the Russian intelligence.

Thus, having expressed his wish to his British employers to return to Austria, Broda had discovered in September 1946 that two sisters, Ina Ehrlich and Vera Stein, with whom he had been acquainted years earlier, were living in Rome, and he had corresponded with Ina. According to MI5's research, she had been born in 1902 in Zagreb, and so was eight years older than Broda, but a comment added to an intercepted letter in February 1947 observed 'She would clearly not object to marrying Broda.'[15] Accordingly, Broda had flown to Rome on 3 March and returned to London eight days later to settle his affairs. He flew back to

Italy on 22 April and the couple were married the following month, moving to Vienna.

Ina was a poet, translator and author of stories for Jewish children, but in 1941 she had led a left-wing women's organization and was forced to flee to Dalmatia. During her marriage, as Ina Jun Broda, she published poems and essays, and translated Serbo-Croat and Italian texts into German. In 1950 her *Der Dichter in der Barbarei* gave an account of her experiences during the Nazi occupation and in 1958 she published *Die Schwarze Erde*, an anthology of Yugoslav partisan poetry.

Broda, who risked a return to Britain only once, briefly in May 1948, later explained to his family that Ina's first husband and child had been murdered by the Croatian Ustaše during the German occupation, and that she had then joined Tito's partisans. However, the marriage was not a success, and ended in divorce in June 1953. Broda died in October 1983, followed later the same year by Ina, never having commented publicly about his espionage.

May also exercised great reticence about his activities, apart from his official statement in which he had admitted having passed classified information to a Soviet diplomat, Pavel N. Angelov, who had called at his apartment on Montreal's Swail Avenue for the first time in April 1945, having telephoned to his laboratory to make an appointment. When the two men had met, Angelov had used the *parole* 'Greetings from Alek' to confirm his *bona-fides*. Thereafter May took papers home at the weekend 'several times' and left them overnight with Angelov so he could copy them in time for their return on Monday mornings. On one occasion May had supplied samples of Uranium-233 and U-235, which had been considered so important that the assistant military attaché, Colonel Pyotr Motinov, had carried it to Moscow by air.

May died in January 2003, having completed the manuscript of an autobiography which, during his lifetime, he had feared to publish because he believed it contained information that might have led to other criminal charges. To his stepson, Paul Broda, he denied that he had ever known Donald Maclean at Trinity Hall, and stated that Engelbert had not played any role whatever in his espionage.[16] As for the precise identity of the individual who acted as an intermediary in 1942, when he began contact with the Soviets, MI5 concluded that Broda had been the most likely candidate, a view expressed in a minute entered on his MI5 personal file in October 1953:

Engelbert Broda might well have been the person who recruited Nunn May for the Russian Intelligence Service. You will remember that one of Nunn May's few admissions was that he was recruited for the RIS [Russian Intelligence Service] only a very short while before he left this country for Canada and that the individual who recruited him was no longer within reach in March 1949 when Nunn May said this Broda was no longer in the country.

MI5 may have been very suspicious of Broda and his associations, but the first indication that Barkovsky had been running an important spy in London with access to atomic secrets was the publication in 1988 of KGB 3rd Department FCD archive material *The Crown Jewels*. Sanitized by Moscow, the disclosure referred to a source identified only as 'K' but can now be seen as an accurate account of the London *rezidentura*'s handling of three atomic spies, being John Cairncross, who had passed a copy of the MAUD Report in 1940, 'K', who became active in January 1941, and a third individual, codenamed KELLY, in 1945. According to Oleg Tsarev,

> Another of the London *rezidentura*'s sources, codenamed MOOR and run by Barkovsky, passed on information about the separation of Uranium-235 and on the efforts made by the Americans and British to find new deposits. A third ENORMOZ source in Britain was KELLY who, like 'K', passed on important atomic documents and in June 1945 supplied more than 35 reports and scientific correspondence on atomic developments.

In 1999 Alexander Vassiliev and his two American co-authors expanded on the unknown atomic spy in *The Haunted Wood*, describing him as an Englishman codenamed ERIC, but it was not until 2009 that Vassiliev, having emigrated from Russia, was able to produce his collection of manuscript notes from the KGB archive which identified ERIC as Engelbert Broda.[17] It was only then that Broda's full role, his espionage, his links with Edith Suschitsky, Klaus Fuchs and Alan Nunn May, could be explained for the first time.

Chapter 9

William Whalen

... seriously but not critically degraded the capabilities
of the US and the Allies to successfully wage general
or limited war

[Damage Assessment, Deputy Chief of Staff, 1966]

Arrested at his home in Dewey Drive, Alexandria, Virginia, in July 1966, 50-year-old Lieutenant Colonel William H. Whalen was identified as a spy by Dmitri Polyakov, a GRU source run by the Federal Bureau of Investigation.[1] Whalen, who had retired from working for the Chiefs of Staff in the Pentagon in 1961, had been recruited originally in 1955 at the Farmington shopping centre parking lot in Alexandria by Mikhail M. Shumaev, listed as the embassy's first secretary, who had later passed the case on to his GRU colleague Colonel Sergei A. Edemski, the assistant military attaché who returned to Moscow in February 1960. Edemski would later be promoted and posted to the Soviet embassy in London.

According to the indictment issued on 12 July 1966, the Soviets had received information pertaining to atomic weaponry, missiles, military plans for the defence of Europe, estimates of comparative military capabilities, military intelligence reports and analyses, information concerning the retaliation plans by the United States Strategic Air Command and information pertaining to troop movements.

Evidence from the US Army's deputy chief of staff asserted that Whalen had 'seriously but not critically degraded the capabilities of the US and the Allies to successfully wage general or limited war'. He was alleged to have received $5,500 at five meetings held between December 1959 and March 1961. Convicted, in March 1967 he was sentenced to fifteen years' imprisonment with the minimum of publicity, and died in prison, survived by his wife Bernardine and daughter Kathy. When polygraphed by the FBI in September 1963, Whalen had broken down and signed a series of confessions, blaming his behaviour on financial problems, which he later attempted, unsuccessfully, to suppress on legal grounds.

Whalen had joined the US Army in October 1940 as an enlisted soldier and spent the war in the United States, not receiving a European posting until May 1945. Reportedly he had received wounds during a training exercise, and then had been commissioned. In 1948 he was assigned to an intelligence staff post, first in Europe and then in the United States, attached to the Office of the Assistant Chief of Staff Intelligence (OACSI), where he participated in PAPERCLIP, the recruitment of Nazi scientists to work on defence projects in the United States, and then in Japan.[2]

Although all the Allies adopted their individual programmes to exploit Nazi scientific developments by identifying and recruiting key personnel, the American version, initiated in July 1945 as OVERCAST (but changed four months later to PAPERCLIP), was by far the best resourced, funded and managed. It has been estimated that during the postwar era some 1,000 technicians were processed in the United States, interviewed about their fields of research, and employed on particular defence projects at various secluded sites where they were segregated and put back to work in their specialist areas. Although PAPERCLIP was considered a secret operation when it was operational, by the time Whalen participated, likely in a supervisory or administrative capacity, the project's existence was less sensitive, but aspects of what it had accomplished, in terms of weapon development, was most certainly highly sensitive in an era when advances in rocketry and guided missiles looked likely to dominate the future of armed conflict. The scientists were offered one-year contracts in the United States and, during their absence, their families were accommodated at a former German cavalry barracks at Landshut, Bavaria. The operation involved all the US armed forces, each of which sponsored their own particular projects, intended to exploit German scientific advances. However, the participation of Werner von Braun and his V-2 missile design team from Peenemunde would become controversial because of the Nazi backgrounds of some of the scientists and their involvement in atrocities committed at the Dora-Mittelbau concentration camp which supplied slave labour for the Nordhausen rocket factory. The PAPERCLIP administration was accused of having been inordinately lax in its vetting procedures, and even of having turned a blind eye to war criminals. Nevertheless, the project, which mirrored the objectives of similar schemes in England and the Soviet Union, was immensely successful.

By May 1948 1,136 PAPERCLIP Germans had been shipped to the US, with 127 rocket specialists working at Fort Bliss, El Paso, and 146 experts at Wright Field, Ohio. German scientists taken to England were accommodated at a branch of the Royal Aircraft Establishment, Farnborough, located at Westcott, where research on rocket motors was concentrated until the cancellation of the *Blue Streak* missile project in 1962.

In 1951 Whalen was transferred to the Army Security Agency (ASA), then with its headquarters at Fort Meade, Maryland, with a subordinate station at Arlington Hall, Virginia. The ASA, together with the service branches, the Naval Security Group and the Air Force Security Service, acted as the signals intelligence collection components of the Armed Forces Security Agency, later to become the National Security Agency. ASA radio intercept sites included a network of stations within the United States, and several covert installations overseas, including Asmara, Chitose, Guam, New Delhi, Peshawar, the Philippines, Sinop and RAF Menwith Hill. The ASA in Europe, based in Frankfurt, encompassed sites at Augsburg, Russelsheim and Seckheim. The precise locations of the ASA stations were kept confidential so as to make the task of observation, and maybe penetration, more difficult, in line with the doctrine that any indication of the ASA's size or activities could be helpful to an adversary. The ASA managed several sites in West Germany, perhaps the best known being the Berlin field station atop the Teufelsburg in the British Sector of West Berlin, a constant target for the Soviets.

During the period that Whalen served in the ASA, the organization took over the electronic intelligence and electronic warfare responsibilities of the US Signal Corps, both topics of considerable interest to the Soviet Bloc. According to Whalen's own admissions, he was in touch with his Soviet contacts in 1959, which suggests that the still classified damage assessment drafted when he confessed includes the possibility of him having compromised ASA data.

Eight years later, in 1959, Whalen moved to the Joint Intelligence Objectives Agency (JIOA) as deputy director. Created in 1945, the JIOA had the status of a subcommittee of the Joint Chiefs of Staff and oversaw the acquisition, collation and distribution of scientific and industrial intelligence on behalf of the armed forces and the US State Department. The JIOA was wound up in 1962.

In February 1952 Whalen had undergone an orientation course in anticipation of his joining Detachment M, OACSI. This unit was responsible for maintaining the security of SIGINT distributed within the

135

US Army, and on 20 May 1952 he was transferred to Tokyo to head the Detachment M office there. He returned from Japan on 2 July 1957 to be appointed Assistant Chief of the OACSI, US Army Foreign Liaison Office, and on 5 July 1959 was promoted to Chief. He suffered a severe heart attack in July 1960 which led to his retirement in February 1961, by which time he had sold his Soviet contacts 17 classified military manuals. Although Whalen's usefulness as an espionage asset ceased upon his enforced retirement on disability grounds, he had been active over a period of five years when he had been in a critical position with access to precisely the categories of material the Soviets most valued, such as US intelligence assessments, Allied nuclear capabilities, the deployment of nuclear war-heads, policy relating to first-strike policy, retaliation and intelligence collection priorities.

Although only the Soviets can be certain of what Whalen compromised, he was certainly in a position to pass details of warfare doctrine and con-fidential position papers relating to the defence of Europe. The key issues of that period of the Cold War, in the era of credible deterrence and mutually-assured destruction, were Allied knowledge of the Kremlin's plans; analysis of Soviet warhead and missile production; the Soviet ICBM arsenal; and NATO retaliation doctrine. At the heart of the dilemma challenging the Allied intelligence community was the bluff and counter-bluff aspects to Allied and Soviet strategies. Put simply, Nikita Khrush-chev had no viable method of delivering nuclear weapons to their targets in the United States at a time when his strategic bombers had insufficient range, and anyway were vulnerable to air and ground defences. Only three ICBMs had been constructed, and there was no confidence that they would perform. These ICBMs, incidentally, were liquid-fuelled and required twenty hours to prepare for launch, so were useless as retaliatory weapons. The Red Banner Navy had yet to develop a submarine-launched ballistic missile. In these circumstances Khrushchev could only make false boasts about his ICBM capability and plan to deploy shorter-range MRBMs and IRBMs closer to their target, a high-risk (but Politburo-approved) policy that would become manifest in October 1962 in the Caribbean.

The American position had been to take Soviet claims about warhead production at face value and engage in an arms race predicated upon the false notions of the 'bomber-gap' and then the 'missile gap'. In reality, the lack of ICBM launch-sites, which anyway were subject to monitoring through telemetry interception, had been exposed by HOMERUN, the U-2 photographic reconnaissance overflights which commenced in July

1956 and mapped the cosmodromes at Plesetsk and Baikonur, and the railway lines serving them.

Khrushchev's bluff was exposed in 1960 by the GRU's Oleg Penkovsky, who delivered IRONBARK, the codename for huge quantities of *Military Doctrine*, the semi-official Soviet periodical in which senior military personnel discussed policy issues with a surprising degree of candour. A 1970 CIA assessment of IRONBARK eloquently explained the source's value.

> Some of the IRONBARK material which Penkovsky passed to us in 1961 and 1962 revealed a sharp military debate concerning Soviet military concepts and organization needed for nuclear warfare. There was general agreement in the writings that the existing doctrine and organization were obsolete and inadequate for the era of modern nuclear weapons. But there was wide disagreement on what changes were necessary and how best to accomplish them. The central issue in the IRONBARK debate in the early sixties was the force structure question of whether nuclear weapons should support massive conventional combat operations in Europe – or replace them.

Penkovsky's great value was his confirmation that the Kremlin had lied about Soviet ICBMs and that the development programme had endured countless failures since the first rocket exploded on the launch-pad in May 1957. Specifically, the GRU officer asserted that there were only three operational ICBMs, and he doubted whether the engine of one of them would ignite. Once fuelled, the R-7A Semyorka variant, with an estimated range of 7,500 miles and designated *Sapwood* by NATO, could only remain at operational readiness for a day without the cryogenic system becoming dangerously unstable. When fired, the on-board navigation system required a down-range signal to correct the trajectory. In these circumstances, where Khrushchev was gambling for time to build a reliable ICBM force, and perfect an underwater launch, information about the opponents' true standing was critical. The first test, in September 1960, of a Northern Fleet submarine-launched missile required B-67, a converted Zulu IV, actually a Type-XXI U-boat derivative, armed with a single missile, to surface first, whereas the US-designed Polaris was fired while the vessel, USS *George Washington*, was cruising at depth. Furthermore, the nuclear-powered *George Washington*, armed with sixteen missiles with a range of 1,400 miles, had entered service in December 1959, the first of forty in the class. The competitive advantage of a nuclear-powered submarine operating undetected, and carrying a phenomenal arsenal, over a noisy diesel-electric that would have to surface for a dangerously long time to erect, prepare and fire the sole R-11FM Scud missile, which had a range of just 105 miles, was obvious. To pose a credible threat to the United States' eastern seaboard, *B-67* would have to sneak past the US Naval Air Station at Kindley Field on Bermuda, through the SOSUS acoustic detection arrays, and then loiter on the surface as the crew undertook the delicate and dangerous task of preparing the missile for launch and fuelling it with an extremely volatile mixture of kerosene and nitric acid.

Even though the Northern Fleet would deploy a further five conventional Zulus over the years that followed the first test launch in September 1955, armed with two missiles each, the imbalance between the superpowers was plain, if it had been understood for what it was, which is where Whalen and his espionage must have been of such great significance to the Kremlin. Did NATO appreciate the true situation? Was Moscow fully informed about Washington's knowledge of the hollow threat of Soviet warhead production? Had the Politburo grasped the challenges of launching a surprise nuclear strike against the United States?

The IRONBARK material circulated in Washington gave the context for Penkovsky's own reporting, codenamed CHICKADEE, which exposed the Potemkin village nature of the Kremlin's bluff. Although Penkovsky himself was taken into custody by the KGB on the very day of President Kennedy's broadcast to announce the imposition of a quarantine on Cuba, he had served his purpose and alerted the CIA, and thereby Washington policymakers, of what was really at stake.[3] Considering the potential for one side or the other to seize the initiative before it was too late, much rested on the intelligence picture. Whether Whalen was a part of this remains a matter of speculation, but while he was in a position to see current reporting, he could not have seen IRONBARK because he retired a month *before* Penkovsky's first visit to England, in April 1961, when he began producing prodigious quantities of intelligence. Nevertheless, Whalen would have known the current understanding of the strategic balance, based on U-2 imagery and the run of R-7 disasters monitored by SIGINT, a subject he must have known well from his ASA experience. Indeed, a priority target for the ASA stations in Turkey had been Kaspustin Yar and other experimental ranges.

Whalen was one of several GRU assets identified by Dmitri Polyakov, who, codenamed TOPHAT by the FBI and ROAM by the CIA, remained active until his retirement in 1980, and was undetected by the Soviets until May 1985 when he was betrayed by the CIA's Aldrich Ames.[4] In this, and similar cases, the FBI's priority was to eliminate a leak without compromising the source. In such circumstances the KGB would have initiated an investigation to understand what had contaminated a valuable asset so as to take the necessary counter-measures to limit the damage. Anticipating this, the FBI would have required a plausible cover-story to protect their precious source which, at the time, remained *en poste* and therefore extremely vulnerable. Certainly Polyakov, who would be promoted to the rank of general, was highly prized by the FBI and CIA, and had served twice in the United States before being posted as military attaché to New Delhi in 1973. However, at the time of Whalen's arrest in 1966, Polyakov had been in Rangoon for the past ten months, a posting that would last four years.

The question of when Polyakov identified Whalen as a spy, or supplied the crucial pieces of evidence that allowed the FBI to track him down, remains unresolved. So too is the precise date upon which Whalen was recruited by the GRU and began supplying information, there being a contradiction between the suggestion that he sold classified material from 1955, and the indictment which reveals a date in 1959. A routine fitness report attached to the damage assessment comments

> Although the investigation reported that he occasionally drank to excess, and that between 1952 and 1955 he had recurrent financial problems, it did not discover evidence that he was a spy.

The titles of the manuals sold by Whalen are also unknown, although reportedly they included information about the Nike and Hawk anti-aircraft missiles. The Nike, built by Bell Laboratories and introduced in 1953, was essentially a wartime-vintage programme operating a radar-guided, line-of-sight weapon capable of destroying a bomber at an altitude of 60,000 feet. It was deployed across the United States at some 200 batteries in a defensive role. The mobile Hawk anti-aircraft system, which entered service seven years later in 1959, was built by Northrop and offered an improved range of 40 miles. At a time when the Soviet nuclear strategy depended on the delivery of free-fall bombs delivered by long-range bombers, American air defence arrangements were of vital interest to the Kremlin.

As for the FBI's cover-story to explain how Whalen was unmasked, a narrative peddled by Peter Kross in *Tales from Langley*[5] asserted that Special Agent Donald A. Gruentzel, who had investigated the Swedish spy Stig Wennerstrom in 1963, had stumbled across some compromising information which had led him to interrogate Whalen at headquarters, where he had been confronted with evidence of unexplained wealth in his bank account.[6]

Of course, the FBI had the best of motives for the deliberate obfuscation concerning how Whalen was caught, or incriminated himself, but one can be sure that the unexplained wealth *canard* is nothing more than that. Generally, one can say that spies are caught by other spies, which is the value of aggressive counter-intelligence, and not by 'the vigilance of colleagues'.

Chapter 10

John Walker

John Walker led one of the most devastating spy-rings
ever unmasked in the US. Along with his brother, son,
and friend, he compromised US Navy cryptographic
systems and classified information from 1967 to 1985.

[Laura Heath, Damage Assessment, June 2005[1]]

John Walker joined the US Navy in May 1955 and held top secret crypto
clearances while serving on two ballistic nuclear submarines, USS *Arthur
Jackson* and *Simon Bolivar*. In October 1967, short of money, Walker sold
some key cards for cipher machines to the Soviet embassy in Washington
DC, thus exposing the Polaris missile fleet's encrypted communications.
Walker's espionage would not end until May 1985, when he was arrested
after a four-hour fruitless search for money left for him at a designated
cache in woods near Rockville, Maryland, by his KGB handler, Alexei
Tkachenko. Significantly, throughout his seventeen years as a spy, Walker
was controlled by the KGB's 16th Directorate, the highly compartmented
communications branch which ran a handful of agents with access to
crypto-equipment, such as Geoffrey Prime in Britain's Government Communications Headquarters, under exceptionally tight security. Indeed,
even after Prime had been arrested in April 1982, the Allied intelligence
community had not realized that the 16th Directorate actually recruited
and managed agents, and had handled Prime until he retired from GCHQ
in 1977.[2] Interestingly, SIS's recently arrived asset in the London *rezidentura*, Oleg Gordievsky, had no knowledge of Prime because he had not
been run by his own First Chief Directorate (FCD). Indeed, if Prime had
not been apprehended on entirely separate sex charges, he probably would
never have been caught. Much the same applied to the Walker spy-ring,
which was largely unknown to the FCD in Boris Solomatin's heavily
penetrated Washington *rezidentura*. Another 16th Directorate asset was

Robert Lipka, a National Security Agency analyst who had been a similar embassy walk-in, back in September 1965, and whose product was emphatically cryptographic in origin. For two years, until August 1967, Lipka passed the KGB thousands of classified documents intended for shredding, and was paid around $27,000. Although only a junior clerk completing his compulsory military service, Lipka's job in the NSA's Central Communications Room gave him access from his posting in 1964 to a vast quantity of documents, few of which he actually read.[3]

Once Solomatin had been convinced of Walker's *bona-fides*, he assigned a trusted Line PR political intelligence subordinate, Oleg Kalugin, to deal with future contacts, and had a naval expert, Yuti Linkov, assess the material. Once satisfied Walker's product was authentic, the entire case was transferred to the 16th Directorate.

To assist his collection efforts, the KGB provided Walker with a Minox camera and a specially constructed device for reading the internal wiring of the KL-74 cipher machine rotors. It is now believed that some of Walker's information was relayed to Hanoi and compromised American battle plans in the region, enabling the North Vietnamese Army to anticipate B-52 air raids and take the appropriate counter-measures. According to the KGB FCD defector Vitali Yurchenko, who had served as security officer at the Washington embassy and therefore had been indoctrinated into the case, and debriefed in August 1985, 'the information delivered by Walker enabled the KGB to decipher over a million messages'. Yurchenko gave evidence to General Richard Stilwell, who headed a commission of inquiry which, after five years of deliberation, made sixty-three separate recommendations to improve security and avoid a similar episode.

During his submarine assignments Walker handled the most sensitive coding equipment, including the key cards used to alter the daily settings on the 37 Series, 14 Series and 7 Series cipher machines. The KL-47 was a seven-rotor machine, using rotors selected from a box of 10, not dissimilar to the German Enigma, and Walker's first delivery to the Soviets included the keylist for the entire month of November 1967. Of Second World War vintage, it was replaced by the KW-7, an online automatic, high-speed encrypted teleprinter that relied upon IBM punchcards to make daily variations. The KW-7 was a grey box, weighing 75 pounds, containing vacuum and transistor components. The early models incorporated a plugboard that required periodic manual rewiring but later date-stamped punchcards were introduced, and these Walker also passed to his KGB controllers, thus enabling them to retrospectively read the traffic generated on the KSW-37 transmitter for reception on the KWR-37. He also used the KY-8 voice scrambler, a device that the Soviets would express no interest in after January 1983. After having served on USS *Razorback* as a radio operator, Walker attended a school to learn repair skills for mending faulty cryptographic equipment until he was posted as the crypto custodian to a combat supply ship, USS *Niagara Falls*, for duty in Vietnam.

Between 1967 and 1974 he effectively compromised the entire Fleet Broadcast System (FBS), the US Navy's sole means of communicating with its vessels at sea, during a critical period of the Vietnam War. The FBS depended on high-frequency shortwave teletype transmissions which were broadcast from four Naval Communications Area Master Stations, one of which was located in each of the US Navy's four theatres of operations (the West and Eastern Pacific, the Mediterranean and the Atlantic).

After his initial approach to the embassy, where he had been received by the security officer, Yakov Lukasevics, who had promptly introduced him to the KGB *rezident* Boris Solomatin in October 1967, Walker would only arrange to rendezvous with his Soviet handlers or exchange secrets for money at dead-drops every six months or so, and the meetings usually took place overseas, in Vienna or Casablanca. He claimed later that one of these meetings, in a Vienna suburb, had been attended by the KGB's chairman, Yuri Andropov.

After his retirement from the US Navy in July 1976, Walker ensured the continued flow of classified material by recruiting a friend, Jerry A. Whitworth, who was serving as a chief radioman aboard USS *Constellation*, then later *Niagara Falls*; finally, he involved his son, Michael L. Walker, a seaman on USS *Nimitz*.

Michael Walker joined the US Navy in 1982 and, upon his assignment as a yeoman to a fighter squadron, began copying classified documents for his father. In November 1983 he joined USS *Nimitz*, having served previously on other carriers. In his memoirs, *My Life as a Spy*[4], John Walker asserted that the Soviets had not been consulted by the North Koreans before the capture of USS *Pueblo*, suggesting that they would have opposed anything that might have prompted the Americans to replace the KW-7. He also claimed that he had been motivated to betray secrets by a policy of government deception dating back to the USS *Greer* incident in September 1941, which effectively brought the Roosevelt administration into the war when *U-853* fired a torpedo at the destroyer, and he further stated that his purpose had been to persuade the Kremlin that the United States would never launch a surprise attack on the Soviet Union. Far from betraying his country, Walker believed he should have been awarded a Nobel Peace Prize.

Walker's espionage, over a period of seventeen years, was the worst case of hostile penetration detected within the US Navy, and there were recriminations within the service and the FBI, which was blamed for ignoring early indicators, such as a drunken denunciation made in November 1984 by Walker's ex-wife Barbara, whom he had divorced in 1976. She insisted her ex-husband had told her he was spying for the Soviets back in 1968, but she was disbelieved. Although initially dismissed as vexatious, an investigation codenamed WINDFLYER was initiated by the FBI's Boston Field Office. Barbara had been persuaded to speak out by her daughter Laura, a soldier who had turned down a 'pitch' from her father. When Laura was interviewed, she corroborated her mother's allegations, and in March the FBI headquarters authorized large-scale surveillance on Walker which quickly uncovered incriminating evidence. The Naval Investigative Service also participated, as Michael Walker also became a suspect. When his father was arrested, he had in his possession twenty-seven classified documents which Michael had removed from the *Nimitz*, and which had been secreted at a dead-drop. Further evidence implicating his brother Arthur and his friend Jerry Whitworth was found during a search of his house. At their trial John and Michael pleaded guilty to charges of espionage. John received two terms of life imprisonment, plus ten years, and his son received twenty-five years. Whitworth, who turned himself in to the authorities in June, was found guilty and was sentenced to 365 years and fined $410,000. Arthur was also arrested and was sentenced to three life terms plus a $250,000 fine.

Asked in 1995 about Walker's impact, Solomatin would confirm that his 'information not only provided us with ongoing intelligence, but helped us over time to understand and study how your military actually thinks'.[5] He explained that Walker and his network had been the Soviets' key source on US submarine missile forces, which was regarded in Moscow as the principal threat to the Soviet Union. He also added that Walker helped both superpowers avoid nuclear conflict by enabling the Kremlin to understand American intentions, an achievement that served to reduce tension at particular moments of diplomatic friction.

From the Allied perspective, it will be impossible to fully appreciate the scale of what Walker did until the Stilwell Commission damage assessment is declassified, but for the present it remains under wraps. In strategic terms, it is, however, possible, based on the quantity of documents, manuals and intelligence reports he is known to have compromised, to estimate his impact. Tens of thousands of secret documents were copied by him and passed to the KGB, which was understandably eager to learn more about US Navy capabilities, weaponry, tactics and doctrine at a time when the Kremlin's defensive stance was based upon an ability to anticipate (and perhaps thereby deter) a surprise, first-strike nuclear attack mounted by NATO, and the ability to deliver nuclear weapons to targets in North America. This vital dimension to Soviet policy depended on three methods. The dropping of free-fall bombs from long-distance strategic bombers depended on obsolete aircraft being able to penetrate American airspace to reach their targets and deliver their ordnance, with the crews confident that they would survive the experience and have the range to land at a safe-haven airfield, or at least do more than hope to survive rescue in mid-Atlantic by pre-positioned submarines deployed for the purpose. The ancient bombers were, as the crews knew only too well, very vulnerable to early detection by comprehensive radar coverage and to attack by either Nike and Hawk missile batteries, or to interception by supersonic fighters. In short, few believed that the Red Army's air fleet was viable.

Nor was there much faith in the second option, Soviet ICBMs that could only be fired from a limited number of heavily monitored launch-sites inside the Soviet Union, which were serviced by a railway system that itself was under constant surveillance. If the ICBMs could be prepared for launch in conditions of secrecy, they might be considered a first-strike weapon, but the lengthy fuelling process ruled out ballistic missiles as a weapon of retaliation.

Finally, and most critically, there were submarine-launched weapons, either nuclear-tipped missiles or torpedoes, that could engage the adversary having evaded detection by aircraft, surface ships, hunter-killer attack submarines and the SOSUS acoustic arrays. Accordingly, much rested on the certainty that sufficient ballistic missile boats could be successfully deployed from bases in Murmansk and Kamchatka to penetrate into the deep oceans and place themselves in range off the US seaboards to either participate in a first-strike surprise attack, or to inflict a lethal retaliatory counter-strike. The most obvious challenges to the Kremlin's submarine strategy were five-fold: the first being the extent and capability of the SOSUS hydrophones, which consisted of a huge passive apparatus, with receivers the size of a double-decker bus, that were linked by underwater cables to heavily protected onshore monitoring sites whose precise locations were classified. All SOSUS capabilities were Soviet collection priorities, and Walker was content to oblige.

Soviet submarines were not only vulnerable to SOSUS. As soon as a boat ventured out on patrol it was the subject of detection and shadowing by Allied attack submarines equipped with advanced sonar and highly classified towed-arrays extending from the boat's stern. Naturally, the exact capabilities of this sophisticated technology was another Soviet collection priority, which Walker duly fulfilled. Even if a Red Banner submarine evaded detection at the outset, and chose a course to avoid SOSUS choke-points, such as the Iceland-Greenland-Faroes gap or the Straits of Gibraltar, it would still have to contend with sonobuoys dropped from hostile maritime reconnaissance aircraft and orthodox sonar carried by surface vessels, the capabilities of which were also matters in which Walker could assist. Put simply, Walker had been in a position to satisfy Moscow's demand for crucial information upon which the entire Soviet nuclear strategy was dependent. He had disclosed current intelligence assessments, revealed operational doctrine, compromised highly sensitive covert eavesdropping operations which took submarines into Soviet harbours and coastal waters, identified the bunkers which accommodated SOSUS sensor terminals, and maybe even undermined double agent operations aimed against the GRU.

As for making the world safer, it could also be argued that the opposite was true because it gave the Politburo support for the proposition that a first-strike plan was viable, a dangerous concept that went to the heart of the principle of deterrence, which had kept the peace since 1945, and offered the Soviets, in the event of conflict breaking out, as the US Director of Naval Intelligence Admiral William O. Studeman described it in his 1986 testimony to the Senate Select Committee on Intelligence, 'powerful war-winning capabilities'. The Committee's report included his evidence presented at Whitworth's trial:

1. I am William O. Studeman, a naval officer presently holding the rank of Rear Admiral. I was commissioned an Ensign in the Navy in 1963, and have served virtually continuously on active duty as a naval intelligence officer since that time. My present position is that of

Director of Naval Intelligence, which I have held since September 1985. As Director of Naval Intelligence, I am responsible for the collection, analysis and distribution of intelligence information within the Naval Service. I am the Navy's sponsor for counter-intelligence programs executed by the Naval Security and Investigative Command, under the policy auspices of the Office of the Secretary of Defense. I offer this affidavit to the Court for use as it deems appropriate in constructing an appropriate sentence for the defendant in this case.

2. The defendant in this case, formerly Senior Chief Petty Officer Jerry Alfred Whitworth, served the United States Navy for 24 years, 18 of which were in the rate of Radioman, rising to the rank of Senior Chief prior to his retirement. The primary function of a Radioman is to provide and maintain the ability of Department of Defense and naval forces to communicate with each other as well as senior and subordinate commands. Unlike the navies of old, virtually all the information required to plan, operate, command, maintain, modernize, repair, replenish, warn, inform and control the military forces of all the services and our allies is exchanged electrically via communication systems, most of which are considered secure by virtue of their cryptographic cover. Electrical distribution of naval messages is an essential backbone activity designed to reach all levels of command in the Navy. This naval communications system is operated by some of our brightest people who are given the tools, training and sacred trust to protect the vital high technology systems and access to sensitive secrets which are placed in their hands. It is important, therefore, to understand the vulnerabilities inherent in naval communications, to understand the concept of cryptographic support to communications security (COMSEC) and to understand how Radioman Senior Chief Jerry Whitworth's violation of his trust as a member of the elite fraternity of naval communication professionals has resulted in unprecedented damage to the Navy and the nation.

3. Cryptographic systems are designed to encipher information so that only the holders of the system will be able to decipher that same information. Contemporary crypto-equipments accomplish enciphering and deciphering on the basis of complex mathematical formulas called 'logic', which are designed as an integral part of the system with changeable additives called 'key'. To decipher an intercepted message, an adversary must know both the logic and the key of the

cryptosystem used to encipher it. Since it is effectively impossible to ensure that the logic of a cryptosystem will not be compromised during the years it remains in effect, the security of our machine cryptosystems depends on ensuring the integrity of the associated key and the personnel who care for the system. 'Key' literally will unlock the secrets contained in encrypted communications. The ultimate vulnerability of cryptosystems and all procedures designed to protect sensitive information lies at the human level. For this reason, personnel chosen for communications-related duties are carefully screened and indoctrinated in the especially sensitive nature of the positions they hold and the fiduciary-like nature of the trust placed in them. No system ever designed can be invulnerable to the corrupt, cleared individual who has access to sensitive information. Thus, we depend on an individual's integrity and deterrence of the law to ensure that this trust is fulfilled.

4. The importance of key was amply demonstrated by the evidence in this trial. The Soviets were clearly willing to pay a high price for key – more than $300,000 for the defendant alone. But the price paid by the Soviets pales in comparison to its worth. Naval intelligence analysis has led us to conclude that the Walker-Whitworth espionage activity was of the highest value to the intelligence services of the Soviet Union, with the potential, had conflict erupted between the two superpowers, to have powerful war-winning implications for the Soviet side.

5. The importance of the individual spy cannot be overestimated in this type of intelligence acquisition. When an adversary covertly obtains the protective key supplemented by large volumes of actual messages, he can potentially read any or all intercepted messages which that key protects. In the case of Navy operational command circuits, this can be literally hundreds of messages per key setting, many of which are vital to the national security of the United States. Normally, the information contained in those encrypted messages could be expected to include, at a minimum, further plans, ship locations and transit routes, military operations, intelligence activities and information, weapons and sensor data, naval tactics, terrorist threats, surface, subsurface and airborne doctrine and tactics, and similar information which could prove of incalculable value to hostile powers. Undetected theft of cryptographic key by persons intent on penetrating COMSEC safeguards can have extremely dire consequences to

148

the defense posture of the nation. History is replete with examples of the benefits and risks associated with COMSEC made vulnerable by espionage or otherwise penetrated for the benefit of one side or another. Such vulnerabilities sustained over time have altered the course of history and can do so again in the future.

6. With respect to this specific case, the sheer volume of encrypted data compromised to the Soviet Union makes it impossible to describe all of that data with specificity. The Court has already heard a few of the specifics during trial; therefore, in paragraphs 7–9, I will simply describe generically the types of information which have likely been traded to the Soviet Union through the years of this espionage enterprise. I will briefly mention some of the more significant aspects of the defendant's activities. I will also provide to the Court certain conclusions I have drawn concerning these compromises. My conclusions are based on my twenty-four years' experience as a naval officer, as both a user and producer of intelligence information, and on my current responsibilities as Director of Naval Intelligence and the Senior Intelligence Officer for the Department of the Navy.

7. Ship location and transit information. This is perhaps the most common type of information transmitted over naval communications circuits. On any given day the transit passages and locations of numerous naval vessels, both US and allied, will be transmitted in encrypted radio traffic. Normally, this type of data is held confidential until the information is no longer valid. The reasons why ship locater information is temporarily classified are three-fold. First, simple prudence dictates that the location of ships of the line be held confidential while that sort of information can enhance their vulnerability. This is especially true during periods of hostility. For example, during the Vietnam era, compromises of this type of information could have been responsible for ineffective air strikes, downed aircraft, abandoned targets and infantry losses. It is also particularly true today when US and allied vessels pose a lucrative target for terrorist attack. Secondly, the location and transit routes of naval vessels can be valuable information leading to disclosure, either directly or by informed analysis of naval doctrine and tactics. This, in itself, could prove to be decisive to the outcome of an engagement at sea. Finally, the rationale that persuades the United States to maintain the confidentiality of ship movements is universally shared by allied nations. Disclosures of

transit movements of our allied navies would be as potentially harmful to them as to our own ships; therefore, inappropriate disclosures of such information resulting from breaches of US security could reasonably be expected to have some adverse impact on both foreign relations and on international military cooperation.

8. US Naval operations information. The volume of communications traffic concerning naval plans and operations is large. As with the previous section, analysis of naval plans and operations information can lead, either directly or by informed analysis, to disclosure of naval exercises, contingency activities, and future combat operations which can be exploited to the advantage of a hostile power. In addition, communications will invariably reveal classified technical information, intelligence data, intelligence surveillance activities or information critical and potentially harmful to the foreign policy of the United States. It would directly reveal substantive information used by the United States in making decisions concerning the security of the nation and its foreign policy. If a hostile power were to obtain that information, it would be possible to turn this newly acquired information to the disadvantage of the United States, either by adopting measures to counter the advantage otherwise available to the United States, or by inserting misleading data into the collection process. An indirect benefit of obtaining this information would be the ability to analyze it for intelligence value, and to inferentially extrapolate the location and concentration of resources dedicated by the United States to obtaining similar information worldwide. Thus, disclosures of specific data can lead to harmful results, both for the specific collection activity involved, and also for similar activities conducted worldwide by US forces and other agencies of the government.

9. Special category (SPECAT) information. Frequently it is necessary to transmit information which is of such a degree of sensitivity that its disclosure must be limited to only those individuals with an absolute need to acquire the data. One method of restricting access to especially sensitive information is to permit its dissemination only within special, restricted channels of communication called Special Category (SPECAT) channels. The defendant was on several occasions in a position to have access to SPECAT communications and had the ability to transfer the information to the Soviet Union. Some examples of operations that are planned and executed through SPECAT channels are:

150

a. Covert Military Operations: Disclosure of communications concerning covert operations jeopardizes the United States' ability to conduct missions vital to national defense and world peace. The risks involve not only extreme embarrassment to our government, but also danger to the lives of the personnel involved.

b. Counter-intelligence Operations: Only through the aggressive pursuit of counter-intelligence initiatives such as double-agent operations, surveillance, and eavesdropping can the United States protect itself from the threat of espionage conducted against our defense establishment. Disclosure of SPECAT communications concerning such operations allows hostile intelligence services to develop counter-measures and techniques to render these operations ineffective.

c. Human Intelligence (HUMINT) Operations: HUMINT is unquestionably the most fragile of intelligence sources, due to the difficulties in recruiting human agents, the ease with which they are lost, the personal danger often involved and because the quality of information is entirely dependent on the abilities of the individual recruited. Disclosure of any information relating to HUMINT operations, even the intelligence reports derived from HUMINT, can lead to loss of the source, personal harm to the agent and the insertion of false and misleading information through the agent once the target organization becomes aware.

10. Based upon an analysis of Whitworth's access to classified information during his participation in the espionage scheme, on the trial testimony, and on debriefings conducted by the Office of Naval Intelligence, we wish to point out certain areas of concern:

a. Mr Whitworth met with John Walker two to four times per year between 1976 and 1985, and supplied Walker with between twenty-five and fifty rolls of Minox film at each meeting. Since the rolls were undeveloped, Walker cannot assure us of their content, but he believes that it was largely photographed key material. The amount of money paid by the Soviets corroborates that belief. Whitworth was originally paid $2,000 per month for the material he supplied, however, this was subsequently increased to $4,000 and then $6,000 per month later in the conspiracy.

b. We also know that Whitworth compromised detailed plans for primary, secondary, and emergency communications circuits which are used by the National Command Authority to maintain contact

151

with operational units. With this knowledge, an adversary can gain significant advantage during crisis events or hostilities.

c. Whitworth also compromised operational military plans, operations orders, and operational message traffic over a significant period of time. For example, he provided the Soviets with a full year of operational message traffic from USS *Enterprise*, including TOP SECRET information. He also compromised the operations order for Fleet Exercise 83-1, a unique exercise conducted near the Soviet coast by three carrier battle groups. We believe that he also compromised the communications plan for all US naval forces in the Indian Ocean and all littoral nations.

11. Most importantly, the activities of Jerry Whitworth, continuing as the principal agent of collection for John Walker, permitted the Soviets to gauge the true capabilities and vulnerabilities of the US Navy. The US Navy is a technology-intensive service, conducting sophisticated and often sensitive operations using highly advanced warfare capabilities. Soviet access to those operations and capabilities provided them with the motivation to dramatically improve the Soviet military posture, and identified the specific steps which could achieve the largest gains relative to the US. It allowed them the focussed insights required to reduce their own vulnerabilities while simultaneously increasing the vulnerability of the US. We have seen clear signals of dramatic Soviet gains in all naval warfare areas, which must now be interpreted in light of the Walker-Whitworth espionage conspiracy conducted over approximately two decades. Mr Whitworth's role was all the more important because of the new directions taken by the US Navy during his years of collection for the Soviets. For example, through Whitworth the Soviets were able to monitor the US Navy's transition to use of satellite systems as its principal communication network.

12. In conclusion, the US Navy and the nation have been seriously wounded by Jerry Whitworth's breach of faith and honor wherein he agreed to sell the secrets with which he was entrusted to a foreign power for personal gain. His misuse of a position of trust in naval communications has jeopardized the backbone of this country's national defense. Recovery from the Walker-Whitworth espionage will take years and millions of taxpayer dollars. Even given these expenditures, we will likely never know the true extent to which our

capabilities have been impaired by the traitorous and infamous acts of Jerry Whitworth.

When he read Admiral Studeman's evidence, Secretary of Defense Caspar Weinberger wanted to petition the judge to set aside the plea agreement made with the prosecution, on the grounds that the negotiated sentences were too lenient, but was eventually dissuaded.

In retrospect, several senior US Naval officers recalled that they had been surprised by the ubiquity demonstrated by the Red Banner Fleet, which in the early 1980s, at the period evinced by Studeman, had showed up in the most surprising of locations. Intelligence-gathering ships would be deployed routinely to monitor the departures of ballistic missile 'boomers' when they commenced a patrol, and other vessels would materialize down-range during missile flight-tests to salvage debris. Similarly, Soviet warships often manifested surprising degrees of aggression, almost as if their commanders had been briefed on the limits set by the current naval rules-of-engagement. Some damage, such as the loss of IVY BELLS technical surveillance on Soviet underwater cables on behalf of the National Security Agency, would later be attributed to an NSA analyst, Ronald Pelton, based on information from the defector Vitali Yurchenko, but at the time too many operations seemed to be going wrong.

Chapter 11

Clyde Conrad

Even if the superpowers had only engaged in a
conventional war in Europe the Soviets would have had a
distinct advantage – a spy in the US Army, Sergeant
Clyde Conrad, had given their Hungarian ally NATO's
complete defense plan for the continent.

[Michael J. Sulick, CIA Deputy Director for Operations, *Spies in America*[1]]

Another spy-ring broken up in 1985, which had also been active since 1967, almost complemented the Walker network by compromising strategically important secrets relevant not to the US Navy but to NATO battle plans for Europe.

The organization, headed by a US Army retiree, Sergeant Clyde L. Conrad, was terminated with his arrest in August 1988 at his home in West Germany. Prior to his retirement in 1985, Conrad had served at the Bad Kreuznach headquarters of the US Eighth Infantry Division, where he had enjoyed access to highly classified military information concerning NATO troop deployments, which he had sold to a Hungarian intelligence officer, Zoltan Szabo, for more than $1.2 million. He recruited some of his subordinates, who also supplied secret documents, and then participated in the illicit procurement of embargoed computer components by exporting them through a dummy company in Canada. The damage assessment completed after Conrad's arrest concluded that he had compromised NATO's entire order-of-battle and plans to defend Western Europe from a Soviet attack.[2]

At the time of the compromise, the Soviet plan to overrun Western Europe had been drafted by Marshal Nikolai Ogarkov, who was appointed chief of the Soviet general staff in 1977. Ogarkov was a highly influential figure who redrew Soviet military strategy and developed a secret plan for a surprise invasion of Western Europe. His principal assistant in reforming the Kremlin's doctrine was General Andrian Danilevich, who drafted a three-volume study innocuously titled *Strategy of Deep Operations (Global and Theatre)*.

The central theme of the document was the launch of a sudden offensive under cover of a supposedly routine Warsaw Pact exercise, but in reality it would involve two million well-equipped troops, supported by 2,000 ground-attack aircraft that in one operation would destroy all NATO's nuclear weapons in Europe and all its airfields. The key objective was to strike decisively within 48 hours so as to prevent NATO's political leadership from retaliating with nuclear weapons. All NATO's planning had relied on air power to stymie Soviet tanks rolling across the plains of north Germany, but Ogarkov called for three massive thrusts, 450 miles wide, reaching into 750 miles of NATO territory. *Spetsnaz* Special Forces would be helicoptered behind the front lines to seize vital bridges, and massive firepower would be concentrated against NATO anti-tank weapon positions. The plan predicted reaching the English Channel in twenty days, without any use of nuclear warheads by either side. The emphasis on surprise and speed was a dramatic departure from the original, established Warsaw Pact scheme to deploy slow Soviet armour to surround NATO strongpoints. These innovative tactics were welcomed by Poland's General Wojciech Jaruzelski, who had been dismayed by the results of an exercise in 1980 which had left Poland devastated by a supposed NATO nuclear strike. A further exercise the following year, ZAPAD-81, appeared to suggest that the Ogarkov approach could be executed successfully.

Marshal Ogarkov's new, ruthlessly aggressive doctrine, which depended on accurate intelligence on all western nuclear installations, was delivered to the US Central Intelligence Agency first by TOPHAT, the GRU General Dmitri Polyakov, and then by the CIA's key asset in Warsaw, Colonel Ryszard Kuklinski, and it shocked the analysts who examined it. Whereas Polyakov had been in touch with the CIA since 1962, Kuklinski had volunteered to spy a decade later, in 1972. Both men had enjoyed access to the most closely held Warsaw Pact deliberations.[3]

The material examined in Washington DC was verified by independent satellite imagery which identified the new secret command bunkers under construction in the Moscow area. The plan amounted to political dynamite, but could not be made public for fear of compromising the CIA's sources. As well as demonstrating the plan's viability, it also suggested the most detailed knowledge of NATO's own contingency plans. How had these fallen into Soviet hands?

The answer was supplied in 1983 by a GRU officer based in Budapest, Lieutenant Colonel Vladimir M. Vasiliev, who became an agent code-named GT/ACCORD for the local CIA station. Very little has been disclosed publicly concerning Vasiliev, who would himself be betrayed in May 1985 by Aldrich Ames, ordered back to Moscow and executed in December the following year. However, Jim Olsen, the former CIA station chief in Vienna, recalls that:

> The CIA received a startling report from one of its well-placed sources behind the iron curtain: a Soviet GRU colonel working with Hungarian military intelligence in Budapest. According to this source the Hungarians were receiving huge quantities of classified documents from the US Army in Germany, including top secret war plans. The documents, he added, were being immediately shipped to Moscow. One document alone was considered so valuable that the unknown agent was paid $50,000 for it in 1978.[4]

After Vasiliev's initial tip the CIA reportedly received additional information when in 1984 an MNVK/2 officer, Colonel Istvan Belovai, used the spy-ring as his 'meal-ticket' to resettlement. Born in 1938, Belovai had been transferred to the service a year after joining the army in 1958. In 1978, promoted to the rank of major, he had been assigned to SNOW-DROP, the analytical unit set up to process material from the US Seventh Army in Germany.

In Belovai's version of events, he realized the secret advantage gained by the Warsaw Pact and feared the Kremlin would exploit the situation. 'I decided to prevent the potential Soviet aggression.'[5] Accordingly, after he was posted to London in 1982 as assistant military and air attaché, Belovai made contact with the CIA in 1984, just before his return to Budapest. Once back in Hungary he maintained contact with the CIA using the codename SKORPION-B but was arrested in July 1985, as he approached a pre-arranged dead-drop, most likely as a consequence of being compromised by Aldrich Ames, and was sentenced to life imprisonment.

Belovai was convicted of espionage and incarcerated, but was paroled by the new, democratically elected post-Communist government in September 1990. Upon his release he moved with his wife and son to the United States, where he proclaimed that he 'was never a traitor. I was Hungary's first NATO soldier.' His declared motivation was his certainty that the Warsaw Pact was preparing for war, his mistrust of Soviet military doctrine and a fear that Moscow's war plans would cause the annihilation of the Hungarian army.

> The Russian military doctrine had offensive character, it was proved, by the locations and concentrations of the armed forces in the territory of Russia and in the territories of the countries occupied by the Red Army in Europe. The strategic build-up of the Warsaw Pact was good only to attack. The Warsaw Pact, on the second day of the war, would have deployed the operational/tactical nuclear missiles (Frog-7, Scud-B, SS-20, 21, 22) against NATO forces. NATO from the beginning had a defensive character, and it never prepared for offensive operations. This was proven by the locations, concentrations of the forces, and the operation plans of NATO.
>
> Both the Russian and the Warsaw Pact's military doctrine emphasized that the Third World War would be carried out by the mass deployment of the nuclear weapons, and the war would be won by that coalition which launched the first nuclear strike. The Russian political and military leadership was determined that on the first or second day of the war they would deploy the strategic and operational/tactical nuclear missiles. The Soviets believed the nuclear war could be won by the Soviet Union. This was a dangerous policy.[6]

According to Vasiliev, who had a liaison role with the Hungarian military intelligence service, the MNVK/2, NATO had suffered a significant penetration over a long period as a consequence of a calculated MNVK/2 strategy which exploited émigrés with vulnerable families still living in eastern Europe. One such individual was a retired US Army officer and Vietnam veteran, Captain Zoltan Szabo, who was found to have recruited a subordinate, Sergeant Clyde L. Conrad, who would be paid an estimated $1 million for selling some 30,000 documents from his division's classified vault.

Szabo, allegedly holding the rank of colonel in Hungary, had emigrated to the United States with his parents in 1957 and had joined the US Army in 1959. He had spied since 1971 and had recruited Conrad in 1975. Originally from Sebring, Ohio, Conrad in turn in 1978 had recruited another US Army NCO, Sergeant Roderick J. Ramsay, who had obtained a security clearance in 1978 when attached to the 8th Infantry Division headquarters in Bad Kreuznach, West Germany. Ramsay had access to a vault of classified material, including NATO war plans, which he sold to his Hungarian contacts. Ramsay also recruited another NCO, 30-year-old Sergeant Jeffrey S. Rondeau, who photocopied hundreds of documents at Ramsay's direction, which another spy, Sergeant Jeffrey E. Gregory, had stuffed into a military flight bag for delivery to the Hungarians.

Yet another member of the network was Kelly Therese Warren, who also served in the 8th Infantry Division between 1986 and 1988 as a G-3 administrative clerk responsible for the custody and distribution of classified papers. Aged 31, she was arrested in Warner-Robbins, Georgia, in June 1997 and was sentenced in February 1999 to 25 years' imprisonment, She was released from a federal penitentiary in 2011.

The network also included two couriers, Sandor and Imre Kercsik, Hungarian-born brothers, and both physicians, who were detained and imprisoned in Goteborg, Sweden. Szabo was arrested in Austria and gave evidence against Conrad, who received a life sentence in Germany and died of heart failure in Diez prison in January 1998. Szabo also named Sergeant Tommaso Mortati, a 42-year-old former US Army paratrooper, who was arrested at his home in Vicenza in August 1988 and later sentenced to life imprisonment. Szabo himself was convicted of espionage but freed in return for his testimony against Conrad. Ramsay was sentenced in August 1992 to 36 years' imprisonment and was released in February 2013. In June 1994 his recruits Rondeau and Gregory were each sentenced to 18 years' imprisonment. Rondeau was released in January 2002 and Gregory in May 2007.

The sheer scale of Conrad's spy-ring was breathtaking, and the military authorities were conscious that without Vasiliev they most likely would not have detected his espionage. As for Colonel Belovai, he was granted US citizenship in 1992 and was vocal in his public statements about the Warsaw Pact's plans to implement Marshal Ogarkov's masterplan for invasion which involved the Hungarian army entering Italy through Austria. He also claimed to have seen documents suggesting the existence of atomic minefields in Germany, controlled by the US V Corps, and plans for an Allied counter-attack codenamed LIONHEART. He also asserted that 'If the Soviets would reach the Rhine River, the US would deploy nuclear weapons. Because what else could they do?' Frustrated that he had not received the recognition he felt he deserved as the 'spy who saved the world', Belovai died in Denver, Colorado, in November 2009, leaving behind an unpublished memoir, *Strike to the Red Empire*.

Chapter 12

Vladimir Kuzichkin

REDWOOD was the greatest KGB defector nobody has
ever heard of.

[Brian Kelley, *Falsely Accused*[1]]

Codenamed REDWOOD by the British Secret Intelligence Service,
35-year-old Vladimir Kuzichkin had a profound impact on the geopolitics
of the Middle East and was single-handedly responsible for scuppering the
Kremlin's plans to organize a Communist coup in Iran, and then have
the new government invite the Soviets to administer the country and its
economy. The conspiracy was to be managed by the KGB and would
result in accomplishing two long-term Soviet goals: possession of Iran's
vast oil assets, and the age-old ambition of access to a warm water port.
The person responsible for coordinating the coup was the KGB *rezident*
in Tehran, General Leonid Shebarshin.

Born in March 1935, Shebarshin studied at the Moscow Institute of
Oriental Studies and in 1962 was recruited by the First Chief Directorate
(FCD). His first overseas posting was to the *rezidentura* in Pakistan, where
he remained for six years.

After a further three years at headquarters, Shebarshin was appointed
deputy *rezident* in New Delhi, and was promoted *rezident* in 1975. He
returned to Moscow in April 1977 and the following year was posted to
Tehran, where he had a front-row seat as the Islamic revolution swept
across the country and replaced the Shah with a hardline theocratic state.

The man chosen by Shebarshin to supervise the Kremlin's coup was a
very unusual FCD officer, who had been a drummer in a Moscow rock-
band.[2] He moved in dissident circles, counted radical poets among his
friends and never joined the Communist Party. He was distinctive in every
way, including his appearance; he was six foot five inches tall, and towered
over others at an embassy cocktail party, or in the street. Indeed, as a
potential agent recruiter and handler anywhere outside Europe, he would

161

be likely to attract attention, and an easy target to keep under surveillance. Undercover operators may be able to change their clothes and alter their appearance with the addition of a hat or spectacles, but there was no remedy for Kuzichkin's very unusual, and therefore memorable, height. Equally unusually, Kuzichkin had been a career Directorate S officer, and not a 'Varangian', the Directorate's term for a KGB officer brought in from the First Chief Directorate.

Kuzichkin had spent five years at Moscow University studying Iran, a period which had included two lengthy visits as a Farsi interpreter, first in the iron ore centre of Bafq, and then in Tehran. After graduating, he had attended an initial interview with Nikolai A. Korznikov of the KGB, whom Kuzichkin later learned was one of Directorate S's four deputy chiefs, and he had undergone the usual two years of training, with a heavy emphasis on languages, at the FCD's Red Banner Institute near Yurlovo, to the northwest of Moscow, where he had been indoctrinated into the secrets of Directorate S by Colonel Pavel K. Revizorov, a retired officer who had once headed the Directorate's First Department, having apparently worked in the field in Canada and the United States. Kuzichkin's English had been perfected by Elena I. Akhmerova, who had taught the ill-fated Yuri Loginov[3], and he had completed his course at the FCD facility on Festival Street, close to the Moscow River metro station. Having been assigned to Directorate S, which occupied the sixth and seventh floors of the KGB headquarters in Dzerzhinsky Square, Kuzichkin had joined the Seventh Department, responsible for Line N operations in Arabia and the Indian subcontinent, headed by Valentin M. Piskunov. After only a short period in the Seventh Department, Kuzichkin had been reassigned to the Eastern subsection of the Second Department, headed by Colonel Ismail M. Aliev, in preparation for his first overseas assignment, to Iran in June 1977. Following six months of intensive briefing, conducted in part by the Eighth Department of the FCD at Yasnevo, headed by General Mikhail Polonik, and the head of the Iranian desk, Colonel Anatoli M. Lezhnin, he was sent to Tehran under visa officer cover to relieve one of the Directorate S representatives, Sasha Yashchenko, who had completed a four-year tour at the embassy *rezidentura*. The other N Line officer in Tehran was Colonel Sergei P. Kharlshkin, who had operated under cover of an administrator at the Soviet Red Cross hospital, but was fluent in Dutch, not Farsi. Upon his arrival, Kuzichkin had learned from Yashchenko that he only ran four local illegals, one of whom was about to be cut loose. Codenamed TIMUR, he had only been recruited because his brother had seemed a useful target, and now he was judged to be an expensive and unproductive liability. Yashchenko also told him that of the fifty Soviet diplomats at the embassy, fifteen were KGB personnel and ten were GRU.

The temporary *rezident* in Tehran, who had presided over the *referentura* on the fourth floor of the embassy, was Colonel Lev P. Kostromin, who had recently arrived from his post as deputy head of the FCD's Eighth Department. He had taken over from Leonid Bogdanov earlier in 1977 following a series of operational setbacks which had been the cause of some dismay in Moscow. In May a local agent in the Ministry of Education named Rabbani had been arrested by SAVAK, causing the expulsion of Evgeni Venednikov, a Line PR officer. In a second incident soon afterwards another Line PR officer, actually the TASS correspondent Boris Checherin, had been compromised and declared *persona non grata*. Kostromin's appointment had been intended to strengthen the *rezidentura*, which had a disproportionate number of new arrivals, including replacements for the heads of the PR and KR Lines. Kostromin's deputy *rezident* was Gennadi Kazankin, a former Directorate S illegal candidate who had been obliged to join the FCD's Eighth Department because of ill health and was head of Line PR in Tehran.

Kuzichkin's approach to the British was equally unorthodox. One morning he simply showed up at the British Interests Section of the Swedish embassy (actually the British embassy during the suspension of diplomatic relations) and asked to speak to Nicholas Barrington, who held the rank of 'Head of Section', which in reality was the role of the acting ambassador. Kuzichkin's selection of Barrington to discuss defection was, it turned out, based on a briefing he had received from Shebarshin, who had identified Barrington, who was unmarried and had a reputation in the diplomatic community of being quite flamboyant, as his counterpart, the local SIS station commander. In fact, not only was Barrington a regular Foreign Office diplomat, but his career path had been obviously conventional, including a period as private secretary to the Permanent Under-Secretary, Paul Gore-Booth, and then to the Foreign Secretary, Michael Stewart. Either Shebarshin had been misinformed, or the KGB's research had been particularly poor, but Barrington, like so many of his Foreign Office colleagues, was quite ambivalent about, if not downright hostile to, SIS, taking the view that the organization had an unlimited capacity for causing trouble and embarrassment to the Diplomatic Service. Appalled that he had been mistaken for a spy, Barrington promptly introduced Kuzichkin to Ian McCredie, and beat a hasty retreat.

McCredie was a young, ambitious SIS officer who had joined just seven years earlier, and had already undertaken one overseas posting, to Lusaka, where he had spent three years. After a short stay at Century House he had been sent to Tehran in April the previous year, when the country was still in turmoil, and his station was considered something of a dangerous front-line position, even if the American embassy hostages had been released. McCredie's predecessors had been tolerated in Tehran by the Shah's regime on the understanding that they should not have any contact with the political opposition of the ayatollahs, and this prohibition had been respected. All had been declared, so McCredie was the first SIS officer for several years to be supposedly unknown to the SAVAK's successor organization, the Ministry of Intelligence (MIS).

The appearance of a 'walk-in' is not always met with unalloyed joy as in many environments the event may be part of an elaborate 'dangle' intended to identify and maybe compromise a target intelligence professional. As it was, SIS was initially sceptical of Kuzichkin, even if he had correctly answered McCredie's initial questions about the structure of the KGB *rezidentura*. Such validation questionnaires were routine, but the unheralded manifestation of potential defectors was not. Accordingly, McCredie's task was to confirm the candidate's *bona-fides*, determine precisely what information was on offer, arrange for a future means of communication, and establish a proposed timescale, if not a motive.

London's reaction to McCredie's news was, predictably, very sceptical. At that time SIS had successfully resettled one KGB officer, Oleg Lyalin, who had defected in London in August 1971, in a joint operation with MI5. Six years later, in June 1978, political asylum was granted to two GRU officers, Vladimir Rezun, and his wife, who had deserted their posts in Geneva. For SIS, which received no Soviet intelligence defectors between 1946 (Grigori Tokaev[4]) and 1971 (Lyalin[5]), apart from Yuri Tasoev[6] in May 1948 who changed his mind after he arrived in London and demanded to be repatriated, defectors are a valued commodity and their scarcity made the prize all the greater, especially when it is understood that two other potential defectors, Vladimir Skripkin[7] and Yuri Rastvorov[8], opened negotiations to defect before they experienced cold feet and withdrew. For no apparent reason, SIS was almost awash with walk-ins. It was currently handling one important KGB penetration, Oleg Gordievsky, who had been recruited (amid great scepticism in London) and had just arrived at his new posting to the London *rezidentura*, where he was expected to be SIS's star asset, and here was another KGB FCD insider volunteering to trust an agency that, years earlier, had suffered hostile penetration at the hands of Kim Philby and then George Blake. Had SIS recovered its reputation and was now considered trustworthy, or was there another, more sinister, explanation? Could it be that the KGB, having detected evidence of penetration within its own ranks, was seeking to insert a trusted agent into SIS so as to run a counter-intelligence game and maybe turn up an indication that it was harbouring a traitor? Apart from suborning someone who already had the necessary access, which would be a near to impossible challenge, the solution was to 'coat-trail' in the hope the adversary would accept a double agent, and then plan to gain an advantage by analysis of his (or her) taskings. This amounted to day one at the Counter-Intelligence 201 course, but was nonetheless effective. SIS's director of counter-intelligence and security smelled a rat, and cautioned McCredie to treat Kuzichkin accordingly. On the other hand, McCredie was very conscious of two dangers: firstly, that he had revealed himself to Kuzichkin, which would be information of value to his *rezidentura* colleagues who, having identified him as an authentic SIS officer, might target him one way or another. Secondly, life in Tehran was dangerous enough without having to deal with MIS street surveillance which could be expected the moment the KGB felt it was in Moscow's interests to compromise him. Accordingly, when McCredie attended his first rendezvous with Kuzichkin, it was a street pick-up staged at a moment when he and his Soviet friend's ostentatious BMW were briefly out of eye-contact with the inevitable surveillance. Subsequent car meetings were held in McCredie's vehicle which was equipped with special apparatus to monitor the radio traffic generated by the MIS mobile teams. MIS agents were interested in Kuzichkin, and tried to follow him whenever he left the Soviet compound, on foot or in a car. According to a pair of MIS defectors who were debriefed by a western agency in a third country, Kuzichkin was easy to shadow but when on one occasion he simply disappeared after turning a corner, every house in the street was later ransacked to find out where he had gone. In fact, this was a classic vehicle pick-up, executed in textbook style by McCredie, who had no need to tutor the KGB officer in tradecraft. Even though the car with British diplomatic plates had been logged in the area, the connection was not made by the MIS controllers.

The issue of Kuzichkin's authenticity would linger for some time, and at least until Gordievsky was asked to substantiate some of his product. Coincidentally, both men had started their KGB careers in Directorate S, but care was taken to ensure that Gordievsky could not guess the source of the information he was asked to verify. When consulted, Gordievsky was positive.

Eventually there would be a dozen of these clandestine encounters, some in cars, other in 'brush-passes', in which Kuzichkin described his abusive wife who taunted him constantly for his lack of libido. This led to the disclosure of his primary demand, which was not resettlement but treatment for erectile dysfunction. This requirement was promptly fulfilled with help from the Royal Air Force, where the medical staff were very familiar with the stress endured by fighter pilots.

Kuzichkin's motives for negotiating his defection were probably more than being trapped in an unhappy marriage, but precisely what drove him to abandon the KGB was never entirely clear. However, his determination to defect was undiminished, and the pressure increased when he refused to risk a long-term partnership, to be maintained in Moscow. Both men would have known that attempting to run agents in Moscow was an extraordinarily ambitious proposition, considering the ubiquitous hostile surveillance and the long, sorry record of ambushes mounted at compromised dead-drop sites, dating back to the arrest of Oleg Penkovsky in October 1962. Quite rightly, Kuzichkin declined the invitation to 'work his passage' by returning to Moscow and continuing to engage in espionage, but he countered with a curious story that was obviously intended to apply pressure on Century House. His narrative was that Shebarshin had decreed that, as a precaution against an occupation of the embassy premises, and therefore the *referentura*, all KGB files were to be copied onto photographic film, and the exposed but undeveloped film placed in canisters which would then be secured in various hiding-places inside the building. According to Kuzichkin, some of his duplicated documents, concealed behind a skirting-board, had gone missing, and this loss would be detected by an audit inspection scheduled soon. He insisted that when the negligence was discovered it would be bound to result in his recall to Moscow and disciplinary action. Although this tale was not entirely believed at headquarters, it was clear that Kuzichkin was anxious to leave Tehran quickly, and he was not going to contemplate putting his life in jeopardy to help out SIS.

Having accepted Kuzichkin's demand to be resettled, SIS had to develop an exfiltration plan which involved him crossing the Turkish border carrying a forged British diplomatic passport. This unorthodox expedient required the approval of the Foreign Secretary, Peter Carrington, who was indoctrinated into the full story by the SIS Chief, Colin Figures. However, by the time all the preparations had been made, Carrington had resigned over the invasion of the Falkland Islands, and had been replaced by Francis Pym, who reluctantly sanctioned the proposed operation but forbade McCredie from accompanying Kuzichkin across the border. Indeed, he was banned from even leaving the capital on the selected day. In the event, Kuzichkin was handed the forged passport and drove to the border at Kipokoy in his own car, which he abandoned on the Iranian side, and then took a bus through the frontier. Although an improbable British diplomat, especially when at one moment he pretended to an Iranian official that he did not understand English, Kuzichkin's forged passport, which included some stamps hastily fabricated at the Tehran station, went unchallenged.

Once through the Turkish customs post Kuzichkin was welcomed by SIS's John Scarlett, who had flown into the country for the operation, and together they drove to Ankara.[9] Later Kuzichkin would recall how his chauffeur had not been able to replace the wheel when a tyre suffered a puncture.

Delivered safely to London, Kuzichkin underwent a lengthy debriefing in which he identified several Directorate S illegals deployed in Canada and Switzerland, who were promptly arrested before the KGB could extract them. This type of information is the hard currency of the international intelligence community and the basis of strong liaison relationships. REDWOOD also participated in a 'dog and pony show' tour of Allied intelligence organizations to impart his knowledge on the topic of KGB Line N illegals, even then regarded as a subject of wonder and fascination. To be able to make REDWOOD available for questions so soon after Lyalin had undertaken similar tours to reveal the secrets of the FCD's legendary Department V, once known as the Thirteenth Department, served to re-establish SIS's tarnished reputation. Added to these contributions was the reporting from the London *rezidentura* which would remain undetected by the KGB for a further three years.

By far the most compelling part of Kuzichkin's testimony was his account of the Politburo's approval of the plan to support a *coup d'état* mounted by the Tudeh Party. Founded in September 1941, the Tudeh

Party had existed at a time when the Soviets occupied the north of the country, and was part of Moscow's strategy to retain control over the country's northern oilfields, and encourage the separation of a supposedly independent Azerbaijan.

In August 1941, three months after the Soviet Union was invaded by the Nazis, the Allies occupied neutral Iran in just five days. At that time the Soviets agreed to withdraw 'not more than six months' after the cessation of hostilities, but then showed a reluctance to do so when the Germans surrendered. Under considerable pressure, the Soviets finally departed in May 1946, but they left behind the Tudeh Party and its underground military organization, the TPMO, which had penetrated the local security and intelligence apparatus. There was also an influential Party newspaper, *Rahbat*, and a growing membership that espoused pro-Kremlin policies, but an attempt on the life of the Shah in February 1949 led to a government ban and the arrest of the Party's leadership. Eighteen months later the TPMO arranged for some of the Central Council to escape from prison, and they later backed the nationalist Mohammed Mossadeq, who was appointed prime minister in July 1952 and proceeded to confiscate assets of the Anglo-Iranian Oil Company. A coup d'etat followed in August 1953 which removed Mossadeq from power and forced the Tudeh Party cadres to go underground to avoid arrest. Much of the party membership was detained and the TPMO's charismatic leader, Captain Khosro Roozbeh, was executed in May 1958.

As opposition grew to the Shah's western-sponsored regime in the 1970s, the Tudeh Party tried to take advantage of the unrest, but played little part in the Islamic revolution of 1979, although it benefited from the general release of political prisoners, among whom were a large number of Tudeh detainees. Reinvigorated, the Tudeh became a major political force and, following Moscow's guidance, initially supported the clerics, but in 1981 plotted a coup which would eliminate the mullahs and establish a Kremlin-controlled administration.

According to Kuzichkin, planning of the coup, to be mounted by the Tudeh leadership, was well advanced, and he was able to identify the entire group of conspirators, together with details of their KGB-financed hideouts and safe-houses. Documented in the REDWOOD dossier, SIS found a circuitous route through which to deliver the damning details to the Khomeini government and ensure it was taken seriously. The chosen intermediary was Pakistan's President Zia Al-Haq, whose Inter-Services Intelligence (ISI) directorate had maintained cordial relations with the ever-suspicious MIS. The REDWOOD material thus reached Tehran with ISI credibility, and triggered a furious response in which the Party was banned, and an estimated 1,000 Tudeh members were arrested and interrogated. Many were executed and Tudeh's secretary-general Nourredin Kianouri and newspaper editor Mahmoud Etemadzadeh were also detained, later in April to be presented on television to read confessions in which they admitted to having acted for the KGB.[10]

Among those detained was Admiral Bahram Afzzali, commander of Iran's navy, who would be executed in 1984. Furthermore, seventeen members of the embassy staff, including the GRU and KGB *rezidenturas*, were expelled in May 1983, accused of 'establishing contacts and taking advantage of treacherous and mercenary agents'. Also, the TASS news agency office was closed, and the consul at Esfahan, Barkhas Artynov, was declared *persona non grata*. The Tudeh Party was decimated and Shebarshin's plot collapsed.

The episode reflected immense credit on SIS, which used the REDWOOD material to greatly improve its liaison relationship with the ISI at a time when British personnel were being 'de-badged' and infiltrated over the border from Peshawar into Afghanistan. More importantly, the regional balance of power had been maintained, and the Kremlin had been prevented from expanding its sphere of influence into Iran.

Kuzichkin himself fared less well, and found it hard to adjust to life in England. Soon after his arrival his medical issues had been resolved by a prescription for entirely worthless placebo pills which, he was advised, had proved effective for RAF fighter pilots. Their efficacy would be proved when he went on holiday to a seaside villa in Morocco, where he met a French girl on the beach and spent the entire week in her bedroom, only emerging occasionally to share meals with his SIS personal protection team. Kuzichkin returned from his vacation fully restored but his morale was affected by an unhappy marriage to an alcoholic whom he eventually divorced. In 1991 he published his memoirs, *Inside the KGB: Myth and Reality*, but his account necessarily had been heavily circumscribed by his SIS sponsors. Bizarrely, the book's release prompted Mehmet Ali Agca, who had tried to assassinate Pope John Paul II in May 1981, to claim that Kuzichkin had been his KGB handler.

Gradually, Kuzichkin's stability declined and at one point, when he was found naked by a police patrol in a motorway service station on the M5, he was detained under the Mental Health Act and treated in a secure psychiatric wing at Melksham Hospital. He died soon afterwards in Weston-super-Mare, Somerset, his true identity still concealed by an alias.

The one person who might have been expected to be disadvantaged by Kuzichkin's defection was the *rezident*, Leonid Shebarshin, who later described the episode as 'the worst in my life'. Perhaps surprisingly, he was shielded by his mentor, Vladimir Kryuchkov, who appointed him his deputy chief of the FCD in April 1987. When Kryuchkov was promoted KGB Chairman, Shebarshin took over the FCD leadership. When, during the August 1991 attempted coup in Moscow, Kryuchkov was arrested, Shebarshin took over the KGB for just two days, and then resigned on 20 September. In March 2012, alone in his Moscow apartment, in failing health after a major stroke, he shot himself.

Chapter 13

Ashraf Marwan

The probability that Egypt will try to cross the canal is
close to zero.

[Israeli military intelligence assessment, 1972]

Ashraf Marwan's name became a matter of controversy in June 2007 when, by some clerical error, it was mentioned thirty-six times in an Israeli court judgment that was placed accidentally on the internet before it had been redacted. The document was to be the final round in a bizarre, long-standing dispute between two senior intelligence officers, the former Mossad director Zvi Zamir and the retired director of military intelligence General Eliyahu Zeira, over the background to the Yom Kippur War of October 1973, a conflict that cost the Israelis 2,800 dead, 8,800 wounded and 293 taken prisoner.

The litigation before Judge Theodore Or had arisen after Zeira appeared on a television show in 2004 and referred to Marwan by name, declaring that he had been a Mossad spy, and a double agent for Egypt in the months leading up to the conflict, when Marwan had been enrolled as a Mossad asset in London in 1969. The issue had arisen over a separate enquiry, the Agranat Commission, which had been empanelled to look into the obvious intelligence failures that had led to the conflict.

The attack by Israel's Arab neighbours took the Israeli Defence Force (IDF) entirely by surprise, and on 18 November a commission of enquiry, headed by the Supreme Court president Simon Agranat, was empanelled by the government to investigate the perceived intelligence failure. Accompanied by another judge, Moshe Landau, the State Comptroller Yitzhak Nebenzahl, and two former Chiefs of the General Staff, Yigael Yadin and Chaim Laskov, Agranat was required to look at what information had been available prior to the war, and what assessments had been made by the various different strands of the Israeli intelligence establishment, and he produced a 40-page interim report on 2 April 1974. This

171

controversial document placed much of the blame on General Zeira; his deputy, Brigadier Aryeh Shalev; Colonel David Gedaliah, the senior IDF Southern Command intelligence officer; and Colonel Yonah Bendman, head of the military intelligence directorate's Egyptian section. Also recommended for dismissal were the chief of the Southern Command, General Shmuel Gonen, and the Chief of the General Staff, General David Elazar.

Most significantly, the Agranat Commission found that there had been plenty of advance intelligence about preparations being made by Syria and Egypt prior to the conflict, but the IDF staff had misinterpreted the situation and concluded that any attack could be handled by the IDF's regular forces, without support from reserves. Crucially, the IDF analysts had made two further miscalculations: firstly, that Egypt would not engage in combat without a strong air force, and secondly that, as in the past, there would be clear advance notice of any major coordinated Arab offensive. This doctrine would become known as the '*konzeptziya*'', and would prove to be deeply flawed, but was partly supported by documents acquired by Mossad's top-level source in Cairo, who had obtained copies of the Egyptian order-of-battle and plans for a coordinated Arab attack codenamed BADR.

The IDF was also found to have been in a poor state of readiness to deal with any large-scale conflict, and Agranat criticized the IDF's monopoly of the intelligence assessment process, recommending that an independent body should evaluate intelligence from all sources. Accordingly, a separate research staff to handle 'political-strategic intelligence' was established in the Ministry of Foreign Affairs, while Mossad developed its own analytical branch.

The Commission also suggested that the prime minister's office should include an intelligence adviser, a proposal originally made in 1963 by the Yadin Sherf Commission when David Ben Gurion had asked for a review of the country's entire intelligence structure.

Although the document released by the Commission in April 1974 was intended to be an interim report, no fuller version was ever published, but it was believed that the Commission had been impressed by the work undertaken by the IDF's signals intelligence organization, Unit 8200, led by Colonel Yoel Ben-Port, which had reported that on 4 October the Soviets had warned their diplomatic missions in Damascus and Cairo to withdraw all but key personnel. Unit 8200, later renamed Unit 9200, was also known as the Central Warning Unit and had provided accurate assessments of the Syrian build-up on the Golan Heights.

Formerly the Israeli military attaché in London, Zamir had been appointed to head Mossad in 1966, and he remained director until his retirement in 1974. He was at the Furstenfeldbruch air base when German police failed to rescue nine Israeli athletes taken hostage at the Munich Olympics, and thereafter established a formidable reputation, having supervised the WRATH OF GOD retribution operation conducted against the Black September terrorist group. Although he had not been a Mossad professional before his promotion, he had been outraged by Zeira's deliberate indiscretion.

Singled out for criticism, Zeira had been infuriated, and had publicly cited the role of a spy near the top of the Egyptian government, who, he alleged, had been mishandled by Mossad. The existence of this elusive source codenamed BABEL (a detail only declassified in 2012) had been hinted at by Agranat, who had taken care to protect his identity, but Zeira named him in his television interview, prompting Zamir to protest at what he saw as a flagrant breach of security. Furthermore, Zamir issued defamation proceedings, and the dispute was assigned to a mediation court presided over by Theodore Or, who ruled in Zamir's favour. Within three weeks of the leak, Marwan was dead, his body found on the ground beneath the balcony of his £4.4 million fifth floor flat in Carlton House Terrace after midday on 27 June 2007.

Ostensibly, Marwan, a chemical engineering graduate from Cairo University, was a director of Redditch-based Ubichem Laboratories, a company engaged in the manufacture of pharmaceuticals, and was a wealthy man. He was born in 1944, the son of a senior Republican Guard officer, and the same year met the President's second daughter, Mona Nasser, then aged 17. They were married in July 1966 and Marwan was absorbed into the presidential administration, working with his father-in-law's aide-de-camp Sami Sharaf, who had strong links to the Mukhabarat. Two years later, in late 1968, Marwan took his wife and newborn son, Gamal, to London, where he was to continue his studies at King's College. However, after a few months, perhaps as a result of adverse reports from the embassy about his lifestyle, Marwan was recalled to Cairo to resume his duties at the Presidential Office, a post he would hold until 1976. When Nasser died unexpectedly in September 1970, Marwan was retained by his successor, Anwar Sadat, who employed him as a foreign policy adviser and personal representative in talks with the Saudis, Libyans and OPEC

(Organization of the Petroleum Exporting Countries). In February 1974 he was appointed to a new post, that of Secretary to the President of the Republic for Foreign Relations, apparently in an attempt to out-manoeuvre the Foreign Ministry. He remained in that position until March 1976, and was subsequently nominated to head the Arab Organi-zation for Industrialization, which had been created by Saudi Arabia in 1975 to promote the development of an Arab defence industry.

In 1973 Marwan alerted his Mossad case officer about Egypt's plan to launch a surprise attack across the Suez Canal, but he was disbelieved. Referred to as 'Top Source', Marwan had been in touch with Mossad since 1969 when he had approached an Israeli diplomat in London, offer-ing to spy. This was his third attempt, as he had made two other bids in other European capitals. Allegedly, Marwan warned in April 1973 that Egypt and Syria planned to start a war on 15 May, and consequently Israel had mobilized, an act that may have served to postpone the offensive. Codenamed BLUE AND WHITE, the IDF's enhanced state of readiness had a severely adverse impact on Israel's economy, undermined the influ-ence of Zeira and Shalev, and increased pressure for an entirely new analysis of Egyptian intentions.

On 4 October he gave another warning, telephoned from Paris, and was debriefed two days later in London by Zvi Zamir, who flew in for the purpose, on the very morning the conflict began.

Zamir thus established a brief but very personal bond with Marwan, who was acknowledged to have performed well over his four years as a Mossad asset. He had been granted the unusual privilege of being assigned the same case officer, identified as Dubi Asherov, and made frequent use of a London safe-house, an apartment in Mayfair. When Mossad had sug-gested replacing Asherov, Marwan had protested vigorously, and an excep-tion was made to the organization's routine tradecraft to rotate their handlers. Marwan's remuneration was alleged to be £50,000 for each meet-ing, which reflected his value as a source, and the sensitive nature of his documents. Although highly regarded by Mossad, which had invested heavily in Marwan, he had ground to recover because of his alert, in April 1973, of an imminent offensive, which turned out to be a false alarm. This incident, which had triggered an IDF mobilization, had served to under-mine the standing of the source known in some compartments as ANGEL.

Marwan himself was deeply affected by the IDF's perceived failures in October 1973 and when he met Zamir again, a few months after the conflict, he complained 'How could you have done this to me?', a remark

174

interpreted by Mossad as Marwan's identification of himself with the Israelis.

When Marwan moved to England permanently soon after Sadat's assassination in October 1981, and the succession of Hosni Mubarak, his usefulness did not come to an end, and he maintained his Mossad contact until a final rendezvous in London's Dorchester Hotel in 2000, when doubtless he was assured that his past relationship with Mossad would remain a secret for ever. No one could have anticipated the spat between the two Israeli intelligence chiefs, and the extraordinary circumstances in which premature disclosure of the Or judgment would compromise Marwan. Even more remarkably, far from exulting over Marwan's death as a traitor's deserved fate, the Egyptian government let it be known that Marwan had acted throughout his espionage career as a double agent on a mission to mislead the Israelis. Was this a desperately improbable attempt at face-saving, or the genuine article? Mossad would conduct no fewer than four internal reviews to satisfy itself that it had not been duped.

President Hosni Mubarak's son Gamal and Umar Soleiman, then director-general of the Mukhabarat, attended Marwan's funeral in Cairo, implying that he had always worked for Egypt, perhaps as a double agent, deliberately passing disinformation to the Israelis. Certainly Sadat ran a very sophisticated deception campaign over a long period to conceal the intention to attack, and the Israeli director of military intelligence, General Eli Zeira, declared that Marwan had been a double agent who had duped Mossad. One ploy was to mount frequent large-scale exercises to lull the Israelis into a sense of false security. Between 1970 and 1973 these prompted four costly major mobilizations in Israel, and in 1973 the Egyptians organized some twenty-two exercises, all for the same purpose.

In retrospect, one can see that there were several indicators in 1973 of imminent conflict. One was the unscheduled evacuation by giant AN-22 transports of non-essential Soviet personnel, mainly advisers' families, from Syria and Egypt, although the actual advisers remained in post. Secondly, EgyptAir aircraft were instructed to divert to Libyan airfields.

Soviet-made SA-6 *Gainful* mobile anti-aircraft missile batteries were supplied to Egypt in considerable numbers, and forty were deployed, mainly along the Suez Canal. Mounted on tracked vehicles, the radar system proved effective, especially at low altitude, against the 160 US-manufactured A-4 Skyhawk and 30 F-4 Phantom jet fighters which had not been fitted with electronic counter-measures or warning devices. Significantly, the SA-6 offered air defence cover into the Sinai, and some of this hardware, together with artillery and even bridging equipment, had stayed *in situ* at the end of the May exercises, and had not been returned to its usual bases.

While the Israelis had correctly assessed the Egyptian air defence strength of 40 SA-2 and 85 SA-3 missile batteries, it had failed to spot deliveries of the more modern SA-6. However, it was aware that the Soviets had supplied some long-range, nuclear-capable Tu-16 medium bombers.

Altogether some forty Israeli warplanes were destroyed by the SA-6 (and a rather larger number of friendly aircraft). Of the IDF's 540 aircraft, a third were shot down in the first few days of the conflict, thus dispelling any lingering belief in Israel's air superiority so firmly established in the 1967 Six-Day War.

One explanation for misplaced Israeli confidence in its early-warning intelligence was a secret source, occasionally referred to as a 'special means of collection', which is thought to have been a COMINT source, a tap on an underground military cable outside Cairo which transmitted voice recordings in undetectable burst transmissions to an Israeli receiving station. Those indoctrinated into the source were assured that it would give five days' notice of any surprise attack. This was but one component of a large Israeli SIGINT spectrum which monitored traffic from inter-cept sites in the Sinai and on Mount Hermon on the Golan. The accepted strategic analysis, the 'concept' would prove to be a fatal example of 'mirror-imaging', which completely misinterpreted the Egyptian position and concluded that the Arabs would never embark on a war they could not win because of Israeli military superiority on land and in the air estab-lished in the 1967 war. This balance of power suggested Israel was safe from attack for at least three years, recognizing that Sadat would only risk conflict when he had other Arab partners.

In April 1973 Marwan warned of the arrival of SA-6 batteries, and in June asserted that the Soviets had committed to the delivery on 24 August of a brigade of nine wheeled erector-launchers and eighteen Scud-B missiles with a range of 160 nautical miles, capable of reaching Tel Aviv from a launch site in the Sinai. On 16 October Sadat made a public state-ment in which he claimed that his country possessed an 'Egyptian-built' missile capable of striking Israel, thereby implying that the ill-fated *al Zafir* ('Victor') project had not been abandoned after the 1976 war, after all.

According to Israeli military intelligence (Aman), the Egyptian crews would require several months of training before the Scuds could be considered operational. In the event, three would be fired by Soviet personnel on 22 October, without any Egyptian involvement. Despite a warhead of 2 tons of conventional explosives, this first operational launch of a Scud missile inflicted little damage and killed five Israeli soldiers on the Canal's eastern bank.

A week later, on 30 October, the CIA reported that aerial reconnaissance had revealed the existence of 'a transporter-erector-launcher unique to the Scud-B missile in an area near the Tura caves some 20 miles south of Cairo, and two resupply vehicles at Cairo international airport, one of which is carrying a probable canvas-covered missile'. Of particular concern was the presence of *Mozhduechenck*, a Soviet freighter suspected of carrying nuclear warheads, which had transited through the Bosphorus to dock at Alexandria on 24 October, having sailed from the port of Okbyabrskoye, near Nikolayev, on the Black Sea.

In September Marwan reported that Sadat had visited Saudi Arabia in August for a meeting with King Faisal, who had promised his support in the form of an oil embargo if the United States attempted to resupply the IDF. At the end of the month the Egyptian media announced a major military exercise on the Canal, codenamed TAHRIR 1, scheduled for a week beginning 1 October. Both events were later to be recognized as preparations for the surprise attack.

In Syria tension had mounted since an aerial confrontation over the Mediterranean on 13 September when thirteen MiG-21s were shot down by the IDF in a dogfight for the loss of a single aircraft, whose pilot parachuted to safety. Two Phantoms and four Mirage IIIs on a photo-reconnaissance mission over Syria were challenged by the MiGs. Apparently as a reaction, the Syrians had poured troops and armour into the Golan, where the number of tanks grew from the 250 seen in April to 850. The two SAM sites photographed in May had grown to thirty-one.

After his apparent retirement from espionage, Marwan based himself and his family in and around London, reinventing himself as a well-heeled City investor, taking stakes in some high-profile businesses, such as Chelsea Football Club, then owned by the property developer Ken Bates. He also advised Lonrho during its controversial attempt to wrest the Harrods department store from Mohammed Al-Fayed, and gained a reputation as a shrewd corporate raider using funds apparently generated by his part-ownership of Egypt's state-owned arms manufacturer, a benefit from his past proximity to Nasser and Sadat. His portfolio included the Castello Son Vida Hotel in Mallorca and numerous other holdings.

There were no witnesses to Marwan's defenestration, which was investigated by the Metropolitan Police as an 'unexplained death'. The first enquiry was conducted by two detectives, Kevin Naidoo and Martin Woodroffe, and a second was undertaken by John Johnson. The evidence accumulated by the police led the coroner, William Dollman, to conclude that there were many unanswered questions, and so the inquest, in the absence of indications of suicide or murder, declined to return a verdict.

Coincidentally, on the morning of his death Marwan had failed to attend a meeting in a neighbouring building with four of his Ubichem PLC colleagues, József Répási, Essam Shawki, Michael Parkhurst and John Roberts. Concerned by his absence, at midday they had telephoned Marwan, who had assured them he was on his way, but running late.

Evidence unavailable to the coroner suggests that responsibility for Marwan's murder lies with two Libyan intelligence officers who undertook the mission ordered in retaliation for the compromise of a plan in September 1973 for a Popular Front for the Liberation of Palestine (PFLP) group to use two *Strela* shoulder-fired missiles against an El Al aircraft at Fiumicino in Rome. The tip was passed to the Italian police who arrested the terrorists at a rented flat strategically located at Ostia, near the airport, and foiled the plot intended to revenge the Israeli shooting down of a Libyan airliner over the Sinai two months earlier, in February 1973. On the basis of Marwan's information, which detailed how the Soviet weapons had been bought from Libya and then smuggled, wrapped in a consignment of rugs, in the Egyptian diplomatic pouch to the embassy in Rome, five men were arrested and their SA-7 missiles were seized.

Libyan revenge killings in London have been frequent and blatant since 1980 when the Gaddafi regime in Tripoli announced a 'stray-dogs' policy to eliminate its political opponents overseas. There followed a global campaign, conducted by Libyan intelligence personnel, to track down and assassinate dissidents. In most examples, two Jamahinya officers travel to the target's location, shoot or stab the victim, and then flee the jurisdiction immediately on any suitable scheduled flight. Among the likely scenarios in Marwan's case is the likelihood that he was threatened with defenestration, accompanied by an ultimatum concerning his family, if he did not jump to his death.

The British failure to arrest or publicly identify the killers may be either operational, with an international arrest warrant having been issued without public announcement, in the hope of catching them should they be

178

unwise enough to travel abroad, or because there are other issues at stake, perhaps relating to the defection in 2011 of the Jamahinya chief Moussa Koussa. Formerly attached to the Libyan embassy in London, Koussa had been expelled in 1980 for publicly endorsing the 'stray-dogs' programme.

From Mossad's perspective, Marwan was never a spy, in the sense that he sold out his country. Marwan preferred to represent himself to his handlers as a patriot who feared the consequences of some of his government's mistaken strategic decisions. Such self-delusion is part-and-parcel of agent management psychology and most probably Marwan was encouraged in that belief by his principal handler, Dubi Asherov, who was later promoted to the post of assistant to Rafii Meidun, the Mossad chief in London in 1970.

Any objective analysis of what Marwan achieved rules out the possibility that the Israelis were misled by a double agent 'game'. The list of the material he passed includes a mass of strategic and operational documents relating to discussions with the Soviet, Syrian and Saudi governments; original Egyptian general staff papers; records of the Egyptian summit held in Moscow in November 1971; Egyptian plans in 1971 to attack Israel to increase political pressure; records of a summit meeting in Moscow in February 1972 at which Sadat disclosed plans to attack Israel at the end of the year; Sadat's decision in January 1973 to mount a limited offensive against Israel; and agreements made by Sadat with President Assad in July 1973 relating to a proposed war to be launched in September or October the same year. At the end of August 1973 Marwan provided the entire Syrian war plan. The totality of this haemorrhage of classified documents was immense, but any single item would have been regarded as an intelligence coup great enough to influence events in the region for several decades.

The Egyptian narrative, painting Marwan as a loyal double agent, does not take account of what he accomplished because no damage assessment was ever initiated. To undertake such an analysis would necessarily have amounted to an acknowledgement that the position taken publicly was a fiction, so for purely political reasons no effort has been applied to the task of measuring the scale of compromise, although it could also be argued that such a review would be next to impossible without Israel's cooperation, a singularly unlikely prospect.

If there is a direct causal link between Marwan's outing as a spy and his death, the issue is not as simple as an inadvertent slip made by a court clerk in Israel. In fact, an Israeli historian, Ahron Bregman, had worked out

Marwan's name on his own, but had deliberately omitted it from his 2000 book *Israel's Wars*[1], which referred to the spy as having been 'Sadat's right-hand man'. Two years later, in his next book *A History of Israel*[2], Bregman went further and described the still-unnamed spy as 'a very close family member of Egypt's President Nasser', a hint that was followed up by the Cairo newspaper *Al Ahram al Arabi*, which interviewed Marwan and obtained a dismissive denial. This confrontation led to Bregman's one-sided correspondence with Marwan on the subject of a proposed further book, and culminated at their meeting in London on 20 October 2003 at the Inter-Continental Hotel on Hyde Park Corner. After several telephone conversations, including one about the Or judgment, they arranged to meet again, on 27 June 2007. Marwan never kept the appointment.

Chapter 14

Gennadi Vasilenko

It is unlikely that Ames could have betrayed the CIA's
interest in Vasilenko, because he was in Rome during the
time of his attempted recruitment and would not have had
access to information concerning that operation.

[Jack Devine, *Spymaster's Prism*, 2021[1]]

The last years of the Cold War and the immediate post-Cold War era
were periods dominated, from an American intelligence perspective, by
the certainty that the Central Intelligence Agency had been penetrated to
a catastrophic degree, and many of the consequences were both obvious
and went unresolved for years. There is little more debilitating for the
senior management of a secret intelligence agency than to go to work
daily, for years, knowing that it cannot keep secrets.

Hostile penetration of a security or intelligence organization is an occu-
pational hazard and the US intelligence community has been especially
vulnerable to self-recruited spies who were in need of cash. This particular
characteristic of the community has long been recognized and has been
the subject of numerous surveys and reviews conducted by counter-
intelligence professionals and academic studies of the motives of individuals who have compromised classified information since the end of the
Second World War.

Broadly, there are two types of counter-intelligence investigations or
molehunts. The first is where there is a *suspicion* that specific information
has leaked, and the challenge is to identify the source. The task is made
more difficult because although there may be firm *evidence* indicative of
a leak, the source may be non-human, such as a lapse in communications
procedure or a breach of physical security at some sensitive site, perhaps
premises inside a diplomatic mission overseas. The second category
involves the definite compromise of a particular item and the determination that a specific individual, or group of co-conspirators, have engaged

in espionage, so the issues centre on the need to gather sufficient legally admissible evidence to adduce in a criminal prosecution. While the second is relatively straightforward, the first presents considerable problems, not the least of which is the lingering doubt that no actual spy has been at work and that an adversary had taken advantage of some other source. For example, throughout the Cold War the cryptographic breakthrough code-named VENONA revealed the existence of hundreds of NKVD and GRU assets across the globe, their real identities protected by codenames, but the intercepts provided clues to the true names of many of them. The source, a veritable treasure-trove of espionage data, triggered hundreds of individual investigations and eventually exposed numerous Soviet agents. Some were neutralized by removal from access to classified information, others fled the jurisdiction to live in safe-havens and thereby became fugitives (Al Sarant and Joel Barr), while a few either declined to make their escape or opted to risk arrest and prosecution (Ethel and Julius Rosenberg). Significantly, when the Soviets grasped the nature of the threat to its networks overseas, they did not issue warnings to explain the likelihood of compromise, but simply advised those thought to be most vulnerable to escape.

The dilemma facing the CIA in 1985 was the knowledge that it was suffering terrible losses, though the operational failures did not immediately suggest a human source. A long molehunt ensued, and in December 1993, seven years after the original leaks were detected, the field of suspects was narrowed to a single person: Aldrich Ames. Although the CIA went to considerable lengths to conceal exactly how Ames had become the focus of an intensive investigation, the truth was that the critical tip-off had come from a still-serving SVR officer, although he himself had not been aware of the significance of his information, which led to Ames's arrest in February 1994.

Ames had inflicted lasting reputational and operational damage to his colleagues and agreed in a plea bargain to cooperate with his interrogators in return for the removal of the threat of execution and a reduced sentence for his Colombian wife, who had been his accomplice. However, over a number of detailed interviews it became clear that Ames could not account for all the items on a long list of CIA failures. Put simply, there was compelling proof, in the form of unexplained losses, which signalled the existence of another Soviet spy, as yet undetected. For instance, the CIA continued to suffer failures at a time when Ames demonstrably had been posted to Rome (between July 1986 and December 1989), and could not have had the required access.

Persuaded that there was a second mole at liberty, a further investigation was initiated by the FBI's Washington Field Office, but it was flawed at the outset because the squad's membership was convinced that their quarry was a CIA officer, and most likely a senior officer with the Counter-intelligence Center. Realizing that it had taken more than eight years to track down Ames, the FBI analysts concluded that any strategy that involved a review of suspect personnel would be equally long drawn-out, and would probably not yield any results if the culprit was, as suspected, a seasoned operator who would exercise his (or her) special skills to cover their tracks. It was also recognized, in terms of tactics, that Ames had not been caught by solid sleuthing. The vital clue had come unwittingly from inside the SVR, and the decision was taken to adopt the same approach and find someone, either still serving or, better still, a recent retiree, who might be expected to have some knowledge of the case.

The CIC's Russian counterpart was Directorate K of the KGB's First Chief Directorate, and latterly its successor, the SVR, and its sole purpose had been to protect the organization from penetration by receiving and managing self-recruited CIA staff who had already decided to betray secrets, most likely for money. In recent years they had achieved considerable success in acquiring such assets. In 1976 David Barnett[2] had approached the KGB *rezidentura* in Jakarta and sold secrets to his contact for the next three years; Ed Howard[3] had defected to Moscow in 1985, leaving behind uncertainty about when he had first approached the Soviets; Hal Nicholson[4] passed classified material to the SVR between June 1994 and December 1996.

These were three cases that the CIC knew about, and there remained at least one undetected. None of the three had been exposed by routine polygraphs, clearance reviews or other security precautions. In each there was a common denominator, albeit one that had been kept under wraps to protect the source. Each of these spies had been betrayed by a Russian: Barnett had been compromised by Vladimir Piguzov; Howard's link to the KGB had been known to Vitali Yurchenko;[5] Nicholson was arrested in November 1996 after a tip-off from the same SVR officer who had inadvertently compromised Ames. Two years later he was responsible for the arrest of a retired NSA analyst, David Boone[6], who had sold secrets to the KGB between 1988 and 1991 for $60,000. The lesson learned by the KGB, which understood the counter-intelligence game quite as well as the

Americans (if not even better), was that knowledge of these assets had been too widely spread. Directorate K realized that Yurchenko had been to blame for blowing not only Howard, but also a former NSA analyst, Ron Pelton, who was arrested in November 1985.

The KGB's solution, the brainchild of Vadim Kirpichenko, was the creation of a specialist unit, working at a very high level, with no permanent staff but a group of trusted agent handlers who could be called upon to manage really important walk-ins. A common thread across the examples of Barnett, Howard, Nicholson, Boone and Pelton (and indeed another NSA analyst, Robert Lipka) was that they all fitted a pattern. They were intelligence professionals who, for mercenary reasons, had simply volunteered to spy. According to Kirpichenko, this rich resource deserved to be exploited professionally, and not left to the *rezidenturas* which were, by their nature, vulnerable to hostile penetration. Although, at the time of the creation of GROUP NORTH, there was no understanding of how Barnett and Nicholson had been detected, the KGB's weakness lay in its exposed front line where its personnel were vulnerable to an orchestrated recruitment campaign conducted jointly by the FBI and CIA, appropriately codenamed COURTSHIP.

As the Soviet Union disintegrated, and a slimmed-down SVR replaced the KGB, a large number of former FCD officers found themselves unemployed, including several who either knew of GROUP NORTH's existence, or had known of colleagues who had undertaken assignments for it. Among the first to disclose some peripheral information about the unit was Alexander Zaporozhsky, a former member of the Addis Ababa *rezidentura* who had been responsible for, as he saw it, earning his retirement pension by compromising Nicholson and Boone.

Zaporozhsky returned from his post in Ethiopia to be promoted to a senior position, that of deputy chief of the FCD's 1st (USA & Canada) Department. What made Zaporozhsky unusual was the nature of his arrangement with the CIA: he would not be responding to the questionnaires that are part-and-parcel of the agent-case officer relationship. He alone would decide what he would communicate, and when he would do so. In other words, he would control the channel, and the CIA would be trusted to build up a bank deposit as a reward for whenever the spy decided to defect or, preferably, simply emigrate without creating problems with the authorities in Moscow which were anyway somewhat distracted in the post-Soviet Yeltsin era. In the event, Zaporozhsky, who had joined the KGB in 1975 at the age of 24, retired from the SVR and in

1998 quietly moved his wife and sons to a safe-house in Haymarket in northern Virginia and then moved to a $400,000 mansion on Willow Vista Way in Cockeysville, Maryland, not as an intelligence defector but as a Russian emigrant seeking to start a mineral water supply company.

Zaporozhsky had earned his new life by helping the CIA, although he was unaware of his own value. In November 1992, asked about the unidentified mole in the CIA, he had suggested that his colleague Vitali Karetkin had flown to Lima to meet an important GROUP NORTH asset. This apparently innocuous information, which might otherwise have been one of several pieces of a counter-intelligence jigsaw puzzle, matched a journey made by Ames to Bogota. At that time there were no direct flights from Moscow to Colombia, so Karetkin had been obliged to fly to Peru and change planes. This was the vital item that sealed Ames's fate, and he was immediately placed under intensive surveillance before his arrest three months later.

At that stage Zaporozhsky had not realized the significance or consequences of his tip about Karetkin, but his relationship with the CIA became known to the SVR, which lured him back to Moscow in November 2001 on the promise of a lucrative security contract, despite the strenuous objections of his CIA handlers. Specifically, he lunched every week with the head of the resettlement unit, Joe Augustyn, who begged him not to take the risk of visiting Moscow. Zaporozhsky countered that he had already made one trip back, to attend a KGB reunion, and the episode had been entirely uneventful. The Russian was convinced he was in no danger. At his trial in June 2003 he was accused of having spied for the CIA between 1982 and his retirement in 1997, and was sentenced to eighteen years' hard labour.

Prior to his arrival at Shemetyevo Airport, where he was arrested, Zaporozhsky had informed the Russian Consulate in New York of his travel plans, and had renewed his passport. While he had waited for his flight at Dulles he had been visited by senior CIA officers who begged him to cancel his plans. What they could not tell him was that they were almost certain that he had been betrayed by the 'second mole' who had been run by GROUP NORTH.

The FBI's expedient of tracking down the GROUP NORTH membership, instead of trawling through lists of potential suspects, was aided by a CIA asset who had been cultivated ever since he arrived at the Washington *rezidentura* in 1979. He had verified Zaporozhsky's credentials when he made his first approach to the CIA in Ethiopia, and he had been run under the codename MONOLIGHT by the CIA's Jack Platt. Born in Siberia in December 1941, Gennadi Vasilenko was five years younger than the case officer deployed to recruit him as part of the COURTSHIP programme, but their genuine friendship was based on a mutual love of sports and shooting. While Platt, a gregarious Texan from San Antonio, was directed to 'develop' the KGB officer, Vasilenko had reported the contact to his *rezident* and received permission to ensnare his CIA counterpart, whose cover as a Pentagon contractor was wafer-thin because a previous posting to Paris had been blown by the CIA renegade Philip Agee.[7] However the relationship progressed, it was the subject of a report to Moscow by the 'second mole' in October 1987 in which Vasilenko was referred to by the codename AE/MONOLIGHT and described as a 'valuable source'. This apparently incriminating text triggered an immediate response from the KGB which summoned Vasilenko from his *rezidentura* in Georgetown, Guyana, to Havana, Cuba, where he was detained and questioned before being shipped back to Moscow on a cargo vessel. Incarcerated in Lefortovo prison, Vasilenko was interrogated for six months, and accused of having been recruited by the CIA. He countered with what amounted to his insurance policy: he had been authorized by his *rezident* and Moscow to cultivate Platt.[8] Furthermore, he had participated in an operation involving the NSA linguist Ron Pelton, who had visited the embassy in January 1980 to sell classified information. Although the *rezidentura* had been delighted by this un-expected 'walk-in', the staff realized that the FBI's physical surveillance on the building would have spotted the bearded man as he entered, so elaborate arrangements were made to change his appearance and smuggle him out. The security officer, Vitali Yurchenko, had asked Vasilenko to shave off Pelton's beard and arrange for him to join a minivan that routinely drove employees home at the end of the working day. Pelton was to lie down in the vehicle, shielded from the FBI's cameras by the other passengers.

Trained as a Russian linguist by the US Air Force, Pelton had served at an intercept site at Peshawar before transferring to the NSA in November 1965. However, he resigned in July 1979, two months after he had filed for bankruptcy, and his financial crisis led him to visit the embassy. Over the next five years Pelton met his KGB handler, Anatoli Slavnov, several times, flew to Vienna twice, in October 1980 and again in January 1983, to be debriefed inside the embassy compound, and was paid $35,000. Although Pelton's information was based on his memory, as he no longer had access to classified information, he had compromised numerous pro-grammes into which he had been indoctrinated while stationed in Pakistan and England. Perhaps the most damaging disclosure was his description of IVY BELLS, an underwater cable-tapping project run in conjunction with the US Navy, which collected communications traffic at Soviet naval bases and in Libyan territorial waters. The distinctively red-haired Pelton would be identified as a spy by Yurchenko during interviews conducted after his defection in July 1985, and the NSA retiree would be arrested by the FBI in November that year. Convicted at his trial in December 1986, he was sentenced to three life terms plus ten years' imprisonment. He would not be released until November 2015.

It was Vasilenko's argument that the proof of his continued loyalty to the KGB was the fact that although he had known about the spy since January 1980, Pelton had not been apprehended until November 1985, a period when he had done immense damage to the NSA. The fact that Pelton had been at liberty over those five years was, claimed Vasilenko, evidence of his integrity. The assertion may have convinced a few, but in October 1988 he was demoted and dismissed from the KGB.

It would not be until 1992 that Vasilenko was able to obtain a passport and travel to the United States, where he was reunited with Platt, now officially retired from the CIA but retained on a consultancy contract. At the end of his visit Vasilenko returned to Moscow, where, in common with so many of his former FCD colleagues, he opened a security company to take advantage of the Russian era of privatization which was accompanied by corruption, graft and protection rackets. Those KGB veterans who could not use their connections to acquire jobs with the new banks, airlines or oil companies created their own enterprises in the private sector. By 2000 Vasilenko was running his own business and was lending office space to his FCD friend Alexander Shcherbakov, who also happened to have been closely involved in GROUP NORTH. Indeed, in the August 1991 coup Shcherbakov had been one of the trusted inner circle who had been called back to the Yasenevo headquarters to transfer especially sensitive files to safe storage, the prevalent fear being that the site might be seized and occupied by demonstrators, as had happened to the Stasi compound in East Berlin two years earlier. Shcherbakov had not only participated in the evacuation of the archive, but purloined one particular collection of documents relating to KARAT, a still active source in the United States, known to the FBI as the second mole.

Meanwhile, the FBI was still in pursuit of the second mole, and was engaged on a detailed study of GROUP NORTH to identify the officers who had worked in the unit, and trace their current whereabouts. This was an extraordinarily challenging project as it involved trying to name the staff employed by a highly secret compartment within another secret organization. Finally, having found a target, the objective was to persuade that individual, who had been selected to work for GROUP NORTH on the basis of their reliability and loyalty, to succumb to some inducement and reveal something about the second mole.

The exact number of GROUP NORTH targets identified and approached remains secret, as does the identity of those who may have assisted the investigators. General Oleg Kalugin, the Directorate K Chief who left Moscow in 1995 and settled in the United States, was obviously one of those asked to cooperate, but he has always insisted that he only ever helped the American authorities on issues concerning spies already known to them, such as the NSA analyst Robert Lipka and the US Army officer Colonel George Trofimoff who, although known to Kalugin, had both been exposed by the defector Vasili Mitrokhin. Under subpoena, Kalugin had reluctantly given evidence in June 2000 for the prosecution at Trofimoff's trial but he had always insisted that he was not an intelligence defector, and received his US citizenship in August 2003 without any intervention by federal agencies. Another 'non-defector' who proved to be helpful was one of Kalugin's subordinates, who, fortuitously, turned out to know a great deal about GROUP NORTH and its membership, but not its agents.

The lynchpin who was able to solve the puzzle of the second mole was Alexander Shcherbakov, who in July 2000 was enticed to New York for a purported business deal, which was actually a staged event where he could be 'pitched' by the FBI's Mike Rochford. Lengthy negotiations followed, but eventually a deal was struck for the sale, reportedly for $7 million, of 'volume 1' of the KARAT file, which was still in Shcherbakov's possession, stored in his mother's garage. The contents of this file – which included a black plastic rubbish bag which had been used as a wrapper for a package of documents delivered to a dead-drop in Virginia, bearing a fingerprint, and a voice-tape of a recorded telephone conversation – clearly identified the second mole, codenamed KARAT, as a senior FBI officer, Robert Hanssen.

Hanssen's espionage for the GRU, then the KGB and finally the SVR extended from November 1979 to the day he was arrested in February

2001. During that period Hanssen delivered classified information to a GRU officer in New York, which included the real identity of an FBI source inside the GRU, Dmitri Polyakov. There followed a hiatus in his espionage until October 1985, when he made contact anonymously with the KGB *rezidentura* in Washington and sold more secrets, estimated in volume to be around 6,000 pages.

The still-classified damage assessment, drafted with Hanssen's co-operation, indicated the breadth of his access and included details of MONOPOLY, a tunnel dug under the Soviet compound at Mount Alto, packed with NSA eavesdropping apparatus to intercept Russian communications, and the 'continuity of government' contingency plans to protect the president and his staff in deep bunkers in the event of a nuclear conflict. He supplied a copy of *The FBI's Double Agent Program* which summarized every current operation, and the 1987, 1989 and 1990 versions of the annual *National Intelligence Program*, which set out inter-agency plans and objectives. Also disclosed were documents circulated by the Director of Central Intelligence, such as *Stealth Orientation* and volume II of *Compendium of Future Intelligence Requirements*. Of strategic significance were two CIA nuclear war assessments for the 1990s; *The Soviet Union in Crisis: Prospects for the Next Two Years*; a copy of the *National HUMINT Collection Plan*; and a technical survey of MASINT (measurement and signature intelligence) capabilities.

In terms of Hanssen's own field, counter-intelligence, he acknowledged having supplied a copy of a summary of defector information listing Soviet intelligence successes; transcripts of meetings held by the inter-agency CI Group; details of Soviet intelligence double agent operations; an FBI memo about a suspected KGB counter-intelligence officer based at the New York *rezidentura*, and another identifying a target for future surveillance; the entire FBI counter-intelligence budget for 1992; details of a 'dangle' operation to be conducted at a military facility with the intention of peddling disinformation, and a CIA report, *The KGB's First Chief Directorate: Structure, Functions and Methods*.

As the recipient of routine but nevertheless highly sensitive information circulated within the intelligence community, Hanssen copied an NSA report concerning a weakness in a Soviet communications satellite that had been exploited by the agency, showed the agency's next target for attack and pointed out which channels had resisted interception. He also supplied the collection schedules for particular sensors sited on US maritime, aerial and satellite platforms. The extent of Hanssen's access was astonishing, and reached far beyond his duties at FBI headquarters. Indeed, some of it handed the Kremlin a strategic advantage, because by identifying the continuity-of-government contingency plans, created for the purpose of an administration surviving a nuclear first-strike attack, it suggested to an adversary that even the protected facilities could be eliminated, thereby undermining the central principle of deterrence.

One of the mysteries cleared up during Hanssen's interrogation, and the examination of his KGB file, was the confirmation that in October 1987 he had been responsible for compromising Vasilenko by alerting the KGB to the true identity of the CIA source codenamed AE/MONO-LIGHT and assessed as 'valuable'. Hanssen had been responsible for Vasilenko's betrayal and now, ironically, he had played a part in ensuring Hanssen's incarceration.[9]

In retrospect it can be seen that the common thread running through the detection of Aldrich Ames and Robert Hanssen was Gennadi Vasilenko, who had played a key role in enabling the CIA to access Zaporozhsky and Shcherbakov. In the latter case, he had even paid a $800 bribe for a valid passport so Shcherbakov could travel to New York.

Vasilenko's situation took a turn for the worse in August 2005 when he was detained on a charge of terrorism, based on the discovery by the FSB of an unregistered hunting rifle and a quantity of ammunition at his dacha outside Moscow. At his trial in May 2006 he was sentenced to three years' imprisonment, but as his release date approached he was rearrested and in December 2007 faced a charge of 'resisting the authorities'.

Vasilenko, for whatever reason, was now in serious danger of disappearing into the Russian penal system, and was being moved around from one prison to another so as to make it next to impossible to find him, engage a lawyer on his behalf or make a family visit. Eventually his son Ilya tracked him down to IK-11, a notorious labour camp near Bor in the Nizhny Novgorod region, 220 miles east of Moscow, where he was suffering daily beatings and, at the age of 66, believed he was unlikely to survive much longer.

When Jack Platt heard of Vasilenko's plight he initiated a campaign within the CIA to find suitable leverage to extract him, and eventually this materialized in the form of a lengthy FBI surveillance of a network of SVR illegals well-established in the United States. The illegals amounted to a large investment on the SVR's part and conformed to all the conventional Directorate S tradecraft so familiar to Allied counter-intelligence agencies. Illegals, by their very nature, do not enjoy the protection of the

1961 Vienna Convention which grants immunity to accredited diplomats, the cover of preference for most intelligence agencies, for whom the loss of an officer overseas means an embarrassing public expulsion, but not an arrest, followed by a humiliating show-trial and perhaps a death penalty.

However, illegals hold considerable disadvantages. Much depends on their own personal initiative and continued ideological motivation. Illegals are exceptional in every respect but require to be maintained and resourced. They must keep the faith and remain committed to their cause, for it would be all too easy for a disenchanted agent to simply relocate and resume a normal life elsewhere, or turn themselves in to the local security apparatus. The Soviets had plenty of experience of the consequences of disaffection, and the only KGB illegal *rezident* to be caught in the United States, Willie Fisher, alias Rudolf Abel, had been apprehended in June 1957 because his deputy, Reino Hayhanen, had feared his recall to Moscow to face disciplinary action. Hayhanen had defected to the CIA and then helped the FBI to find Fisher in New York, where he was posing as an artist. Fisher would be released in a spy-swap in February 1962 for the U-2 pilot Gary Powers. When interrogated by the FBI, Fisher refused to make any incriminating admissions, apart from acknowledging that he was a Soviet intelligence professional. Similarly, when the KGB illegal *rezident* in London, Konon Molody, was arrested in January 1961, he also remained largely silent, although he did offer to defect if he was released to fetch his family from Moscow. He was swapped in April 1964 for the SIS courier Greville Wynne, who had been detained in Budapest in October 1962.

Together Fisher and Molody played into the KGB's narrative of the 'great Chekist' in which the committed ideologue undertakes perilous missions in the west at considerable personal and family sacrifice, all for the sake of the Party, but can always be confident that 'the Centre' will engineer a rescue should the need arise. This was, of course, a myth but it served a purpose and became highly relevant in July 2010 when the FBI rolled up ten SVR illegals in the United States and made them available for a spy-swap which resulted in Gennadi Vasilenko and three other Russians being exchanged in Vienna.

The FBI operation, codenamed GHOST STORIES and coordinated from the New York Field Office, had been initiated in 2000 based on information from a Directorate S source, Alexander Poteyev. For the following ten years the FBI had discreetly monitored Poteyev's illegals, read some of their encrypted messages transmitted over the internet and periodically conducted covert searches of their homes. Watching them, either physically through the deployment of the Special Surveillance Group, or electronically via remote-controlled concealed cameras, led investigators to their contacts and, most importantly, identified the SVR illegal support officers working under diplomatic or consular cover. In July 2010, as the FBI prepared to intervene, the network had grown to a dozen and included an elusive paymaster, Pavel Kapustin, who travelled under numerous aliases, including 'Christopher Matsos'. Of the twelve illegals under scrutiny, two were living under their own legitimate identities, and had not been seen to engage in any illegal act. Accordingly, as plans were made to detain the eight illegals who were already well-known to the FBI, a scheme was prepared to entrap the pair, Anna Chapman in New York and Mikhail Semenko in Arlington, who thus far had not been seen to break the law.

However, before the GHOST STORIES arrests could be actioned, the CIA had the task of exfiltrating Poteyev and Shcherbakov from Moscow. The arrests would be bound to lead the SVR to conclude that its network had been betrayed from within, and Poteyev was an obvious candidate, not least because a decade earlier he had been posted to the New York *rezidentura*, when there would have been an opportunity for his recruitment. Secondly, the entrapment method adopted to incriminate Chapman and Semenko involved the use of a secret *parole* or password which was instantly traceable back to Poteyev. Accordingly, there was a requirement to carefully coordinate the timing of the arrests with the moment that Poteyev had reached a safe-haven. Similarly, there was a perceived duty to extract Shcherbakov, who would be vulnerable if he remained within the FSB's grasp.

The precise timing of the intervention was complicated further by two other issues. Most of the illegals routinely returned to Russia for a bi-annual period of leave, and one couple, Andrey Bezrikov (alias Donald Heathfield) and his wife Elena Vavilov (alias Tracey Foley) had already made their travel plans and were scheduled to leave the country imminently.

On Saturday, 26 June, as soon as confirmation had been received that the exfiltrations had taken place successfully, Chapman and Semenko were induced to commit an act preparatory to espionage, as required by statute, and were arrested the following day. By Sunday evening all eleven targets were in custody. Fortuitously, Kapustin turned up unexpectedly two days later at Larnaca in Cyprus, where he was detained on an international arrest warrant citing money-laundering charges. That particular aspect of the planned operation failed, as Kapustin was released on bail and fled the jurisdiction.

On 4 July, once the eleven detainees were safely in custody, the CIA's Director Leon Panetta telephoned his SVR counterpart, Mikhail Fradkov, to negotiate a spy-swap, and an asymmetrical deal was struck before the Russians noticed the disappearance of Poteyev and Shcherbakov. In the prisoner exchange ten of the illegals were to be delivered to the SVR in Vienna in return for the release of Zaporozhsky and Vasilenko. Fradkov's suggestion that Ames and Hanssen also be included in the swap was brushed aside by Panetta, and to make the agreement look more plausible to the SVR, and help conceal Vasilenko's significance, two other Russian convicts were added as pawns: a GRU officer, Colonel Sergei Skrypal, who had confessed to having spied for the British, and an academic, Igor Sutyagin, who had been imprisoned for leaking arms control data to a London-based journal.

Upon their release Zaporozhsky was reunited with his sons Maxim and Pavel, his wife Galina having died while he was in prison, and resumed his life in the United States. For his part, Vasilenko was welcomed to resettlement in northern Virginia by Jack Platt, the man who had probably saved his life.

Notes

Note: All MI5 documents listed here are in The National Archives.

Introduction

1. Dulles, A., *Great True Spy Stories* (New York: Harper & Row, 1968). Dulles resigned in November 1961 after eight years as Director of Central Intelligence, and then in 1963 published *The Craft of Intelligence* (New York: Harper & Row, 1963) which had been written largely by his staff before his retirement. For many years afterwards both books were recommended reading for new CIA officer trainees.
2. Richard Sorge was a German journalist and Soviet spy executed in Tokyo in November 1944. See Matthews, O., *An Impeccable Spy* (London: Bloomsbury, 2019).
3. Codenamed GEORGE WOOD, Fritz Kolbe was a German diplomat who passed Nazi secrets to Allen Dulles in Switzerland from August 1943. His biography, *A Spy at the Heart of the Third Reich*, was published by Lucas Delattre (New York: Atlantic Monthly Press, 2005).
4. Ronald Seth's 1952 autobiography, *A Spy Has No Friends* (London: André Deutsch), is largely supported by his declassified MI5 personal file at KV2/378 and his SOE file at HS9/1345.
5. Klaus Fuchs' MI5 personal file is at KV2/1252.
6. Ursula Kuczynsky's MI5 personal file is at KV5/43. Her husband's personal file is at KV2/2610.
7. Erich Vermehren's MI5 personal file is at KV2/956.
8. TATE was the MI5 double agent Wolf Schmidt, alias Harry Williamson. His MI5 personal file is at KV2/62. See also Jonason, T. & Olsson, S., *Agent TATE* (Stroud, Glos: Amberley, 2011).
9. A Polish airman, BRUTUS was Roman Garby-Czerniawski, author of *The Big Network* (London: George Ronald, 1961). His MI5 personal file is at KV2/72.
10. GARBO was Juan Pujol, author of *GARBO* (Weidenfeld & Nicolson, 1985). His MI5 personal file is at KV2/40.
11. Alan Foote wrote *Handbook for Spies* in 1949 (London: Museum Press) with his MI5 interrogator, Courtney Young, and it was published by a former MI5 officer, Desmond Vesey. His MI5 personal file is at KV2/1616.
12. Igor Gouzenko wrote his memoir, *This was my Choice* (London: Eyre & Spottiswoode) in 1948.
13. Julius and Ethel Rosenberg. The best analysis is contained in Weinstein, A. & Vassiliev, A., *The Haunted Wood* (Random House, 1999); Haynes, J.E., Klehr, H. & Vassiliev, A., *Spies; The Rise and Fall of the KGB in America* (London: Yale University Press, 2009); Feklisov, A., *The Man Behind the Rosenbergs* (New York: Enigma, 2001)

14. Anatoli Golitsyn released *New Lies for Old* (London: Bodley Head, 1984), edited by SIS's Arthur Martin and Stephen de Mowbray; and *The Perestroika Deception* (London: Edward Harle, 1996), but his memoir, *Checkmate*, remains unpublished.
15. Oleg Penkovsky's career is covered in Duns, J., *Dead Drop* (London: Simon & Schuster, 2014), and Schechter, J. & Deriabin, P., *The Spy Who Saved the World* (New York: Scribner, 1992). Both are based on declassified CIA files.
16. John Vassall published his memoir, *Autobiography of a Spy* (London: Sidgwick & Jackson) in 1975.
17. George Blake published his memoir, *No Other Choice* (London: Jonathan Cape) in 1990.
18. Kim Philby published his memoir, *My Silent War* (London: McGibbon & Kee) in 1968. See also Philby, R. with Peake, H., *The Private Life of Kim Philby: The Moscow Years* (London: St Ermin's Press, 1999).
19. Anthony Blunt's biographies include Costello, J., *Mask of Treachery* (New York: William Morrow, 1998) and Carter, M., *Anthony Blunt: His Lives* (London: Pan, 2002).
20. A Swedish Air Force officer, Colonel Stig Wennerstrom, was arrested in June 1963 and sentenced to life imprisonment after having confessed to espionage for the Soviets. He was paroled in 1974 and died in March 2006. Four biographies, all in Swedish, have been published.
21. A senior NATO official, George Paques was sentenced in Paris to life imprisonment in July 1964 on espionage charges. He was released in 1970.
22. The Canberra NKVD *rezident* Vladimir Petrov defected in 1954 and published his memoir, *Empire of Fear* (New York: Praeger) in 1956.
23. A senior Polish Army staff officer, Ryszard Kuklinski defected from Warsaw in 1981. He was resettled in Tampa, Florida, where he died in February 2004. In December 2008 the CIA released eighty-two documents relating to martial law that had been passed by Kuklinski.
24. A CIA analyst and spy for the Chinese, Larry Wu-Tai Chin committed suicide after his conviction on espionage charges in February 1986.
25. A Soviet aeronautical engineer, Adolf Tolkachev was executed in Moscow in September 1986 after he had been convicted of spying for the CIA. See Hoffman, D., *The Billion Dollar Spy* (New York: Doubleday, 2015).
26. An SIS agent inside the KGB, Oleg Gordievsky was exfiltrated from Moscow in 1985 and published his memoir, *Next Stop Execution* (London: Macmillan) in 1995. See also Macintyre, B., *The Spy and the Traitor* (New York: Crown, 2018).
27. A retired KGB archivist, Vasili Mitrokhin defected to London in 1992 and published *The Sword and the Shield* (London: Basic Books) in 1999 with Professor Christopher Andrew. He later wrote *KGB Lexicon* (London: Frank Cass, 2002) and *The World Was Going Our Way* (London: Basic Books, 2005). Mitrokhin died in January 2004.

Chapter 1: Walther Dewé

1. Landau, H., *The Spy Net* (London: Biteback, 2015).
2. Judd, A., *The Quest for C* (London: HarperCollins, 2000).
3. Morgan, J., *The Secrets of rue St Roche* (London: Allen Lane, 2004).
4. Jeffery, K., *MI6* (London: Penguin, 2009).
5. Landau, H., *The Secrets of the White Lady* (New York: GP Putnam's Sons, 1935).

Chapter 2: Christopher Draper

1. Liddell correspondence, in the Hans Thost personal file, at KV2/952.
2. See also Batvinis, R., *The Origins of FBI Counterintelligence* (Lawrence, KS: University of Kansas Press, 2007). See also Witt, C., *Double Agent CELERY: MI5's Crooked Hero* (Barnsley, Yorks: Pen & Sword, 2017).
3. Jessie Jordan's MI5 personal file is at KV2/3532.
4. Gertrud Brandy's MI5 personal file is at KV2/356.
5. Walter Simon's MI5 personal file is at KV2/1293.
6. My Eriksson's MI5 personal file is at KV2/537.
7. Vera von Schalberg's MI5 personal file is at KV2/14. Her co-conspirator Anna Chateau-Thierry's personal file is at KV2/357.
8. Arthur Owens, codenamed SNOW, was MI5's first double agent of the war. His MI5 personal file is at KV2/444. See also Roberts, M., *SNOW* (London: Biteback, 2011).
9. Draper, C., *The Mad Major* (Los Angeles: Aero Books, 1962).

Chapter 3: Olga Gray

1. Hemming, H., *M: Maxwell Knight, MI5's Greatest Spymaster* (London: Penguin, 2017).
2. Percy Glading's MI5 files are at KV2/1020 and KV3/234.
3. Dickson, G., *Soho Racket* (London: Hutchinson, 1935).
4. Knight, M., *Crime Cargo* (London: Philip Allan, 1934); *Gunman's Holiday* (London: Philip Allan, 1935).
5. Bingham, J., *Night's Black Agents* (London: Penguin, 1961). Also *The Double Agent* (London: Panther, 1966) and *Brock and the Defector* (London: 1982).
6. Mole, W., *The Hammersmith Maggot* (London: Eyre & Spottiswoode, 1956).
7. 'Vigilant', *The Secrets of Modern Spying* (London: J. Hamilton, 1930).
8. 'Vigilant', *Richthofen: Red Knight of the Air* (London: J. Hamilton, 1933).
9. Tom Driberg was expelled from the CPGB in 1941 after he was identified to Moscow as MI5's source codenamed M/8.
10. Mikhail Sokolov's MI5 personal file is at KV2/2572.
11. Eric Camp's MI5 personal file is at KV2/2572.
12. Bob Stewart's MI5 files are at KV2/2507 and KV2/1180.
13. Masters, A., *The Man Who Was M* (HarperCollins, 1986).
14. William Morrison's MI5 personal file is at KV2/606.

Chapter 4: Arnold Deutsch

1. MI5 interviews conducted with Walter Krivitsky at the Langham Hotel, January 1940.
2. Arnold Deutsch's MI5 personal file is at KV2/3328.
3. 'Bumptious' was a term used independently by Olga Gray, in reporting on a conversation with Percy Glading, and by Krivitsky.
4. See Massing, H., *This Deception* (New York: Duell, Sloan & Pearce, 1951); and Poretsky, E., *Our Own People* (Ann Arbor, MI: University of Michigan Press, 1970).
5. Vasili Zubilin was the alias adopted by Vasili Zarubin. He had been in the United States throughout the 1930s as an illegal and in January 1942 was posted to the Washington DC *rezidentura*. He was recalled to Moscow in August 1944, having supervised the spy ring that had penetrated the ENORMOZ Allied atomic weapons programme.

6. Excerpts of Philby's 1963 confession are in Deutsch's MI5 personal file at KV2/4428.
7. Crucially, Philby omitted any reference to Anthony Blunt or John Cairncross.
8. Philby identified Orlov as having been in London with Deutsch, yet Orlov, then in the FBI's protection in Ann Arbor, had never mentioned his period in London as the NKVD's illegal *rezident*. See Gazur, E., *Secret Assignment: The FBI's KGB General* (London: St Ermin's Press, 2001) and Costello, J. & Tsarev, O., *Deadly Illusions* (New York: Crown, 1998).
9. Paul Hardt's MI5 personal file is at KV2/1008.
10. See also West, N. & Tsarev, O., *Crown Jewels* (London: HarperCollins, 1998).
11. *Ibid.*

Chapter 5: Renato Levi

1. Roberts, Captain C.H., *History of CHEESE*, SIME Special Section, February 1943, at WO 169/24893.
2. See West, N., *Double Cross in Cairo* (London: Biteback, 2015).
3. See Holt, T., *The Deceivers* (London: Weidenfeld & Nicolson, 2004); Bendeck, W.T., *'A' Force: The Origins of British Deception During the Second World War* (Annapolis, MD: Naval Institute Press, 2014); and Crowdy, T., *Deceiving Hitler* (Oxford: Osprey, 2008).
4. See Payne Best, S., *The Venlo Incident* (London: Hutchinson, 1951).

Chapter 6: Richard Wurmann

1. The HARLEQUIN personal file is at KV2/268. Wurmann's real name has been redacted throughout.
2. *Ibid.*
3. GLIST was a local compartmentalized codename for the ISOS cryptographic source.
4. Liddell referred to HARLEQUIN in his diaries on 10 February 1943 referring to his naturalization; on 17 April 1943 concerning a special report for the Prime Minister; and on 12 May 1943 when Wurmann 'packed up' and ceased his cooperation.
5. HARLEQUIN personal file.
6. *Ibid.*
7. WATCHDOG was Waldemar Janowsky, an Abwehr agent landed in Canada by U-boat in November 1942.
8. DRAGONFLY was Hans George, who was recruited in 1939 by the Abwehr in Holland.
9. FATHER was a Belgian pilot, Pierre Arend, who arrived in England in June 1941.
10. HARLEQUIN personal file.

Chapter 7: Al Sarant

1. Feklisov, A., *The Man Behind the Rosenbergs* (New York: Enigma, 2001), p. 133.
2. Al Sarant's FBI file no: 65-59242.
3. See Feklisov, *The Man Behind the Rosenbergs*.
4. Weinstein & Vassiliev, *The Haunted Wood*.
5. See Haynes, Klehr & Vassiliev, *Spies; The Rise and Fall of the KGB in America*.
6. Harry Steingart's FBI file no: 65-25385. For the Seborer brothers, see Klehr, H. & Haynes, J.E., 'On the trail of a Fourth Spy at Los Alamos', *Studies in Intelligence*, vol. 63, no. 3 (September 2019).

7. The Cohens were released from prison in 1969 in exchange for Gerald Brooke, a lecturer imprisoned in Moscow.
8. The National Security Agency VENONA Project, available at: www.nsa.gov.
9. Al Sarant's FBI file.

Chapter 8: Engelbert Broda

1. Broda's NKVD file, cited in Tsarev, *The Crown Jewels* (London HarperCollins, 1980) as 'K', p. 233.
2. *Ibid.*
3. *Ibid.*
4. Engelbert Broda's MI5 personal file is at KV2/2350.
5. *Ibid.*
6. Josef Lemmel's MI5 codename was changed from KASPAR to LAMB, probably to avoid confusion with a technical source in the CPGB headquarters in King Street, actually a microphone codenamed TABLE and the KASPAR.
7. Lemmel, J., *The Indestructible*. Privately published in Austria for his family.
8. Fuchs became a suspect for the Los Alamos spy who appeared in several VENONA texts under the codenames REST and CHARLES. He would be interrogated in September 1949 based on the FBI's analysis of the intercepts.
9. Broda's MI5 personal file.
10. Edith Suschitsky's MI5 files are at KV2/1012 and KV2/4091.
11. Alex Tudor Hart's MI5 personal file is at KV2/603.
12. Georg Honigmann's MI5 personal file is at KV5/113.
13. See Tsarev, *The Crown Jewels*.
14. Wright, P., *SpyCatcher* (New York: Viking Penguin, 1987), p. 127.
15. Engelbert Broda's MI5 personal file.
16. Broda, P., *Scientist Spies: A Memoir of my Three Parents* (Market Harborough, Leics: Troubadour, 2011).
17. The unidentified source 'K' was referred to as codenamed ERIC by Nigel West in *Mortal Crimes* (New York: Enigma, 2004). Alexander Vassiliev named ERIC as Engelbert Broda in *Spies* (London: Yale University Press, 2009).

Chapter 9: William Whalen

1. Dmitri Polyakov volunteered to spy for the FBI in January 1962 at the end of his second posting to the GRU's New York *rezidentura* within the Soviet mission to the United Nations. See Dillon, E., *Spies in the Family* (New York: HarperCollins, 2017).
2. Jacobsen, A., *Operation PAPERCLIP* (New York: Little, Brown, 2014).
3. Penkovsky was arrested by the KGB in Moscow on 22 October 1962 so therefore was unavailable to influence the Cuban missile crisis.
4. Although Robert Hanssen is now known to have identified Polyakov as a spy, the GRU officer was not arrested until 1985, when Aldrich Ames confirmed the allegation.
5. Koss, P., *Tales from Langley* (New York: Adventures Unlimited Press, 2014).
6. Stig Wennerstrom, who had been posted to Washington between April 1952 and March 1957, was identified as a spy by Michal Goleniewski in 1959. Wennerstrom was arrested in June 1963.

Chapter 10: John Walker

1. Heath, L., *An analysis of the Systematic Security Weaknesses of the US Navy Fleet Broadcasting System 1967–74 as exploited by CWO John Walker* (Georgia Institute of Technology, 2005).
2. Geoffrey Prime served at GCHQ from 1962 until 1977. He had begun spying for the KGB in January 1968. He was arrested in 1982 and sentenced to 35 years' imprisonment. He was released on parole in March 2001.
3. Robert Lipka spied for the KGB from September 1965 until his retirement two years later. He was arrested in February 1996 and was sentenced to 18 years' imprisonment. He was released in September 1997 and died in July 2013.
4. Walker, J., *My Life as a Spy* (New York: Prometheus, 2010).
5. Solomatin interview with Pete Earley, *Washington Post*, 1995.

Chapter 11: Clyde Conrad

1. Sulick, M., *American Spies* (Washington DC: Georgetown University Press, 2020).
2. Herrington, S.A., *Traitors Among Us* (Novato, CA: Presidio, 1999). See also *The Official History of the Clyde Conrad Case* (Defense Human Resources Activity, US Department of Defense); Williams, D.L., *DAMIAN and MONGOOSE* (New York: Wheatmark, 2011).
3. Kuklinski, R., *A Secret Life* (New York: Public Affairs, 2004).
4. Olson, J.M., *To Catch a Spy: The Art of Counterintelligence* (Washington DC: Georgetown University Press, 2021).
5. Istvan Belovai's memoir, *Strike to the Red Empire*, remains unpublished.
6. *Ibid.*

Chapter 12: Vladimir Kuzichkin

1. Brian Kelley, *Falsely Accused* (unpublished memoir).
2. Kuzichkin, V., *Inside the KGB: Myth & Reality* (London: Andre Deutsch, 1990).
3. Carr, B., *Loginov, Spy in the Sun* (Cape Town, SA: Howard Timmons, 1969). Loginov subsequently turned up at the US embassy in Budapest and, his true identity revealed, was resettled by the CIA in Alexandria, Virginia, under his own name. He died of cancer in 2015.
4. Codenamed EXCISE, Grigori Tokaev's Foreign Office file is at FO 1093/550.
5. Oleg Lyalin's file is at FO 168/4587. See also Wright, *SpyCatcher*, p. 342.
6. Codenamed CAPULET, Yuri Tasoev defected in Operation HOUSE PARTY. His file is at FO 1093/548.
7. Vladimir Skripkin's attempted defection is described in Anatoli Golitsyn's unpublished memoir, *Checkmate*.
8. Yuri Rastvorov defected to the CIA in Tokyo in August 1954 after he had been promised resettlement in Canada by SIS. When he learned that he would be going to England first, he backed out of the agreement, citing penetration in London.
9. John Scarlett, later JIC Chairman (2001–2004) and SIS Chief (2004–2009).
10. See Barrington, N., *Envoy: A Diplomatic Journey* (London: Bloomsbury, 2013). See also his official assessment at FCO 160/220/8.

Chapter 13: Ashraf Marwan

1. Bregman, A., *Israel's Wars* (London: Routledge, 2016).
2. Bregman, A., *A History of Israel* (London: Red Globe, 2002). See also Bregman, A., *The Spy Who Fell to Earth* (CreateSpace, 2016).

Chapter 14: Gennadi Vasilenko

1. Devine, J., *Spymaster's Prism* (New York: Potomac Books, 2021).
2. David Barnett was betrayed by Vladimir Piguzov and was arrested in 1979. He was sentenced to 18 years' imprisonment and was paroled in 1990.
3. Edward Lee Howard defected to Moscow in 1985. See Howard, E.L., *Safe House* (New York: Enigma, 1995). See also Wise, D., *The Spy Who Got Away* (New York: Random House, 1988).
4. Harold Nicholson was betrayed by Alexander Zaporozhsky and was arrested in November 1996. He was sentenced to 23 years' imprisonment but in 2006 was re-arrested with his son Nathaniel and convicted of re-establishing contact with the SVR. He was sentenced in 2010 to a further eight years' imprisonment and is scheduled for release in 2023.
5. Vitali Yurchenko obtained political asylum in the United States in August 1985 but redefected to Moscow in November, having compromised an NSA retiree, Ron Pelton, and a mole in Australia codenamed JABAROO.
6. David Boone was betrayed by Alexander Zaporozhsky, was arrested in October 1998 and sentenced to 24 years' imprisonment. He was released in January 2020.
7. Philip Agee resigned from the CIA after eleven years in 1967 and was recruited by the Cuban intelligence service. He published a series of KGB-sponsored books, including *Inside the Company: A CIA Diary* (London: Penguin, 1975) exposing CIA operations and personnel. He died in Havana in January 2008.
8. See Dexenhall, E. & Russo, G., *Best of Enemies* (New York: Strand, 2018).
9. Hanssen FBI Complaint, February 2001.

Index

Morgan, Janet, 196
MORRIS, *see* Abraham Glasser
Morrison, Philip, xxi, 106–7
Morrison, William, xxi, 34, 197
Mortal Crimes (West), 199
Mortati, Tomasso, xxi, 159
Morton, Jack, vii
Mossad, 171–5
  Chief of, *see* Zvi Zamir
Mossadeq, Mohammed, xxi, 168
Motinov, Pyort, 130
Moussa Koussa, xi, 179
Moxon, Margaret (Peggy), xxi, 53
Moxson, Peter, 112
Mozhduechenck, 177
MRBM, *see* Medium Range Ballistic
  Missile
Mubarak, Gamal, 175
Mubarak, Hosni, xxi, 175
Mueller, Georg, 51
Mukhabarat, 173
Münster Verlag, 37
Murder by Numbers (Dickson), 30
Mure, David, vii
Mutch, Walter, 41
MUTT, *see* John Moe
My Life as a Spy (Walker), 143, 200
My Silent War (Philby), 196

Naidoo, Kevin, xxi, 178
Napoleonic War, 1
NARA, *see* National Archives and Records
  Administration
Nasser, Gamal Abdel, 173, 177, 180
Nasser, Mona, xxi, 193
National Advisory Committee on
  Aeronautics, 109
National Archives and Records
  Administration (NARA), vii
National HUMINT Collection Plan, 189
National Security Agency (NSA), 100,
  135, 183, 199, 201
NATO, *see* North Atlantic Treaty
  Organisation
Naval Communications Area Master
  Stations, 143

Naval Investigative Service, 144
Naval Security Group, 135
Naval Security and Investigative
  Command, 147
Nebenzahl, Yitzhak, xxi, 171
New Lies for Old (Golitsyn), 196
New York Field Office, 191
New York *Rezidentura*, 100–1, 109, 192,
  199
New York, SS, 19
Next Stop Execution (Gordievsky), 196
Niagara Falls, USS, 143
Nicholson, Harold, xxii, 183–4, 201
Nicholson, Nathaniel, 201
Nicossof, Paul, xxii, 63, 69–70, 72, 75
NIGEL, *see* Michael Straight
Night's Black Agent (Bingham), 30, 197
Nike anti-aircraft missile, 145
NIL, *see* Nathan Sussman
Nimitz, USS, 143–4
NKVD, *see* Soviet intelligence service
No Other Choice (Blake), 196
Nobel Prize, 145
Nordhausen rocket factory, 134
Normandy (1944), 60
North Atlantic Treaty Organisation
  (NATO). 137, 145, 155–8
North Vietnamese Army, 142

OACSI, *see* Office of the Assistant Chief
  of Staff Intelligence
Oak Ridge, 103
Oberkommando der Wehrmacht, Cipher
  Section (OKH/Chi), xii
Odeon Theatres, 40–1
O'Donoghue, John, xxii, 109, 112
Office of the Assistant Chief of Staff
  Intelligence (OACSI), 134
Office of Naval Intelligence, 102, 151
Office of Strategic Services (OSS), vii
Ogarkov, Nikolai, xxii, 155, 159
OGPU, *see* Soviet intelligence service
OKH/Chi, *see* Oberkommando der
  Wehrmacht, Cipher Section
OKW Intelligence Liaison (Ic), 87
OLD, *see* Saville Sax

Rabagliati, Euan, vii
Rabbani, xxiii, 163
Rabbat, 168
Radio Direction-Finding (RDF), 68
Radio Security Service (RSS), 20, 83
Raev, Aleksandr (LIGHT), xxiii, 106
RAF Martlesham Heath, 32
RAF Menwith Hill, 135
Ramsay, Roderick, xxiii, 158–9
Ramsbotham, Peter, vii
Ranczak, Hildegard, xxiii, 73
Rantzau, Nikolaus, *see* Nikolaus Ritter
Rastvorov, Yuri, xxiii, 164, 200
RAYMOND, *see* Ignace Reiss
Razorback, USS, 143
RCS, *see* Royal Corps of Signals
RDF, *see* Radio Direction-Finding
Red Banner Fleet, 116, 136, 153
Red Banner Institute, 162
REDWOOD, *see* Vladimir Kuzichkin
Regional Security Liaison Officer
     (RSLO), 126
Reich, Wilhelm, xxiii, 37
Reichswehrministerium, 16
Reiff, Ignaty, *see* Ignace Reiss
Reiss, Ignace, xiii, 38
RELAY, *see* Joseph Chinilevsky
Répási, Jozsef, xxiii, 198
Reuter's, 128
Revizorov, Pavel, xxiii; 162
Rezun, Vladimir, vii, xxiii, 164
Ribbentrop, Joachim, xxiii, 85
Richthofen: Red Knight of the Air (Vigilant),
     31, 197
Riis, Iib (COBWEB), vii
Risso-Gill, Christopher, viii
Ritter, Kathleen, viii
Ritter, Nikolaus, xxiii, 19
ROAM, *see* Dmitri Polyakov
Roberts, John, xxiii, 178, 198
Roberts, Madoc, 197
Robertson, Dennis, 45
Robertson, Joan, vii
Robertson, T.A., vii, xxiii
Rochford, Mike, xxiii, 188
ROF, *see* Royal Ordnance Factory

Rommel, Erwin, xxiii, 59, 68
Rondeau, Jeffrey, xxiii, 159
Roosevelt administration, 143
Roozbeh, Khosro, xxiii, 168
Rosenberg, Ethel (ETHEL), xxiii, 13,
     102, 111
Rosenberg, Julius (ANTENNA;
     LIBERAL), xxiii, 13, 99, 102–5, 109,
     112, 182, 194
Ross, Louise, 106–7
Ross, Victor, 106–7
Rossetti, Clemens, xxiii, 73
Rothschild, Tess, vii
Rothschild, Victor, vii
Royal Air Force (RAF), 9, 17, 23, 166
Royal Aircraft Establishment,
     Farnborough, 135
Royal Aircraft Establishment, Westcott,
     135
Royal Canadian Air Force, 34
Royal Corps of Signals (RCS), 72, 78
Royal Flying Corps, 9
Royal Naval Air Service, 9
RSS, *see* Radio Security Service
Ruhel, Josefine, xxiii, 37
Rumrich, Gunther, xxiii, 18
Rumrich, Gustav, xxiii, 18
Russelsheim ASA site, 135
Russian Federal Security Service (FSB),
     190, 192
Russian military intelligence service
     (GRU), 133, 139, 141–2, 163, 182,
     186
Russo, Gus, 201
Ryde, Michael, vii

SA, *see* Sturmabteilung
SA-2, 176
SA-3, 176
SA-6 *Gainful*, 175
Sadat, Anwar, 173, 175–7, 179
Sapwood, 137
Sarant, Al (HUGHES), xxiii, xxx, 99, 105,
     182–90, 198
Sarant, Louise, 115
Saros, Philip, *see* Al Sarant